Sermons, Essays, and Extracts, by Various Authors

PREFACE.

THIS publication, consisting of Sermons, Essays, &c. on various important subjects, is presented to the public with an earnest desire, that it may aid the cause of truth, and be conducive to the divine glory in the salvation of men. The subjects particularly considered are of primary importance; and it is hoped that the contents of this volume will be read by many, with an impartial desire to know and embrace the truth, and with much instruction and consolation.

- The subject of the two first sermons is one, which has not been so frequently discussed, either from the pulpit or the press, as many others, and for this reason is less familiar, and less clearly understood than many others, even by persons of sound understanding, and ardent piety. This subject is thought to be illustrated in these discourses, in a judicious, scriptural, and convincing manner.

- That is doubtless the most evangelical exhibition of any divine truth, which is best suited to convince of sin, to shew the sinner, that he is justly condemned before God, and wholly without excuse, in his impenitency and unbelief; and which is, therefore, best suited to bring down the loftiness of man, that the LORD alone may be exalted. Such it will be found, by every candid reader, is the exhibition of the truth, which is attempted in these discourses. But this is submitted to the reader's judgment.

Of these two sermons, the *London Evangelical Magazine* gives the following account:

" Very considerable controversies have been agi-
tated respecting the *manner* in which unconverted sinners should be addressed in the gospel ministry. And
though this is most certainly a very important article,
yet there is a great want of unanimity of sentiment respecting it. Perhaps injudicious views of several Calvinistic doctrines have had an unhappy influence upon
the minds of some. It must be owned there are characters in the ministry, and such as are zealous for the
leading truths of the gospel, who in the pulpit have little or nothing to say in a way of *direct address* to the
unconverted part of their auditory. Nay, some go so
far as to contend that this is no part of their work.—
How such can reconcile their *creed* with the *example*
of Christ, the *commission* he gave to his disciples, and
the *practice* of the apostles, to say nothing of the *conduct* of the prophets of old, it is not our province to determine. While that text, " *Go preach the gospel to
every creature,*" stands in our bibles, we must beg leave
to think and act very differently.

It is readily owned, that the discourses before us do
not immediately handle this subject : yet they discuss
a question most intimately connected with it. In the
introduction, after remarking the impotence and helplessness of men in themselves, and their entire dependance upon divine grace for salvation, the preacher observes, that " there is a difficulty in the minds of many,
how to reconcile this total helplessness of sinners with
the sincerity of the *gospel call,* or with the justice of
men's being condemned and punished for their impenitence and unbelief." Several ways in which some
have endeavoured to solve the difficulty are pointed out,
and their insufficiency shown. He then adds, " After
what has been said, I think there is no way of attempting to clear up this mystery left, but by showing that

there are two essentially different senses, in which men are said to be incapable of doing things." He farther explains his idea, by saying, " The one consists only in the want of a heart, or disposition, or will to do a thing : while the other consists in, or arises from want of understanding, bodily strength, opportunity, or *whatever may prevent* our doing a thing when we are willing, and strong enough disposed and inclined to do it." To these he applies the terms of *natural* and *moral* inability. To *state* and *illustrate* this distinction ; to show that men certainly labour under *one*, or the *other* of these kinds of inability to comply with the gospel, *until* they are made the subjects of *effectual* divine grace, more particularly to consider and evince the *moral* impotence of sinners, and endeavour to make it appear, that there is ordinarily *no other* incapacity in sinners, to comply with the gospel, but that which is of the *moral* kind, employ the preacher through two long sermons. At the close, several important inferences are drawn, and, among other matters, the manner in which a ministerial address to the unconverted should be conducted, is introduced

These sermons are evidently the result of close thought, and contain much strong reasoning. The subject is interesting, and the manner in which it is treated is serious. Several marginal notes are added by the author ; one especially, upon the nature of true love to God, which begins on the 28th page, we beg leave to recommend to the most serious attention of the reader."

Of the Sermons and Essays, which are designed to illustrate the doctrine of the atonement, it is expected also, that every reader should judge for himself— The subject is evidently of the first importance. " The sufferings of Christ for sin," says a late writer, " characterize the gospel scheme, and distinguish it from all others. The atonement made by them, adds to the christian religion its chief superiority, and lays the only foundation of hope for all who have just views of the divine law, and the moral state of man. All the doctrines of the gospel will derive their peculiar complexion from the manner in which the doctrine of atonement is explained. A mistake here will be peculiarly injurious, and will infallibly lead into error in every part of divinity. Atonement is the great sun in the centre of the system. Blot it out, and you are lost forever. Not a ray from any other quarter will dart through the gloomy prison of sin, to cheer its disconsolate inhabitants, to disenthral them from their chains, and enlighten their path to freedom and glory."

Correct views of the atonement shed light, consistency, harmony and beauty divinely charming over the other doctrines of the gospel.

However interesting the subject, it is one on which those are not perfectly united, whose piety is apparently unquestionable. In the Discourses and Essays on this subject, the writers have occasionally exhibited a small diversity of sentiment. This must generally have arisen from the different errors, which they designed to expose, and which were more particularly contemplated, in their respective arguments, and illustrations. While they have presented no essential difference of sentiment, they have honestly and faithfully declared to others, what they believed to be the "truth as it is in Jesus."

May the blessing of God accompany His truth, that it may be a savour of life unto many souls; and to Him shall be all the glory forever.

THE PUBLISHER.

CONTENTS.

comply with the gospel, they will never feel their dependence on Him who alone is able to work in them "the whole good pleasure of his goodness, and the work of faith with power." Nor will they feel disposed, or see the occasion they have, to "give unto God the glory," which is indeed "due unto his name," in their salvation. Accordingly, the depravity, blindness and deadness of mankind, in things of a spiritual nature, and their utter inability to comply with the gospel, as well as to obtain salvation by the deeds of the law, are much inculcated and insisted on in the sacred scriptures.

But then, there is a difficulty in the minds of many, how to reconcile this total helplessness of sinners with the sincerity of the gospel call, or with the justice of men's being condemned and punished, for their impenitence and unbelief. And indeed it does seem as if men could not be to blame, for not doing impossibilities: nor should we, in other cases, think there was much kindness or sincerity in offering a favour on conditions that were known to be impracticable.

There is scarce any one, I believe, that has ever thought much about religion, but what has, at one time or other, felt himself pinched with this difficulty. And it is wont to have a most pernicious influence upon the minds of sinners in general; but more especially when they come to be under awakenings, and begin to enquire, "what they shall do to be saved." According to what they hear in sermons, yea, and according to what they read in their bibles, they are at a loss to see how the ways of the Lord can be equal. "The carnal mind," they are told, "is—not subject to the law of God, neither indeed *can* be." And that, "they that are in the flesh *cannot* please God." They are therefore under a *necessity* of sinning, yea, of doing nothing else but sin. And yet, " every transgression and disobedience," is to receive a most dreadful " recompence of reward," the wrath of God being " revealed from heaven against all ungodliness and unrighteousness of men." And no relief, no deliverance from wrath, is to be hoped for through the gospel, but upon impossible conditions : Such conditions as no natural men, no one who is dead in trespasses and sins ever did, ever will, or can comply with. And yet a non-compliance with these conditions exposes to an amazingly aggravated, additional condemnation ; insomuch that it will be more tolerable for Sodom and Gomorrah, in the day of judgment, than for those who enjoy the light of the gospel, and do not embrace the salvation it offers.

But how these things are consistent with reason ; how they can ever be reconciled with the goodness or the justice of God, they are greatly at a loss. Such a .view of the matter seems to them to make the *most high* indeed, what the slothful servant said, a hard master, " reaping where he has not sown, and gathering where he has not strewed." Or, like the cruel Egyptian task-masters, requiring the full tale of brick without allowing the necessary straw ; requiring that of his creatures which he knows exceeds their utmost strength, and then they are beaten ; yea, must be punished with everlasting destruction, for not doing what they would do with all their hearts ; but it is no more in their power, than it is to make a world.

Now, until this difficulty can be fairly got over in the minds of people, it seems impossible they should, in their consciences, justify God, or condemn themselves as he condemns them. Or that they should understand, either the justice of the divine law, or the grace of the gospel. It is therefore certainly highly necessary,

That is, they suppose, if sinners will seek and pray, use the means of grace, and do the best that persons under their circumstances, and having such hearts as they have, *may* do; God will not be wanting on his part, or leave them to perish: That if they exert all the strength, and make a good improvement of all the assistance they have, they shall have more and more given them; till in the end they are enabled to obtain mercy, and to lay hold on eternal life. That although there are no absolute promises to such earnest and sincere, though feeble efforts of the unregenerate, yet certainly there are many very precious encouragements; which may indeed, securely enough be relied. on. So that, on the whole no sinner is under any *real* impossibility, of *any kind,* of obtaining salvation. For every one, let his impotence be as great as it may, can certainly do what he can. And if upon his doing *this,* God will not fail to help, as to what he *cannot* do; then every one *may* be saved, whatever sin and weakness, or depravity he labours under, notwithstanding. Nor do they see how we can vindicate the divine justice, or fairly cast the blame of the sinner's perdition on himself, without supposing such a universal sufficiency of grace as this.

Now, if this can be made out to be really the case, that all are actually, and in every view, *enabled* to do those things which are certainly connected with eternal life, there will be no difficulty, perhaps with any one, to see that the ways of the Lord are equal. For according to this there seems to be no respect of persons with God, even in the distribution of his *freest favours,* any more than in his *judicial proceedings.* The difference between him that is saved, and him that perish·heth, *not* originating from any inequality in the bestowment of divine grace; *but* solely from the better improvement one sinner makes of the same grace, than another does.

But, I am afraid, it will be as hard to reconcile this way of solving matters with the scriptures, and with the truth of fact, as it is the former, with reason. Certainly the scriptures seem to speak a language quite different from this. In them we are taught, " That it is God that maketh one man to differ from another, for the better, and not he himself. That it is not of him that willeth, nor of him that runneth, but of God that sheweth mercy," and " that he hath mercy on whom he will have mercy; and whom he will he hardeneth." And in our text, our Saviour accounts for the murmuring and opposition of the unbelieving Jews, by making this observation to his disciples upon it; " no man can come unto me, except the Father who hath sent me, draw him." By which he evidently meant to intimate, that the conduct of his opposers, considering what human nature was, was not to be wondered at. That they acted no otherwise than all other men would, if left to themselves as they were. That those who now followed and obeyed him, would never have come to him, or become his disciples, had it not been for a gracious divine influence upon their minds, which was not granted to those murmurers and opposers; had they not been effectually drawn by him in whose hand are the hearts of men, and who turneth them as rivers of water are turned. We are plainly taught in this text, taken in the connection in which it stands, as we are also in a multitude of other places, that men do not first distinguish themselves, by hearkening to the calls of the gospel; but it is God that makes one to differ from another, in this respect, by his sovereign and distinguishing grace. The point of *doctrine,* therefore, that I shall insist upon from the words is this:

That none are *able* to comply with the gospel, but those who are the subjects of the special and *effectual* grace of God; or those who are *made willing,* and actually *do* comply with it.

What I have in view, in the following discourse, is not only to confirm this doctrine, but to endeavour to set it in such a light as to obviate the forementioned difficulty, of salvation's being offered on impossible conditions, and men's being condemned for not doing that which they are incapable of. And, after what has been said, I think there is *no* way of attempting to clear up this mystery left, but by showing that there are *two essentially different senses,* in which men are said to be *incapable* of doing things: or, by having recourse to the distinction of *natural* and *moral inability.* Accordingly, the method I propose, is,

1. As clearly as I can, to *state and illustrate this distinction.*

2. To show, that men certainly labour under *one,* or the *other,* of these kinds of inability to comply with the gospel, *until* they are made the subjects of *effectual* divine grace.

3. More particularly to consider and evince the *moral* impotence of sinners. And,

4. Endeavour to make it appear, that there is ordinarily *no other* incapacity in sinners, to comply with the gospel, but that which is of the *moral* kind.

1. Then, It is to be observed, for the clearing up this subject, that there are *two very different kinds* of *inability;* so different, that the *one,* however great, does not lessen moral obligation in the least; whereas the *other,* so far as it obtains, destroys obligation, and ~s away all desert of blame and punishment entirely.

These two kinds of inability, as I hinted, have commonly been distinguished, by calling one a *natural*, the other a *moral* inability. Which distinction may be briefly stated thus. *Moral inability* consists only in the want of a heart, or disposition, or will, to do a thing. *Natural inability*, on the other hand, consists in, or arises from, want of understanding, bodily strength, opportunity, or *whatever may prevent*, our doing a thing, when we are willing, and strongly enough disposed and inclined to do it. Or, in fewer words, thus: Whatever a man could not do, *if he would*, in this, he is under a *natural* inability; but when all the reason why one *cannot* do a thing, is because he does not choose to do it, the inability is only of a *moral* nature.

This distinction takes place equally with regard to both *evil* and *good* actions. Thus, for instance, the divine Being *cannot* do evil ; not because he wants opportunity, or understanding, or strength, to do, with infinite ease, whatever he pleases ; but only because he is not, and it is impossible he ever should be, inclined to do iniquity. He is so infinitely and immutably holy, wise, just, and good, that it is impossible he should ever *please* to act otherwise, than in the most holy, righteous, and best manner. Hence though we read that " with God *all things* are possible," and that he can do *every* thing ; yet elsewhere we are told, " he cannot *deny himself ;*" and that it is impossible, " for God to lie."

On the other hand, satan is incapable of doing right, or of behaving virtuously, in any one instance, or in the least possible degree. But this is not because he wants natural abilities ; for undoubtedly in that respect, he is far superior to many that are truly virtuous. His being incapable of any thing but infernal wickedness, is altogether owing to his being of such an infernal disposition.

And it is not uncommon to speak of incapacity in mankind, both as to doing good and doing evil, in this two-fold signification. Some persons we say are incapable of doing a *mean thing*. Not that we think it is above their *natural* capacity; but it is beneath them; they abhor, or they would scorn to do it. Others are incapable of several sorts of villainy, not through any want of good will to do it: they only want a convenient opportunity, or sufficient ingenuity.—And just so it is in regard to doing good. Some have it not in the power of their hands; others have no heart to do it. One is of a truly generous spirit, and nothing but his own poverty keeps him from being what Job was, a father to the poor, the fatherless, and him that has none to help him.—Another is rich, and might be a great benefactor and blessing to all around him; but he has no heart to devise liberal things. He is *deaf* to the cries of the poor, *blind* to their wants, and *dead* to all the generous feelings of humanity and compassion.

Some are so feeble and infirm that they can do scarce any bodily labour; though they are extremely free and willing to lay themselves out to the utmost that their strength will bear, and often go beyond it. Others are strong and healthy enough, and might get a good living, and be useful members of society; but such is their invincible laziness, that their hands refuse to labour, and they can hardly get them out of their bosoms.— Some are effectually kept from shining, or being very useful, in any public sphere in church or state, through the weakness of their heads: Others, as effectually, by the badness of their hearts. Some are incapable of being taught, by reason of natural dulness: others only because they are of an unteachable spirit, and full of self-conceit. Some are blind for want of eyes ; but it is an old proverb, that none are more blind than those who *will not* see.

These examples are sufficient to illustrate the distinction I am insisting on, and to make it evident, that by *incapability*, we often mean something very different from want of natural capacity. We may also perceive from these instances, that there is a real necessity for using such words as *capable, incapable, cannot,* &c. in this diversity of signification, in which we see they are used, in common speech, as well as in the scriptures. For whenever any thing, whether in ourselves or without us, is really absolutely inconsistent with our doing a thing, we have no way fully and strongly enough to express that inconsistence, but by saying we are *unable, we cannot*, it is *impossible*, or using some word of like import. And now it is certain that want of a heart, or inclination to do a thing, may be, and is, as inconsistent with our doing it as any thing else could be. Covetousness is as inconsistent with liberality as poverty, and may as effectually hinder a man from doing deeds of charity. Indolence is as inconsistent with industry, as bodily weakness and infirmity. The want of an upright heart and a public spirit, is as inconsistent with the character of a good ruler, as the want of wisdom and understanding. And the want of all principles of virtue must be as inconsitent with acting virtuously, as even the want of those intellectual faculties which are necessary to moral agency. And so on the other hand as to doing *evil* things. There is no possibility of doing them, that is, knowingly, designedly, and as moral agents, without an evil disposition. Our free and moral actions are, and must be, as invariably guided and dictated by our minds, as they are limited and bounded by our natural power. That is, every one must act his own nature and choice; otherwise he does not act himself; *he* is not the agent. And if, when we would express this sort of necessity, we should not use the same phrases as are made use of in cases of natural ne- cessity; but, for fear of a misunderstanding should carefully avoid saying a man *cannot*, whenever we mean only that he has not such a heart as is necessary, and only say that he *will not*, in all such cases; our language would often sound odd, being out of common custom, which governs the propriety of words; and not only so, but it would not be sufficiently expressive. Should we be afraid to say it is *impossible* for a man to love God, or come to Christ, while his heart is altoge- ther wicked and full of enmity against God and Christ; people would be ready to think we imagined this might sometimes happen, and that there was no real impossibility in it of any kind. Whereas there is as real, and as absolute an impossibility in this case, as in any supposable case whatever. To be more guarded therefore, than the scripture is, in this matter, would be to be unguarded. The apostle demands, " *can* the fig-tree, my brethren, bear olive berries? either a vine, figs?" And the prophet, " *can* the Ethiopian change his skin? or the leopard, his spots? Then may ye also do good, who are accustomed to do evil." And our Saviour says, " a good tree *cannot* bring forth evil fruit; neither *can* a corrupt tree bring forth good fruit. A good man out of the good treasure of the heart bring- eth forth good things. And an evil man out of the evil treasure bringeth forth evil things." There is *as cer- tain* and never-failing a connection in this case as in any natural connection whatever. Which ought by no means to be dissembled, but openly maintained. But then it is certainly of a *quite different*, and even a di- rectly opposite nature, to all intents and purposes of moral agency. And it is of the last importance, in my apprehension, that this also should be maintained and manifested to every man's conscience.

Because a man *must* act according to his own heart, or as he pleases ; does this destroy his freedom ! It is the very thing in which all free agency consists. The pulse *can* beat ; the limbs can move in some bodily disorders, or when one that is stronger than we takes hold of them ; whether we will or no. But God does not consider *us* as accountable for such actions as these. And we should, and that not without reason, think it very hard, should he blame or punish us for them. For an honest and good man's pulse may beat as irregularly as the worst villain's in the world. Or his hands, in a convulsion, may strike those around him, in spite of all he can do to hold them still. Or one may be carried by force along with a gang of thieves, and be taken for one of them, though no man hates such company and actions as theirs, more heartily than he does. Such involuntary actions every one sees a man is not, and ought not to be accountable for. And the reason is, no bad inclination of ours, or want of a good one, is *necessary* in order to them. They are *so free*, as to be independent of *us*, and out of our power. If all our actions were like these ; no ways necessarily connected with our disposition, and choice, and temper of mind, we could not be accountable creatures, or the subjects of moral government. If a good tree could bring forth evil fruit, and a corrupt tree good fruit ; if a good man, out of the good treasure of his heart, could bring forth evil things, and an evil man, out of the evil treasure, good things ; the tree could never be known by its fruit. It could never be known by a man's actions, any thing what his heart was. So that,

B

if they were dealt with according to their works, the most upright and well disposed would be as liable to be punished; and the most ill-natured and ill-disposed, as likely to be rewarded, as the contrary. Whence all moral government must be at an end.

Certainly, if we are justly accountable, rewardable, or punishable, for any actions; if any actions are, or can be, properly *our own*, it must be such as are dictated by ourselves, and which *cannot* take place without our own consent. An inability, therefore, to act otherwise than agreeably to our own minds, is only an inability to act otherwise than as free agents. And that necessity which arises from, or rather consists in, the temper and choice of the agent himself, and that which is against his choice and his very nature, are so far from coming to the same thing at last, that they are directly contrary one to the other, as to all the purposes of morality, freedom, accountableness, and desert of praise or blame, reward or punishment.

And this is agreeable to the sense of all mankind, in all common cases. A man's heart being fully set in him to do evil, does not render his evil actions the less criminal, in the judgment of common sense, but the more so: nor does the strength of a virtuous disposition render a good action the *less*, but the *more* amiable, and worthy of praise. Does any one look upon the divine Being, as less excellent and glorious, for being so infinitely and unchangeably holy in his nature, that he " cannot be tempted with evil," or act otherwise than in the most holy and perfect manner? Does any one look upon the devil as less sinful and to blame, because he is of such a devilish disposition, so full of unreasonable spite and malice against God and man, as to be incapable of any thing but the most horrid wickedness? And as to mankind : who is there that does not make a difference between him that is incapable of a base action, only by reason of the virtuousness of his temper, having all the natural talents requisite for the most consummate villainy: and him that is incapable of being the worst of villains, for no other reason than only because he does not know how? Does any one think that only the want of a will to work, excuses a man from it, just as much as bodily infirmity does? Or, do we any of us ever imagine, that the covetous miser who, with all his useless hoards, has no heart to give a penny to the poor, is for that reason equally excusable from deeds of charity, as he who has nothing to give?

We certainly always make a distinction betwixt want of natural abilities to do good, and the want of a heart; looking upon the one as a *good* excuse, the other as *no* excuse *at all*, but rather as that in which all wickedness radically consists. A natural fool no one blames for acting like a fool. But "to him that knoweth to do good, and doth it not; to him "it is sin," in the sense of all mankind, as well as in God's account. "If there be first a *willing mind*," we always suppose it ought to be accepted according to that a man hath, and not according to that he hath not." But the want of a willing mind, or not having a mind to do well, is universally considered as a crime, and not as an excuse. Nothing is more familiar to us, than to distinguish in this manner. Nor can any man of common sense help judging thus.

Now this distinction is as applicable to the case before us, as it is to any other case. Some may be unable to comply with the gospel, through the want of those powers of mind, or those bodily organs, or those means of grace, without which it is impossible to understand the character of Christ, or the way of salva-

tion through him.   In either of which cases, the inability is of the *natural* kind.   Others may have all the
outward means, and all the *natural* faculties, which are
necessary in order to a right understanding of the gospel ; and yet, through the evil temper of their minds,
they may be disposed to make light of all its proposals
and invitations, and to treat every thing relating to religion and another world, with the utmost neglect and
indifference.   Or, if their fears of " the wrath to come,"
are by any means awakened, and they are made with
much solicitude to enquire " what they shall do to be
saved," still they may be utterly disinclined to submit
to the righteousness, or the grace of God, as revealed
in the gospel.   They may be still, " such children of
the devil, and enemies of all righteousness, as to be
irreconcilably averse to all the right ways of the Lord."
They may have " such an evil heart of unbelief, to depart from the living God," as is absolutely inconsistent
with consenting to the covenant of grace, or " believing to the saving of the soul."   Now, when this is the
case, the inability the sinner is under, is only of a *moral*
nature.

  We may now pass on to the
  2d. head, viz. To show that all who are not the subjects of the special and effectual grace of God, must
certainly be unable, in one or the other of these senses,
to come to Christ, or comply with the gospel.

  Those, many of them at least, who dislike the distinction now explained, and some who seem in a sort
to admit of it, suppose all men have, and must have,
every kind of ability to do their duty, and to obtain salvation.   But, I apprehend, it will be very easy to make
appear, that this certainly is not the case.   A variety
of scripture arguments, and a multitude of texts, might
be adduced here, were they needed.   But that *all* have

not, *both* the fore-mentioned kinds of ability to comply with the gospel, either of themselves, or by the help of common grace, is as evident as any thing needs to be, merely from the fact, that many do not do it, but actually live and die in impenitence and unbelief. By common grace is meant, that grace which is given to sinners in general, those that are not saved, as well as those that are. They who believe that all are in every sense able to work out their own salvation, through the gospel, would not be thought to frustrate the grace of God. They do not suppose sinners are able to do this *of themselves,* but that some divine assistance, some working of God in them, both to will and to do, is really necessary in the case. But then they suppose, all this needed grace, whatever it be, is given to sinners without exception: and hereby they account for God's commanding all men every where to repent and believe the gospel. "I grant, indeed," says an ingenious Arminian writer,* "that by reason of original sin, we are utterly disabled for the performance of the condition, without new grace from God. But I say then, that he gives such grace to all of us, by which the performance of the condition is truly possible, and upon this ground he doth and may most righteously require it." Here by the way, it is worthy of particular remark, what notions many are obliged to entertain of divine grace, in order not to reflect upon the divine justice. To require *perfect holiness* of creatures so enfeebled and depraved as we are, they suppose would be evidently one of the most *unreasonable* things in the world. Therefore God has been *graciously* pleased to send his Son to obey and die in our room, that we

* Dr. Stebbing, on the operation of the Spirit.

might not be " under the law, but under grace." But
then the covenant of *grace* is not gracious enough to
be entirely just ; because by reason of original sin, we
are utterly disabled for the performance of the condition upon which salvation is still suspended.   To remedy the unreasonableness of this, *new grace* from
God is required.   Accordingly, " he giveth *more grace*."
" He gives such grace to all of us, whereby the performance of the condition is truly possible ; and upon
this ground he doth and may most righteously require
it !" Thus, not only the obedience and death of Christ,
but likewise all the grace of the Holy Spirit which is
necessary to salvation, is found no more than barely
sufficient to screen the ways of God to men, from the
just imputation of unreasonableness and unrighteousness!*   It is certainly difficult to conceive, how any
man, who really views things in this light, however
much he may talk of free grace, can ever feel himself
any more obliged and indebted to God, than if he had
only dealt with us in a righteous manner from first to
last, never requiring more of us than we were able to
do, and so no occasion or room had been given for any
grace in the affair.   And yet this view of the matter is

* According to this representation of the matter, I desire it
may be attentively considered, whether this, which is called
grace, does in any thing really differ from *debt* in the strictest
sense ?   If it would be an unrighteous thing in God, to require
a compliance with the gospel, without bestowing all that grace
which is necessary in order to a compliance ; then since he
does indeed require such a *compliance*, would it not be an unrighteous thing in him to withhold such *grace* ? Hence (things
being circumstanced as they are) this *grace* which all are
made partakers of, is no more than what all may claim as their
just due.   And therefore, does not the whole come to this at
last, that this *common grace*, which is so much contended for,
is not *common grace*, but, *common debt* ?

really as friendly to the grace of God, as any conceivable one which proceeds upon the principle that nothing more can be justly required of us, than we have a moral as well as natural power to do.

But what I had more especially in view here, was to enquire how it comes to pass that any in fact do not embrace the gospel, if that grace is given to every one which is sufficient in all respects to enable him to do it. If we want the faculties of body or mind, or the opportunity and means, which are necessary in order to obtain the knowledge of the truth, those difficulties must be removed; and if we want a heart to take pains to know the truth, or to love and embrace it when discovered, that difficulty also must be removed, or else we are not, in every sense, *enabled.* It is not, in all respects, truly possible that a sinner should come to Christ, till every thing that is inconsistent with his coming is removed out of the way. It is truly impossible that any one should cordially embrace the gospel, so long as he has not such a heart in him ; though it would be impossible in a very different sense, if he had not external light, or natural powers sufficient. And now, if God gave that grace to all of us, whereby we were enabled in both these senses to comply with the gospel, the infallible consequence would be, that we should all of us actually do it. To say that a man has both natural and moral ability to do a thing, is the same as to say that nothing in nature is wanting in order to his doing it, but only his own good will, nor *that neither.* Or, that he both could do it if he would, and is sufficiently willing to do it. And whenever this happens to be the case, I believe, it is not very likely, the thing will after all not be done. If in the instance before us it is really thus ; if sinners not only could come to Christ if they would, but they have likewise all that willingness of mind, which is necessary in order to their actually coming, what in the universe can ever be assigned as the reason why in fact they do not come? This must certainly be an event, absolutely without any cause.

The truth is, when people puzzle themselves upon this subject, and insist, we are not accountable, and cannot be blamed, any further than we have a moral as well as a natural power to do otherwise than we do, what their minds run upon is only natural power after all. They may say they know what we mean by *moral* power, viz. that disposition to do a thing which is necessary towards our doing it; and they mean the same. But however, when they get into the dispute, they get bewildered, and lose sight of the distinction. *They* do not suppose an impenitent sinner, going on still in his trespasses, has a *present*, *actual* disposition, and a sufficiently strong one, to hearken to, and obey the gospel. But something like this seems to be in the bottom of their minds, viz. that he must be *able* to be disposed ; or he must have such a disposition as *would* be sufficient, if he was disposed to make a good use of it. Now this is only to use the word *disposition* improperly, and to conceive it to be a mere natural power ; a price in our hands which may be used well or ill, and which will turn to our benefit or condemnation, accordingly as we are disposed to improve it. The disposition they think of, is not in the least degree virtuous, nor any ways necessarily connected with virtuous conduct. But it may lie still, or go wrong, and will do so, unless a man is disposed, and exerts himself, to make it act and keep it right. The sinner is not helped out of his difficulty in the least, by having such a disposition as this. Yea, should we go farther and say, the impenitent sinner might have a heart to embrace the gospel, if he would take proper pains in order to do it; and he might do this if he was so disposed; and he might be so disposed if he would try; and he could try if he had a mind for it. Yet, if after all, he has not a mind to try, to be disposed, to take any proper pains, to get a heart, to embrace the gospel, or do any thing that is good; he is still in as bad a situation as any body supposes him to be in. There is no more hope of his coming to good so long as this is the case with him, no more possibility of it; nor do we say any thing more in his favour, than if we had only said as the scripture does of the fool, "that there is a price in his hand to get wisdom, " but he has no heart to it." Pushing the sinner's moral depravity and impotence back in this manner, may get it out of sight of those who cannot see above two or three steps, but this is all the good it can do. There is still a defect in him *somewhere;* and such a one as will prove his everlasting ruin, unless removed by such grace as he has never yet experienced.

It must for ever hold true and certain, that if sinners do not come to Christ, it is either because they could not if they would; or else because, on the whole, they are not willing. And if, in the room of coming to Christ, we should substitute some lower and preliminary condition of grace and salvation, it would be just the same case. Suppose it were using means, praying and seeking in the most engaged manner the unregenerate sometimes do; all do not come up to this; and the reason certainly is, they are under a natural or else a moral inability of doing it. Either they could not seek in this manner, if they would, or else they are not inclined to do it, but on the contrary are disposed to employ their time and thoughts about other things. So that bringing down the conditions of the gospel lower, in consideration of the depravity of men ; or supposing common grace, whereby all are enabled to come up higher than they could of themselves, removes no difficulties, at least not those designed to be removed, unless the way of life is supposed to be level to the inclinations of all men ; or that all are, in fact, made willing, and are actually saved.

On the whole, I think the *principle*, that God can in justice require of his creatures, only what he gives them a *moral*, as well as *natural* power to do, must be given up.   Otherwise we are reduced to a necessity of supposing all the blame, if any are lost, must lie entirely on God, and not on them.   And as to those who are saved, they can have nothing to say in his praise, but only that he has been barely just to them.   That having given his Son to obey and die, to deliver them from his law, which was an infinitely unreasonable one, for fallen creatures to be under ; and having given his Spirit to enable them to come up to the otherwise impossible terms of the gospel, he has on the whole, dealt not unrighteously by them.   If, therefore, we think, there is any way to vindicate the righteousness of God in the damnation of any ; or that any thing can fairly be said to the praise of the glory of his grace, in the salvation of them that are saved, we must suppose he is not obliged in justice to give all men *both* those kinds of ability that have been spoken of.   And if we believe that any, in fact, do not obtain salvation, we must conclude they *are not* in both these senses, enabled to obtain it.   Which was all I undertook to prove under the second head.   The

3d. Thing proposed was, to consider the *moral* inability of sinners in this matter.

There is not so much need of labouring to confirm this, that unregenerate sinners have not such a heart in them, as is necessary in order to a compliance with the gospel; because proving the preceding and subsequent proposition, will infer the truth of this. If there is certainly an incapacity either of the natural *or* moral kind, as has now been shown; and if there is certainly no *natural* incapacity, as I am to make appear under the next head; then certainly there must be a *moral* one. Besides, I have time to treat this head but very concisely, considering the importance of it.

It may be proper to be observed here, that the disinclination of sinners, as to some things which are pre-requisite to a compliance with the gospel, is different in different persons. Though even this difference, I suppose, is owing to divine grace, or to God's doing more for one than for another. In the *openly vicious* and *immoral* sinner, there is a prevailing inclination to persist in his dissolute and immoral practices. And there is reason to conclude, that *none* of this character would ever reform, and that *all* would be of this character, if left to their own heart's lusts, without any divine restraints.

In *secure* and *unawakened* sinners, there is no disposition to attend to the concerns of their souls, and seriously consider the state they are in, or to make any solicitous enquiry about the way of salvation. They "make light of these things, and go their way, one to his farm and another to his merchandize." And such is their attachment to the vanities of time, and their aversion to attend to the things of another world, that there is no reason to think, any one of this character, would ever become serious, thoughtful, and engaged about his eternal well-being, if left entirely to himself.

In the *awakened* sinner, though earnest in his enquiries, there is still an utter want of an honest openness of mind, to admit a conviction of the truth. "He

that doeth evil hateth the light, neither cometh he to
the light, lest his deeds should be reproved." . He
whose "inward parts are very wickedness," will always
hate to see, and, if he can possibly help it, never will
believe what he really is.   Hence awakened sinners
very often, never do, and if left to themselves none of
them ever would, "know the plague of their own
hearts."   While they think they are doing all in their
power to increase their convictions, they are all the
while inwardly striving with all their might, against
conviction, and trying to find some plausible ground to
think well of themselves, and to establish a righteousness of their own.   Nor will they ever be sensible how
" deceitful and desperately wicked" their hearts are,
and how hopeless their case is, in themselves, till a conviction of it is forced upon them by the most overbear-
ing and irresistible evidence.

And even in the *convinced* sinner, whose mouth is
most effectually stopped, who is forced to see that sin
is alive and has full dominion over him, and that he is
indeed dead; in him who has the fullest conviction of
every necessary truth, that ever any *unrenewed* sinner
had; there is still, if nothing farther is done for him,
no disposition heartily to approve of the law, or comply with the gospel; no disposition to repent truly of
any of his transgressions, or to receive and be dependent on Christ alone for pardon and salvation; no genuine desire to be saved from *sin*, or to be saved from
wrath in that way, in which God's justice can be vindicated, or his grace exalted. But after all his convictions, there remains still in his heart, a most fixed, inveterate, and unconquerable opposition to all these
things.   Nor will he ever be cordially reconciled to
God, by the mere force of truth in his conscience, any

more than the wicked will be at the day of judgment, or the damned in hell.

That no light, or conviction of the understanding, which the *natural* man is capable of receiving, can be sufficient to draw, or drive him into a true compliance with the gospel, is very evident from what is said concerning the necessity of regeneration. When Nicodemus came to Christ, wanting information about the way of life, our Saviour soon let him know that mere instruction, even by a teacher come from God, was not all that was wanted. Yea, that a man could *receive* no instruction about the kingdom of heaven, to any saving purpose, unless something else was done for him first. See John iii. 3. " Jesus answered and said unto him, verily, verily, I say unto thee, except a man be born again, he cannot see the kingdom of God." And again, to explain the matter farther, ver. 5. " Except a man be born of the Spirit, he cannot enter into the kingdom of God." The necessity of such a change as is meant by being born again, or born of the Spirit, turns upon the truth of man's being by nature, under a *total* moral depravity. Accordingly, our Saviour immediately adds, " That which is born of the flesh, is flesh ; and that which is born of the Spirit, is spirit." That is, a man has nothing truly spiritual or holy in him by the first birth ; but every thing of this kind comes by the renewing of the Holy Ghost. Agreeably to this, the apostle Paul says, Rom. vii. 18. " I know that in me (that is, in my flesh ; in my nature as far as it is unrenewed, and as it was by the first birth) there dwelleth no good thing." And in Romans viii. he says, " The carnal mind," the mind we have as born of the flesh, " is enmity against God ; for it is not subject to the law of God, neither indeed can be." He adds, " So then, they that are *in the flesh* cannot please God."

C

This is the reason we *must be born again.* If there was any thing spiritual in us, as born of the flesh, there would be no necessity for this second birth. If we were not by nature *dead* in trespasses and sins, there would be no occasion for our being *quickened,* by divine power and grace. If sinners were at all inclined to that which is good, they would not need to be *created* unto good works. If a man had not *wholly* lost the divine likeness, there would be no need of being *created* again " after God, in righteousness and true holiness." If the " heart of the sons of men" was not altogether depraved, to the very bottom of it, there would be no necessity of " the old heart's being taken away, and a *new* one given." If men's alienation of affection from God, did not arise from *unlikeness* to him, but only from ignorance and misapprehension about him, no *change of nature* would be at all necessary. Mere light in the head, mere conviction of the understanding, would then produce a cordial reconciliation. Yea, if a man has any degree of righteousness and true holiness, nothing but convictions can be wanting in order to his complying with the covenant of grace, and entering into the kingdom of God. He would no sooner be convinced of the holiness and righteousness of God, but he would feel his heart drawn forth in love to him. He would no sooner be convinced that the law was holy, just, and good, but he would be pleased with it, and loathe himself for all his transgressions of it. He would no sooner be convinced of the unparalleled zeal which Chirst hath shewn in the cause of righteousness, and how he has magnified the law and made it honourable, but he would be charmed with him, and see him to be " the chiefest among ten thousand and altogether lovely." He would no sooner be convinced of the holy tendency of all his doctrines and all his

laws, but he would cordially embrace and cheerfully
obey them. He would no sooner understand that his
design was. to save his people from their sins, but he
would receive him, with all joy and thankfulness, as
his Saviour and Lord.

But, if the hearts of men are totally depraved, entirely destitute of righteousness and true holiness, the
case will be quite otherwise. A holy God, a holy law,
a holy Saviour, a holy gospel, will not surely, then appear lovely in their eyes, but the contrary. Nor will a
clearer understanding and conviction of what they
really are, excite complacency and satisfaction in them,
but the greater aversion and dread. They cannot, in
that case, be cordially united to Christ, until *his* character or *theirs* is essentially changed. They cannot be
drawn to him, unless by force, and against their wills,
till either *he* ceases to be what he is, or *they* are made
new creatures. For " an unjust man is an abomination
to the just ; and he that is upright in the way is an abomination to the wicked." And, " what fellowship
hath righteousness with unrighteousness ? And what
communion hath light with darkness ? And what con-
cord hath Christ with belial ?"

Can a man whose heart is wholly corrupt, and unholy, choose the holy Jesus for his Lord and Saviour,
and cordially embrace the pure and holy doctrines and
precepts of the gospel? Can one who is really and at
heart, wholly in love with the service of satan, enlist,
with any sincerity, into the service of Christ, all whose
work and business is, " to destroy the works of the
devil ?" Can one who is all the while " an enemy in
his mind to God," yea, whose " mind is enmity itself
against God," be delighted with the character and
ways of his well-beloved Son, who is the " brightness
of the Father's glory, and the very image of his per-

son ?" Can one who is not subject to the law of God, neither indeed can be, voluntarily submit to the Mediator, or cordially acquiesce in his conduct in being obedient even unto death, to condemn sin and do honour to the divine law ? Can any one who is an enemy to all righteousness, be pleased with Christ in this view of his character, pleased with him " for his righteousness sake," and for the zeal he has shewn to " magnify the law and make it honourable ?"

This is the reason the Father is well pleased in him as Mediator. And " all that come unto God by him," must be pleased with him in this view also. There can be no true reconcilation between God and man, unless both parties acquiesce in, and are suited with what the Mediator has done, and that considered in the same point of light. God is well pleased, indeed, with the love Christ has shewn for lost men. For the Father was always as benevolently disposed towards this fallen world, as the Son was. But yet had he not as Mediator, shewn a proper regard to truth and righteousness ; had he not " condemned the sin of men," and " given unto God the glory that was due unto his name," the holy governor of the world could not have acquiesced in his mediation. " The Lord was well pleased for his righteousness sake." And if we are not pleased with him in *this* view, but merely for the sake of his kindness and love to men, we do not come into his plan of reconciliation and peace.*

* If that view of the amiableness of Christ, and that well-pleasedness with his mediation, which is implied in a compliance with the gospel, had nothing more in it than only seeing it to be a beautiful thing in him to feel so much interested in *our* welfare, and willing to do and suffer so much to save *us* from misery and ruin ; then indeed no change of nature in the most depraved creature would be necessary in order to it. We may be as wholly selfish and regardless of God's glory

To conclude this head, and the present discourse. If the moral depravity of unregenerate sinners was fully understood, it must undoubtedly appear that this alone is sufficient to account for all that is said in the

as any sinner ever was, and yet be greatly charmed with the meditation of Christ, viewed *only* in the favourable aspect it has upon our interest. And, undoubtedly, thousands have been fatally deceived in this manner; taking this for a discovery of "the glory of God in the face of Jesus Christ," and the effects of it for conversion and sanctification. For such a view of Christ and of God through him, will, under certain circumstances, produce a sort of repentance, love and obedience, in one who was, and continues to be, entirely void of real holiness. Let a sinner only have an impressive sense of the dreadfulness of damnation, and of his danger of it, and in the midst of this have the love of Christ, and what he has done and suffered for sinners, come suddenly into his mind, in a manner that makes him believe, or at least strongly hope, he is one of the happy number for whom Christ laid down his life; and is it possible but that he should be filled with comfort and joy, and have his affections greatly drawn forth towards such a kind and almighty Saviour? And when he comes now to view God in Christ, as his reconciled God and father, he will naturally feel quite otherwise affected towards him too. When he believes God has loved him with an everlasting love, and elected him from eternity to be a vessel of mercy and an heir of glory; his enmity against him will hereupon naturally subside: he will naturally be ashamed and grieved that he has had such unworthy thoughts of him, and has behaved so unsuitably towards him. And such an apprehension of his new state, and of God's great goodness, may produce a lasting alteration in his life. He may be very zealous in religion; and possibly very regular in his morals likewise. Here then is faith, repentance, love, and new obedience, without the least occasion for any conformity to God in true holiness from first to last. Such things as these are the natural growth of the human heart, under such rain and sun-

scripture concerning their inability, and to make the grace of the Holy Ghost as necessary as that makes it. If they have " an evil heart of unbelief," wholly inclined " to depart from the living God," such a

shine. There is no need of any alteration in the soil, or of any foreign seed sown in it.

This may be more clearly conceived by the help of a similitude. Let us then suppose a king that is strictly just in his administration, forbidding on very severe penalties all unrighteousness among his subjects, and very thorough in seeing justice executed on all offenders. A number of his subjects, who are viciously inclined, are uneasy under such restraints, and grow disaffected to their sovereign, and at length form a conspiracy to dethrone him. But before they are quite ripe for executing it, their plot is happily discovered. They are taken and brought to judgment; found guilty, and condemned to die. Their hatred against their prince is hereby greatly increased. One of them, however, is exceedingly dejected in spirit, at the thoughts of his approaching execution. For some time he remains in prison with the rest, in fearful expectation that every day may be his last. But in the midst of his greatest anxiety, a messenger at last arrives with a gracious pardon. He is delivered from prison and from death. Yea, his offended sovereign has set his heart so peculiarly upon him, that, instead of having him executed with his fellow criminals, he is determined to make him a particular favourite at court, and raise him to honour and wealth, far exceeding his former condition before he became a rebel and a traitor. How great the surprize! How insupportable the joy, upon hearing all this! The wretch's enmity and hatred is quite overcome. Especially if he now understands that the king had always a particular kindness for *him*, and never designed any penal laws should be executed upon him, let him do what he would. He is filled with the most admiring sentiments of his injured gracious sovereign, and loves him above all men in the world. But hardly dares look up to him, he is so ashamed of his former temper towards him, and the black design he had meditated against his crown and life. All this does not suppose any alteration in the rebel's real character.

heart will effectually and for ever " turn them aside, so that they cannot deliver their soul." Nor would better natural abilities than they have, be of the least service to them. If ever they come to good, it must be by

All this may be, and undoubtedly will be, though his vicious disposition, which first gave rise to his disaffection to his prince, still remains in its full strength. There is no need of his becoming a new man, a friend to righteousness and an enemy to iniquity, in order to his becoming in this manner, a warm friend to his royal patron and benefactor, considered merely as such. He may be so all his days; may be one of the foremost in his commendation, at least in extolling the great things he has done for him; and he may behave excellently well when under the king's eye, or when he expects he will hear of it, with a view to please him, and yet be at heart as unrighteous a creature as ever he was, even to his dying day.

Now such a kind of reconciliation to God will naturally take place in a sinner if he is only effectually terrified with the thoughts of " dwelling with devouring fire, and inhabiting everlasting burnings;" and then gets a hope of God's love. There is no need of being born again, nor ever having any thing of the moral likeness of God, in order to it. Yea, there is no need of conviction in order to such a conversion as this. I mean a conviction of the equitableness and moral fitness of the divine administration. Light, concerning the holiness and justice, wisdom, or general goodness of God, is not what produces such a change as this; nor is it any way necessary in order to it. Accordingly persons of this kind of piety have commonly no great concern to know what God is in himself, but *only* what he is to them. They have no notion of entering much into the nature and ends of his law, or of the gospel, and seeing into the divine character and glory as thereby exhibited. These are matters of empty speculation with them; things which vital piety hath nothing to do with. They know as much about God's general character; as much about the things the Psalmist prayed that his eyes might be opened to behold; as much about " the things the angels desire to look into" as ever they expect or desire to know.

he have divine power at his service, according to his utmost wish, it would not be to change his heart, but to enable him to act it without control. If, therefore, sinners only knew what hearts they have, this alone would bring them to despair of help from themselves, let their natural powers be ever so good, and make them see that if ever they are saved it will be no thanks to them*.

Sinners inwardly imagine, that if they were only dealt fairly with, they should do well enough. If they perish, they think it will be owing to the fatal influence of some dark decree, or to God's requiring more of them than they *can* possibly do, let them exert themselves ever so faithfully. But he that imagines thus, knows not "the plague of his own heart." "He that trusteth in his *own heart*, is a fool."

* Should we even suppose a self-determining power in the will, those who are dead in sin would not be able to help themselves by it. For who is there to put such a power into action the right way? *They* will not do it. And a self-determined determination, contrary to a man's heart, were such a thing possible, would be no more thanks to him, than the having his heart changed by divine power. It can never be by their own power or holiness, that they are first determined to that which is good, when, by the supposition, they *have no* holiness, and all their power is employed in opposition to it.

× or any understanding

SERMON II.

The natural Ability of Men to understand and embrace the Gospel considered; and the Subject applied.

JOHN vi. 44.

No man can come to me, except the Father which hath sent me, draw him.

THE general observation raised from these words, was to this effect,

That no man is able to comply with the gospel of Christ, without the effectual grace of God.

A principal thing I had in view was to clear this doctrine of the common objection in men's minds against it, as if it represented the Most High, as being insincere and unrighteous in his dealings with sinners. Offering them salvation on terms he knows they cannot comply with; and then condemning and punishing them for their non-compliance with such impossible conditions. Accordingly I undertook, in the first place, to explain and illustrate a distinction of *two kinds* of inability; and to shew that men are, not unfrequently, both in common speech, and in the holy scripture, said to be incapable of actions to which they have an aversion, or which they have not an inclination to perform, as well as of things which they

. could not do, if they were so disposed. As likewise, that there is a real occasion for using this and the like expressions in such a manner. There being, indeed, an absolute impossibility of a man's acting otherwise than agreeably to his own heart, as well as there is of his doing things which exceed his natural strength.

Secondly; I endeavoured to shew, that sinners, while they actually neglect the great salvation, are certainly unable, in one or other of these senses, to embrace it. That so long as they do not come to Christ, it must be true that they want, either such natural ability, or else such an heart as is necessary in order to their coming to him.

Thirdly; I considered the moral depravity of sinners; shewing that they have such an evil heart to depart from the living God, that until their natures are changed it is impossible they should come to Christ, or choose him and his salvation.

We come now, to the

4th and last head proposed; viz. To prove that sinners labour under *no other* impossibility of complying with the gospel, but *only* what arises from their *disinclination* to it; or from the badness of their hearts.

I do not mean, however, nor would I be understood here, to assert this of every individual of the human race. There are undoubtedly great multitudes in the world, who are at present, not under external advantages to obtain that knowledge of God, and of the way of salvation through Jesus Christ, which is absolutely necessary in order to the exercise of faith in him. There are some who were born in heathenism, and never enjoyed the light of divine revelation; there are others who have not the use of natural reason; and there are others who have not, nor ever had, the sense of hearing. I am not now speaking concerning those who

are under these and such like circumstances. What
I here undertake to evince, is only, that persons who
have ordinary intellectual powers, and bodily senses,
and are arrived to years of discretion, and live under
the light of the gospel, labour under no *natural ina-
ability* to obtain salvation : But that if they cannot comply with the revealed way of life, it must be owing entirely to their disinclination to it, or to the badness of
their hearts.

There are multitudes that evidently do not view the
matter in this light. It is needful therefore that this
point be laboured a little particularly.

1st Argument I shall make use of for the confirmation of it is, that it is not God's way to require *natural*
impossibilities of any of his creatures ; and to condemn them for not doing what they could not do if they
would.

God commands none of us to fly above the clouds,
or to overturn the mountains by the roots ; or to do
any such kind of impossibilities. Yea, we are particularly told in his word, that "if there be first a willing mind, it is accepted according to that a man hath,
and not according to that he hath not." If a man has
but little estate, it is not expected or required that he
should give away a great deal to pious or charitable uses.
If a poor widow casts in two mites, when it is all she has,
it is as well accepted as if it were *two millions*. If a
man has never so little strength of body or of mind, a
willing exertion and good improvement of that little is
all that is required of him. This is exceedingly evident from those summaries of the whole law, which
we have both in the old testament and in the new.—
Moses says, Deut. x. 12. "And now, Israel, what
doth the Lord thy God require of thee, but to fear the
Lord thy God, to walk in all his ways, and to love him,

D

and to serve the Lord thy God, with all thy heart, and with all thy soul?" And our Saviour, in answer to the question of the scribe, " which is the great commandment in the law ?" says, Matt. xxii. 37—40, and Mark xii. 30. " Thou shalt love the Lord thy God with all thy heart, and with all thy soul, and with all thy mind, and with all thy strength. This is the first and great commandment. And the second is like unto it. Thou shalt love thy neighbour as thyself. On these two commandments hang all the law and the prophets."

It is evident from these passages, that the whole law, in the highest perfection of it, is level to some kind of capacity which men still have in the present fallen state. We are not to suppose, indeed, it is their moral capacity ; or that all the Lord our God requires of us, is only to love and fear and serve him, as much as we are disposed to do. This would be no *law* at all. It would be a dispensation from all law ; a liberty for every one to walk in the way of his own heart, and treat the Deity just as his inclination leads him.— We are not to suppose a perfect law can come down any lower, than to require a perfect heart, and a perfectly good improvement of all the talents and strength we have. And it is evident, neither Moses nor our Saviour understood the divine law as requiring more than this. To love and serve God with all the heart, soul, mind and strength, cannot mean more than to the utmost extent of our natural abilities, be they greater or less. Some men are not capable of so high a degree of love to God as others, though they are equally upright and well disposed ; because their mental powers are not so great ; or their advantages to get the knowledge of God have not been so good. In like manner some cannot *do* so much for God, for want of opportunity, &c. Now all proper allowances are made in the divine law for things of this nature. The more

any one has of intellectual or bodily strength, or outward advantages, the more is required of him; and
the less any one has of these, the less is required. As
to loving our neighbour as ourselves; this is undoubtedly equally in the power of the weak and of the
strong, of him that is capable of higher and lower degrees of affection, provided he is equally upright, disinterested and impartial.

On the whole, I think it is exceedingly plain and evident, thatGod, in his holy and righteous law, requires no
impossibilities of any of us,but what become so by reason
of our present evil temper of mind, and unwillingness
to exert the natural strength we have in the manner we
ought. And now, if we have natural powers sufficient
for understanding and doing our whole duty; and nothing hinders any of us from coming up to all that sinless perfection, which is required in God's perfect law,
but only our own wicked hearts; I conclude few will
think any thing else hinders sinners of ordinary capacity, who enjoy the outward means of grace, from repenting and complying with the gospel.

2d Arg. That sinners, who enjoy the external light
of the gospel, are not under a *natural* impossibility of
complying with, and obeying it, may be drawn from
what the scriptures plainly teach, and what is generally believed, concerning the great difference that will
be made betwixt such sinners, and those who never
heard of a Saviour, as to their final condemnation and
punishment.

Our Saviour let those cities, where he had chiefly
preached and wrought his miracles, know that their
final doom would be much the heavier for it; and that it
would be more tolerable for even Sodom and Gomorrah,
in the day of judgment, than for them. But this, and
what is commonly said about the great guilt of gos-

pel sinners above others, surely supposes that there is some difference between them and the heathen, as to a possibility of their understanding the way of life, and obtaining salvation. It supposes the former have a real price in their hands which the latter have not. But if the gospel sinner is under a *natural* inability to repent and believe in Christ, an inability arising from any thing else besides his own heart, this could not surely be the case. Why should one who is, and always has been, so weak or disordered in his intellect, as to be incapable of understanding the gospel, be thought a greater sinner for living in a christian land? We do not think this is the case as to ideots, or quite delirious persons. We do not think they will have more to answer for than the heathen will. But if we believe a natural impossibility is required of men in this case, because their natural capacity was impaired or lost by the fall, then for the same reason we might expect, that the heathen who never heard of the gospel, and natural fools who can understand nothing about it, would be punished for not embracing it, as much as any. For they would not have been under those disadvantages had it not been for the apostacy.

3d Arg. It is expressly attributed in scripture, to the evil hearts of men, as the sole cause of impenitence and unbelief under the gospel.

And it ought to be particularly observed, that this is done with professed design to set aside the plea of ignorance which sinners are so exceedingly apt to harp upon ; and to let them see that they are without excuse, " This is the condemnation," our Saviour says, " that light is come into the world ; and men have loved darkness rather than light, because their deeds are evil." In another place he says, " if ye were blind ye had not had sin ; but now ye say we see, therefore your sin remaineth." And again, "if I had not done among them the works which none other man did, they had not had sin: but now have they both seen and hated both me and my Father. Now they have no cloke for their sin." That is, if they had not had those powers of mind, or those means of conviction that were necessary, it is true they would not have been to blame, it would have been no sin in them, not to have believed in and received me as their Messiah. But now their understandings are good enough; and when means, powerful and sufficient external means, have been used with them; their unbelief and rejection of me, can be owing to nothing but the desperate wickedness of their hearts. It is *knowledge* and not *ignorance* of my character, that is the spring of their hatred. Or if any of them are ignorant, it is their own fault. There is light enough, only they hate it, and will not come to it.

4th Arg. That it is not owing to weakness of the understanding, or any *natural* defect, that sinners in general under the gospel are not saved, is evident from the *inferior* abilities of many of those who actually obtain salvation.

It is not men of the strongest and brightest genius, and they only, that understand and embrace the gospel; but they are persons of very ordinary powers of mind, as often, if not oftener than any. "Ye see your calling, brethren," says the apostle to the Corinthians, "how that not many *wise men* after the flesh—are called. But God hath chosen the foolish things of the world, and the weak things to confound the mighty." &c. And our Saviour says, "I thank thee, O Father, Lord of heaven and earth, because thou hast hid these things from the wise and prudent, and hast revealed them unto babes. Even so, Father, for so it seemed good in thy sight." Though God bestows the special influences of his grace, just where and when he pleases, or as seemeth good in his sight, yet he has doubtless always a sufficient reason for fixing upon the particular object of his sovereign mercy, exactly as he does. We are not to conceive of it as a blind partiality, but a wise sovereignty that is exercised in this matter. The reason why not many of the noble and honourable are called, but rather the base and such as are despised, is, we are told, that no flesh should glory in his presence. And the reason why it seemeth good in the sight of God, to hide these things from the wise and prudent, and to reveal them unto babes, may be, and undoubtedly one reason of it is, that hereby it may be made evident; it is not owing to the superior strength of man's natural powers, that they discover the strait and narrow way which leadeth unto life ; nor to their weakness, in respect of natural abilities, that they do not. If babes are able to see the suitableness and glory of the gospel way of salvation, unquestionably wise men might, were it not for something besides weakness of understanding, or any deficiency in the intellect merely. It is evident from hence that natural weakness can be no insuperable bar in the way of men's obtaining salvation, unless they are weaker than babes.

5th Arg. At least this will be undeniably evident, if we consider *what is done* for a person when *these things are revealed unto him ;* or when he is made to see " the things of the Spirit of God, as they are spiritually discerned."

God does not reveal any new truths, not contained in his written word ; nor does he give any new faculties to persons, or enlarge their natural powers of body or of mind, when he enables them to obey and believe the gospel. But what he does for them is, to alter the temper and disposition of their hearts. If we found all that became real christians, however weak before, were immediately afterwards persons of genius and abilities superior to all other men, we should, indeed, have reason to suspect, that the unregenerate wanted better understandings, rather than better hearts, in order to their being able truly to know Jesus Christ, and the way of life. But this is not the case. It is the *heart*, and not the *head* that is created anew, when one becomes a good man. We find the natural powers of men are the same after regeneration as before; and often far inferior to many of their neighbours, who have experienced no such change. It is true, the wisdom of good men runs in another channel; they are wise to do *good*, and apt to get *divine* knowledge; but that is only because they have a taste for these things, and are disposed to take pains about them. " The children of this world are, in their generation, *wiser* than the children of light." They prosecute their own schemes, and make proficiency in what they turn their hands to, and set their hearts upon, beyond what good men do in the things of virtue and religion. What makes good men see the glory of God, which others can perceive nothing of, is not their having more speculative knowledge about the divine character, than others have, or are capable of; but their being conformed to God in temper and in heart; conformed to him " in righteousness and true holiness." This, indeed, makes divine things, and all things of a moral nature, appear in quite a new light; and hence they are said to be *renewed in knowledge.* He that is altogether unholy, let his head be ever so clear, and his speculative knowledge ever so great, cannot have all that perception of holiness, which the weakest saint has, who feels the operation and power of it in his own heart. There is no knowledge like that we get by experience. A man that has never felt a particular kind of pain, we say, can have no idea of it; so of parental affection, one who has never experienced it, knows not what it is. The same may be said of all kinds of sensations and affections; the experiencing them gives a knowledge of them that can no otherwise be obtained. And this holds true with respect to holy exercises and affections as much as any other. Hence, those who are made " partakers of a divine nature," or who have " put on the new man which after God is created in righteousness and true holiness," are capable of a kind of knowledge of God which is peculiar to themselves. Accordingly the apostle John says, " Every one that loveth is born of God, and knoweth God. He that loveth not, knoweth not God, for God is love." 1 John iv. 7, 8. He who is acquainted with the feelings of universal benevolence, in his own breast, has a different idea of him who is good unto all, and whose tender mercies are over all his works," than he whose heart is contracted, and who is truly good to none, has, or is capable of. Particularly he who is conformed in heart to God, sees a beauty in his character and government, which no one of an entirely opposite temper can possibly discern. The reason is, whatever any one regards and is zealous about, he is necessarily pleased to see others regard and be engaged in promoting. Thus if a man values his own particular interest or reputation, as every one does, he is thence unavoidably pleased to see others tender of it, and disposed to promote it. And if a man is benevolently concerned for the public interest, he will in like manner be peculiarly delighted to see others public spirited and zealously aiming to secure and advance the general good. The entirely selfish soul feels as if his own private happiness was the most valuable, yea, the *only* valuable thing in all the universe. Hence if he can only believe, God has set his kindest love on *him*, from eternity; and sent his only Son from his bosom to die for *his* sake (whether necessary or unnecessary, wise or unwise, right or wrong, it matters not;) this gives him the most exalted, the most glorious conception, of the parent and Lord of all worlds, that his narrow soul can possibly contain. But to him that is born of God, and assimilated in temper to his father who is in heaven, things will appear in a quite different light.— To him who is made to be in any measure of a true, a God-like public spirit, an impartial, infinite disposition to maintain universal order, to promote universal good, is the grand, the infinite beauty.

To have the spirit of Christ, or the same mind that was in him, is, in like manner, the only thing which can enable a person to have that sense which all saints have, of the greatness and glory of his redeeming love. Hence it was the apostle Paul's prayer for the Ephesians, "that they being rooted and grounded in love, might be able to comprehend with *all saints*, what is the breadth, and length, and depth, and height; and to know the love of Christ which passeth knowledge." Eph. iii. 17, 18, 19.

And to have a heavenly, that is, a holy temper and spirit, is necessary in order to have a true understanding of any thing heavenly; any thing of " the inheritance of the saints in light," or what "God hath prepared for them that love him." This the apostle very particularly and largely takes notice of, in 1 Cor. ii. 11—15. "For what man," says he, " knoweth the things of a man, save the spirit of man which is in him?" The *spirit of man;* the narrowness, pride, and various corrupt affections by which mankind are actuated, would be very incomprehensible to us, did we not feel, and had we never felt, any thing of the same in our own breasts. We should be perfectly amazed to see how men act, not being able to conceive what inward feelings or principles should excite them to behave in such a manner. *The things of a man;* the enjoyments which fallen creatures so fondly doat on, and so eagerly pursue, to one who never had any thing of their spirit, would be inconceivable; how there could be any thing gratifying or agreeable in them, to any mortal, it would be impossible for him to discern.— " So the things of God knoweth no man, but the spirit of God." The enjoyments of religion and of heaven can no more be perceived to have any thing amiable in them, by one who is entirely destitute of a divine and heavenly temper. " Now we have received, not the spirit of the world, but the spirit which is of God; that we might know *the things that are freely given to us of God:*" That is, the holy delights and entertainments provided for saints in a future world. " Which things also we speak, not in the words which man's wisdom teacheth, but which the Holy Ghost teacheth; comparing spiritual things with spiritual." In describing these future glories and felicities we do not make use of such language as a carnal taste would suggest, or as would be thought the true sublime by the wisdom of this world; but we speak of them in a manner to which we are led by the spirit of holiness. To give us the most elevated ideas of the joys to be expected in heaven, we compare them, not with the idolized possessions and delights of time and sense, but with those spiritual enjoyments, those holy delights, experienced, in some low degree in this lower world. " But the natural man receiveth not the things of the Spirit

f God: for they are foolishness unto him; neither

can he know them, because they are spiritually discerned." The unrenewed sinner having nothing spiritual in him to compare spiritual things with, being a stranger to spiritual joys, or the feelings and pleasures of a truly virtuous mind, they will necessarily seem empty, out-of-the-way things to him, nor can he perceive their true excellence and worth, because their being perceived thus, depends entirely upon the spirit and temper a man is of.

It appears from these passages, that it is neither the having new truths suggested, that are not contained in the scriptures; nor the having the understanding convinced of the truths contained in them; nor the having new faculties of mind given, or the old ones enlarged, or mended, or any-how made better, that enables a man to see God, or Christ, or heavenly things, as saints see them. But that a foundation is, and can be laid for this, only by a man's becoming a saint, or having a new spirit given him; *the spirit which is of G*-*d.*

In a word, whatever is said by some about rectifying the natural faculties, it is very generally agreed, that regeneration is not a *physical* change, but a *moral* one. That it consists not in making men *great,* but in making them *good.* That the new creation is nothing else but the moral image of God, consisting in righteousness and true holiness. But if these things are so, then certainly all the inability that *is* removed, and consequently all that *wants* to be removed, by the renewing of the Holy Ghost, is entirely of a *moral* nature. An inability which altogether consists in the want of an honest and good heart.

6th Arg. This way of conceiving of the impotence of fallen man, does not frustrate, but tends most of all to advance and magnify the GRACE *of* GOD.

Undoubtedly that view of the inability of man, which is most easily and fairly reconcilable with the justice of God, ought to be embraced, provided it does not derogate from the freeness and richness of divine grace in the sinner's salvation. Now I presume there are few, but what are sensible of some difficulty in reconciling God's requiring natural impossibilities, with any notions we have of justice. As if he should require a man to fly, or lift a million weight, or make a world. And should suspend his salvation on the condition of his doing such things as these, which are evidently beyond the capacity of any man, let his disposition be as it will. And should say he had no cloke for his sin, in not doing things of this nature. And that for his not complying with such a merciful proposal of salvation, it should be more tolerable for Sodom and Gomorrah, in the day of judgment, than for him. I say, I believe there are few, but must be sensible of some difficulty in seeing into the reasonableness and justice of this. But then perhaps they may think there is no way to leave room for such a display of divine grace, as we are taught there is in the salvation of men, without supposing something like this to be in fact the case. They may think there can be no necessity of the grace of the Holy Ghost, on supposition sinners can comply with the gospel, whenever they are disposed to do it. But any apprehension of this kind must arise from a very favourable opinion of the goodness of the sinner's disposition. As if he was so willing to use his talents, and improve the price put into his hands aright, that God has no way sufficiently to display his grace towards him, but by requiring things of him, which the holiest creature in the universe, under his circumstances, could not perform. If men are ill-disposed, they so far stand in need of grace to enable them to do that which, without any such divine help, they would find no difficulty in, if they are well disposed. And is it not easy to see, that it will require as much power, and more grace, to change a sinner's heart, than to alter a man's head, or enlarge any of his natural faculties?

The sot who has lived in a course of intemperance from twenty to threescore years, is still under no inability to reform, but *only* what arises from his own appetite and inclination. He might still refuse the glass, and become a sober man, without the advice or help of any one, if his own will was not wanting. But yet no one would think it a less unpromising undertaking to go about to reclaim such a person, than to cure one of a bodily infirmity in which the patient's will had no hand, and which he could not get rid of himself, let him be ever so heartily and steadily, and strongly desirous of it. Suppose such an one, that had had all motives, fetched from this world and the world to come, repeatedly urged upon him, in the tenderest and most forcible manner by all his friends, but without the least effect. Should one at last find means to persuade him into a thorough and lasting reformation, would he not be thought to do as great a thing, as he that should cure one of a natural infirmity that had long baffled the skill of all the physicians?

Moral sickness may be as hard to cure, and require as powerful means, and as able a physician, as natural sickness. And if a man is dead in the moral sense, that is, has lost all principles of true virtue entirely, he is as absolutely beyond the reach of all means, as to their bringing him to life again, as one that is dead in the natural sense. Moral means can only work upon such moral principles as they find to work upon. They cannot produce a *new nature, new principles* of action,

E

any more than natural means can make new life for themselves to work upon in a dead carcase. Cultivation and manuring may make a bad tree grow, and bear fruit, after its kind. But can never make a thorn bear figs, or a bramble-bush, grapes. Let what means will be used, so long as the tree is evil, the fruit will be so likewise. If mankind have lost the moral image of God entirely, it is easy to see that nothing short of a new creation can restore it to them. If they are *dead* in trespasses and sins, the quickening them must be an instance of the working of God's mighty power, in a supernatural manner, like that of raising Christ from the dead. And without a work of this kind, whatever means are used with them, they will never have the least spiritual life, or real holiness.*

* Obj. Regeneration is frequently represented in scripture, as being effected *by means.* Men are said to be born again by the word of God, 1 Pet. i. 23. To be begotten by the word of truth, James i. 18. And Paul says to the Corinthians, " In Christ Jesus I have begotten you through the gospel." But how is this to be reconciled with making the quickening of sinners properly a supernatural work ?

Ans. Almost all the supernatural works recorded in the scriptures, are represented as wrought by means, as much as regeneration is. The red sea was divided by Moses's rod, and the river Jordan by Elijah's mantle. It was by smiting the flinty rock in the wilderness, that the waters were made to flow out of it like a river. Moses brought forth this water, as much as Paul regenerated the Corinthians. It was by throwing a stick into the river, that the young prophet's ax was made to swim ; and by washing seven times in Jordan, that Naaman was healed of his leprosy. It was by prophesying over a valley of dry bones, as represented in the vision of Ezekiel, and calling to the four winds to breathe upon them, that they were converted into a living army. It was with clay made of dirt and spittle, that our Saviour opened

And now does not the admitting such a total moral depravity suppose room and necessity enough for the grace of the Holy Ghost in the salvation of men, without supposing any deficiency in their natural faculties?

But let us compare the two hypotheses, that of a natural inability, and the contrary one which I have now been endeavouring to prove, and we may easily see which gives the highest conception of the grace of God. Those who conceive sinners labour under a *natural* incapacity to come to Christ, place the defect in the understanding. They suppose that ignorance and mis-apprehension is the primary cause of all our enmity and opposition to God. And consequently, that as soon as the understanding comes to be rectified and rightly informed, we of course become reconciled in heart to the ways of God, and pleased with the character and mediation of Christ. This seems to suppose we always had been conformed to God's real

the eyes of one that was born blind. And by calling with a loud voice, that Lazarus was made to hear, and come out of his grave, after he had been dead four days.

Now to suppose that regeneration is effected by means as much as these things were, is not inconsistent with its being properly a supernatural work. But that it is effected by the power of means, is what the scriptures are far from leading us to conceive. It would be thought very remarkable, if any one should undertake to explain the connection betwixt the means used, and the effects wrought, in those instances now mentioned, in as natural and intelligible a manner as some have attempted to do, betwixt light in the understanding, and the production of grace in the heart of a totally depraved sinner. But yet I apprehend, any of those things may be as rationally accounted for, from the known laws of nature, as regeneration can; and that the plain account of scripture as much obliges us to think the former were effected by the power, or natural tendency, or proper causality of means, as that the latter is.

character, in the temper of our minds; and that all
we had been quarrelling with, and enemies to, was
only a false idea of God; or such a character as no
one *ought* to love. As if a very righteous man should
be prejudiced against, and greatly engaged in opposing
another, that was really as righteous and good a man
as himself. But he had been mis-informed about him,
and conceived him to be quite a different man from
what he really was. Now as soon as his understanding
comes to be truly enlightened, or his mistakes are removed, and he gets a thorough acquaintance, the good
man loves the good man of course, without any change
of character in either. But shall we view the enmity
of the carnal mind against God in this light, in order
to have the most exalted idea of divine grace, in the
salvation of such a carnal person? Shall we suppose
that the reason, and the only reason why he is not, neither indeed can be subject to the law of God, is because he does not, neither indeed can understand it?
Or because, through the weakness of his natural powers, he understands it so, as it would be wicked to
obey it, and no truly virtuous and upright mind could be
subject to it, or suited with it *in his sense* of it? In that
case all that is necessary to be done by the divine Spirit is, to inform us rightly concerning the holy nature
and ways of God; and let us know that all our hatred
of him is owing to a *mere mis-understanding;* and that
he is really just such a being as we all naturally love;
even altogether such an one as ourselves. Can there
be a necessity of any thing supernatural, in bringing a
sinner " out of darkness into God's marvellous light,"
if this is all that is implied in it? Yes, it will be said, a
supernatural work upon the *understanding* is still necessary. Though light alone will produce all the
change of heart that is wanted; yet not *objective* light

merely, but what may perhaps be called *subjective*
light. That is, the understanding itself must be strength-
ened, or enlarged, or brightened, or somehow made
better; otherwise the external light, however clear,
will shine in darkness, and cannot be comprehended.

Now if this is the supernatural work of the Spirit
which persons are the subjects of when they are born
again, it is of the same nature as if a natural fool should,
by a miracle, have reason given him.* But is this the
way to advance the grace of God most in our salvation?
Is it the most wonderful instance of rich grace, to give
an intelligent mind to one whose heart was so good,
that he only wanted to have reason enough to understand the gospel, and he would embrace it most cordially as soon as ever it was proposed to him? Does
the grace appear so great in this, as in changing the
heart of one who was an enemy to the *true God?* One
that might have had light enough, only he hated the
light and would not *come* to it? Or one that had had
the light of conviction forced upon him, and had both
seen and hated, both the Father and the Son, both the
law and the gospel?

* It is apprehended this representation of the matter will
be thought unfair, if not quite ridiculous. Men do not mean
to be made natural fools of neither. The weakness, and
blindness, and want of abilities so much complained of, is
nothing of this kind. They would be thought to have as
much wit, as much reason and good sense, as the best, notwithstanding all their darkness of understanding. Nay,
they may exceed even a Locke, or a Sir Isaac Newton, in
clearness and strength of mind, and yet have such weak in-
tellects as to be incapable of understanding truly, the plainest
principles of the oracles of God. Thus the reputation of the
head and the heart are equally taken care of; while the poor
defect, which must bear the blame of all the sin in the world,
is crowded into a corner of the soul, which no soul has, and
therefore, which no one cares how much is said against.

Let any one think how he would address himself to God, with a view to magnify the riches of his grace in saving him. Would he think, that lessening his former *natural* abilities as much as possible, was the way to do this most effectually? Would he acknowledge that man by the fall had lost his rational powers, and was become no wiser than the beasts of the field, and of no more understanding than the fowls of heaven; and therefore that he had been utterly incapable of knowing what a kind of being God was, or what his law required, or getting any just notions concerning Christ and the way of salvation? That no one, whose mental powers were so weak, or so much disordered as his had been, could ever possibly get a true understanding of any of these things? And if God had not been graciously pleased to give him a better *head*, he must inevitably have been lost for ever? Is this, I say, the acknowledgment one would make with a view to glorify sovereign grace, in bringing him out of darkness into marvellous light?—Or would he not rather acknowledge the goodness of God, in giving him rational powers in his first formation, and so rendering him capable of acting a higher and happier part than the mere sensitive creation; capable of serving and enjoying God as a rational creature? Would he not acknowledge that, though God might justly have deprived him of all the peculiar dignities and advantages of the rational nature, for *his own*, and not merely for *Adam's* abuse of them, yet he had not done it? That he had not been denied the use of reason, or the opportunity and means of knowing God as many had been? But, that under all these advantages to know God, he had not glorified him as God, nor been thankful. That he had shut his eyes against the clearest light, turned a if ear to the most gracious calls, and hated the best of Beings ; hated him, not for what he is not, but for what he is ; for his righteousness, for his holiness ; for those very things for which angels and saints, so much admire and love him. And that the more he knew of God and Christ, the more he hated them ; and should for ever have done so, had not divine grace most astonishingly interposed in favour of so vile a wretch, and changed his nature, given him quite another spirit.

It is strange if any *should* seriously think, that displaying abroad their natural weaknesses and infirmities, and alledging these as the only causes why they have not known, or done better than they have, is the way to humble themselves most before God, and to do the most honour to his grace in their salvation.

Those who hold to *natural* inability, and suppose all that sinners want, is to have their understandings rectified, thereby virtually and really, though I suppose not designedly deny *moral* depravity altogether. Should we however suppose sinners are depraved, and even totally depraved, in the temper of their minds ; but that they are so impaired in their natural powers too, as to be incapable of understanding and complying with the gospel, if their hearts were good : this natural inability *in addition* to the moral, would not lay a foundation for a larger and fuller display of divine grace in their salvation, but the contrary. Suppose mankind, when they lost the moral image of God, had lost their reason too, and become fools in the natural sense ; and that when their understandings were restored, they were renewed in the temper of their minds also ; then it is easy to see, they would never have had opportunity to *discover* their moral depravity, as when they had understandings good enough, and have known God, but in works have denied him, being abominable, and disobedient, and to every good work reprobate. It would not appear to themselves, or to any but the Searcher of hearts, what an evil disposition they had been of, and what a moral change had been wrought in them. And consequently, the divine grace toward them, if it was in reality as great, would not be *manifested* so much. But, indeed, the grace of God in the salvation of men, on that supposition, would not in reality *be so* great. The better understandings any have, and abuse, the greater is their guilt; and consequently the greater the grace that saves them.

All that now remains is the *improvement* And,

1. From what has been said, I think it follows, that there is no foundation for conceiving of sinners as being to blame and inexcusable for *part* of their neglect of the great salvation, and not for the *whole* of it; or that they may reasonably be exhorted to do *part* of what is implied in coming to Christ, but not the *whole.* Some seem to suppose that unregenerate sinners are not to blame for not doing things, which imply real holiness, and which cannot be done without it; as repenting truly of their sins, believing in Christ, loving God, &c. But that for not doing other things which may be done without any holiness of heart, as reforming externally, praying, &c. they are altogether inexcusable. But is not this evidently a distinction without any just foundation? Either the *natural* abilities of men must be the measure of their duty, and whatever is short of this, is sin; or else their duty is to be measured by their *moral* ability, and they are to blame no farther than they fall short of doing what they have a heart to do. Now if we are under obligation to do well to the utmost of our *natural* power, and no abatement of duty ought to be made, on account of an evil heart, or the want of a good one; then sinners are ¬ blame and altogether inexcusable, in not forsaking

sin heartily, as well as externally; in not believing in
Christ, loving God, and being cordially obedient to his
will. For none of these things are impossible to such
as are well disposed. But if *moral* power is the measure of duty; if want of a disposition to do other ways
than a man does, renders him excusable and not to
blame; then *all* are excusable, *none* are to blame. The
thoughtless and secure, the prayerless and profane, the
most profligate and abandoned, are as excusable, as
little to blame as any others. For the inclinations of
the worst of men, it may, without any great stretch of
charity, be supposed, are as bad as their actions are.
They are none of them any more wicked than they are
disposed to be; nor have any of them a moral power
to be any better. The dissolute and immoral might
reform, it is true, if they were so inclined. The careless sinner might become serious and thoughtful about
his salvation, might read and hear, meditate and pray,
if he were so disposed. But it is as true, that sinners
might come to the saving knowledge of the way of life,
might repent and believe the gospel, were they so disposed; nothing but a heart is wanting in both cases.
" The vile person *will speak* villainy, and his heart *will*
work iniquity, to practice hypocrisy, to utter error, &c."
We are told that, " the heart of the sons of men is full
of evil." And what they will do, if left to themselves,
we are also told, see Rom. i. 27, 31. " God gave them
over to a reprobate mind;" that is, left them to act
their own minds without restraint; and what was the
consequence? " They were filled with all unrighteousness, fornication, wickedness, covetousness, mali-
ciousness, full of envy, murder, &c." The scandalous
sinner will not become externally reformed without
restraining grace; nor will the secure sinner seek and
pray, and use the means of grace, unless he is awaken-

ed ; any more than a man will come to Christ, without
the drawing of the Father. The drunkard has not a
moral power, that is, a sufficient inclination, to forsake
his cups, while he does not forsake them ; nor the
lewd person to forsake his lewd practices ; nor the
murderer to hold back his hand from shedding of
blood, any more than the natural man has to embrace
the gospel.

There is therefore no propriety in exhorting the
unregenerate, to do *only* such things as are consistent
with an entirely depraved and wicked heart, as if nothing further could be expected of them at present,
any more than there would be in exhorting the most
abandoned of mankind, to do only what is consistent
with their disposition and course of life, because nothing better can be expected of them, till they are better disposed, or are under greater restraints.

Accordingly, there is no such compounding with the
natural man, for what he can do, without a heart to do
any thing that is good, to be met with any where in the
sacred scriptures. God's *present* demand upon every
one of us is, " Give me thy heart." He does not say,
give me thy external obedience only, make a decent
show of seeking and serving me, and it shall suffice
for the present ; for as for thy heart, I know, " there
is no hope, it hath loved strangers, and after them it
will go." The law requires truth *in the inward parts ;*
yea, it demands a perfect heart. " Thou shalt love the
Lord thy God, with all thy heart, and with all thy soul,
and with all thy mind, and with all thy strength ; and
thy neighbour as thyself." Not merely thou shalt
seek and pray for this temper, towards God and man,
but thou shalt *have it.* The New Testament preachers
of salvation through Christ, say, " Repent and believe
the gospel ; repent and be converted that your sins

may be blotted out." The sum of their preaching, "both to Jews and also to the Greeks," was, "Repentance towards God, and faith towards our Lord Jesus Christ." Not testifying, as the manner of some is," that if sinners will do what they can (meaning what their wicked hearts will let them do, what the carnal mind, which is enmity against God, may consent to) they will not be left to perish; but God will undoubtedly have pity on them, and afford them farther help.

Certainly, if the divine law is just, no man can justly excuse himself, or be excused, short of a perfect heart, and a perfect life. And if the gospel is true, there is no safety for any sinner, no ground of dependance that God will have mercy on him, or ever show him any favour, short of Christ, and an actual interest in him by faith. "He that believeth not, is condemned already, because he hath not believed in the name of the only begotten Son of God. He that believeth not the Son, shall not see life; but the wrath of God abideth on him. He that believeth not shall be damned."

It is extremely obvious, that the scriptures every where treat the impenitent and the unbeliever, with as little ceremony as any sinners whatsoever. And it is exceedingly evident, I think, from what has now been said, that reason affords no plea in their favour, but what will equally excuse any sinner in the world, in being as he is, and in doing as he does. If the want of a good heart, is a good plea, every sinner, and every imperfect saint, may avail himself of it to his complete justification. Those who are sanctified but in part, cannot be blamed for being but imperfectly holy. Those who have no true holiness at all, cannot be required to have any, or be blamed if they act as well as they can without it. And, by the same rule, not so much as an external reformation can be required of

those who have no mind to reform. Nothing can be
said to the purpose of excusing sinners on account of
the badness of their hearts, unless we would undertake
to maintain this general principle, that the duty of every
one, must be only according to every one's disposition.
But if this principle is true, every one must easily see,
there can never be any such thing as neglect of duty,
or desert of punishment, or need of grace, in the universe.*

* It has been objected that the phrase *moral inability*, is
used in these discourses, and by many of late, in a different
sense from that in which it has formerly most commonly been
used by divines and philosophers ; and in so large and loose a
sense as has a tendency rather to darken counsel by words
without knowledge. That under this general name we include, and confound together, things of a very different nature, and which ought to be carefully distinguished. That
there is a wide difference between a mere *unwillingness*, or
the prevalency of a contrary inclination in particular instances, and the want of a *principle* from which it is possible a
certain kind of actions should be done, let what motives will
be exhibited, and what pains will be taken. For instance,
between the inability of the drunkard to forsake his cups,
while he does not forsake them, and the inability of the natural man to embrace the gospel.

To this it is replied. In these discourses, under moral inability to that which is good, is meant to be included all that
impotency which consists in *moral depravity ;* whether in
principle or exercise : whether in privation, that is, the want
of moral rectitude only, or in any positive lusts and corruptions ; and whether native or contracted ; whether removable
by moral suasion, or not without a new creation. Now under this general notion of moral impotency, it is granted
there are several things included which in some views are of
distinct consideration, and upon some subjects may be of importance to have carefully distinguished. But these differences, it was, and is still conceived, do not affect the present
enquiry. In every supposeable instance, sin, as far as it pre-

2. From what has been said it may appear, that there is no force in that common plea in the mouth of sinners, namely, "That they did not bring their depravity upon themselves, but were born with it. If their hearts are altogether sinful, they did not make them so, nor is it any of their fault; they have only such hearts as were given them, without their choice or consent." Now, in arguing thus, they evidently view a wicked heart, in no other light than as a mere weakness, which a man would not choose, but cannot help. They consider it as a thing not at all faulty in its *own nature;* so that if they are to blame on account of it, it must be

vails, is inconsistent with the prevalence of its opposite, viz. duty, or holiness; and involves a real impossibility of its opposite's taking place, so far as *it* takes place. Whether depravity is total or partial, native or contracted, transient or permanent, still as long as it continues, and as far as it goes, it implies a kind of impotency and a real impossibility, in regard to having or doing certain opposite things. And if it is of the nature of *moral* depravity—if it is in itself, *anomia,* a *moral* evil, the impotency—the impossibility implied in it, does not in any measure exculpate or excuse, in one case any more than in the other. The divine grace or the manner of divine operation requisite to reform the profligate, and to renew the unregenerate, is different, essentially different.— But as to the question about excusing (the only thing under present consideration) there is no difference; since all the difficulty to be overcome, in either case, is of the nature of moral depravity.—The terms *natural* and *moral* it is true have been used in a number of different senses on different occasions, and there are few words but what have been so. The sense in which they are here used is not however new. Nor is the meaning of natural and moral inability in these discourses, any more large or loose or indeterminate, than the meaning of natural and moral good, or natural and moral evil; natural and moral perfections, or natural and moral infirmities.

F

for something previous to it, and quite of another kind.
Concerning innocent natural infirmities, we justly
judge in the above manner. Thus if a man is sick we
do not blame him for it; we know bodily sickness is no
moral evil. But if we are told the man brought his
sickness upon himself, by intemperance, or some bad
conduct, then we blame and condemn him for that bad
conduct; that was a moral evil, though his sickness is
not so. Now those who make the above plea, reason
just in this manner about *sin itself;* as if it were no sin,
merely to *be a sinner;* or to commit sin when one has
an inclination to do it. But that the *bringing a sinful
disposition upon ourselves,* had we done this, would indeed have been a very wicked thing.

Hence it seems to many, as if the poor sinful children of men, were only as it were under a fit of sickness, which Adam brought on himself and them, by
doing an evil deed which he might easily enough have
avoided, in as much as he was perfectly holy; but that
we his miserable offspring, being by nature sinners,
are under a necessity of sinning, and therefore cannot
be to blame for it. It seems as if *Adam* was in reality
the only sinner, and his *first* sin the only sin of the
human kind; because that sin was committed while
man had not an imaginary, but a real, a *moral* as well
as *natural* power to abstain from all sin. That is, the
first sin did not arise from, or consist in, any defect of
the will; and herein consists the sinfulness of it. If
Adam did not sin before he had any inclination to sin,
and while he was strongly enough inclined to the contrary, it is easy to see, he had just the same excuse for
his first sin, as we have for any of ours. Let his first
sin be placed where it will, whether in actually eating
the forbidden fruit, or in hearkening to any teminta-
tions to do it, or in being off his watch, or in whatever

any one pleases; still we must suppose it committed while his heart was perfectly good, else he did not sin without this boasted excuse of all other sinners—want of a moral power to do otherways. Thus by forgetting that sin is in *itself* sinful, we are led to look for something else that is so, not in sinners, but in perfectly innocent beings! We conceive Adam to blame, because of the uprightness of his heart; and ourselves blameless, because our hearts are so wicked! For in this way we certainly bring nothing but perfect holiness into the account, as an aggravation of Adam's sin, beyond those of his posterity.

The very first idea we can have of sin, is a depraved and wicked heart; and if this is not a blameable thing *in itself*, there is no danger of finding any thing that is so. Could we entirely confound all distinction betwixt natural and moral evil, and so betwixt natural and moral inability, as being things *essentially* different, we should be secure enough from the accusations of our own consciences. And in matters of religion, men generally do confound these things, so far as to feel very easy, and very much as if there *was no sin*. But let a neighbour be very unkind and injurious to them, and they presently see a difference. This does not look to them, just as if he was only lame, and unable to go out of their way; nor do they lay the blame upon Adam, but upon the malicious and unrighteous wretch himself; nor does their being told it is in his *very nature* to be so, make them think much the better of him.

3. If the distinction now insisted on was well understood, and clearly kept in view, it would appear in like manner, that a sinner's not being able to change his own heart, is really nothing in his favour. Here some may be ready to think lies the grand difficulty after all

What they wanted to know, was, not whether sinners *would* be able to comply with the gospel, or to obey the law, if their hearts were good ; but whether it is in their power to have such an heart in them. For what does it signify what a man could do, if he had that which he has not, and can by no means obtain ? 'Sinners do not see how it is their own fault, that they have such bad hearts, and do nothing from gracious principles. provided it is not in their own power to alter themselves in this respect.

Now if a wicked heart was not a *moral evil*, but a thing of the same nature as a weak head, a bad memory, or an infirm constitution, this would be the case. A man is not to blame for having these, provided he cannot help it. But if a wicked heart is a thing of a criminal nature, a thing quite different from any such natural weaknesses, then there is no force in the above reasoning. If to have a heart to hate and oppose God and our neighbour, instead of loving them as we are required, is a moral evil ; as certainly it is, and the sum of *all* moral evil ; then to say a man cannot alter in this respect, is only to say, he cannot help being a most vile and inexcusable wretch. To be unalterably in love with sin, does not surely render one less *sinful*, but the more so. Surely the more wicked a man's heart is, the more faulty and blameworthy he is.

But the fallacy whereby sinners elude their consciences in this matter, lies in a secret supposition that they could not change their hearts, nor would they be changed, though they should ever so *sincerely* and heartily, and *uprightly try* to do it ; which would indeed be a very hard case. If a sinner honestly, and from a truly virtuous disposition, tried to the utmost of his natural power to alter his wicked disposition, *but it would* not alter, he was as bad as ever after all ;

it would seem indeed that he was in a very pitiable situation, but not very faulty. Yea, it would be difficult to see wherein he was *at all* to blame. And that something like this is the real view which multitudes have of the matter, is very evident.

Let us put the case (as people would have it) that sinners were, in all respects, able to change their own hearts; only it must take some time, a *month* suppose; and they must apply themselves very diligently, very faithfully to the work, all that while, in order to accomplish it. There is a sinner, however, that neglects his opportunity and spends the whole month in sin, without ever using any means, or making the least attempt to get a good heart. Is he not to blame now for this? Most certainly he is. But why so? Why so! Does not every one see that such carelessness in a case like this, such indifference about becoming good when it was entirely in one's power, must be inexcusable to the last degree? To continue thus in sin, when there was no manner of necessity for it; surely this can never be justified. But another sinner was much better disposed. He seized the favourable opportunity, and applied himself with the greatest imaginable diligence; and at the month's end, actually became a good man. Now was *he* to blame, during this time that he was thus faithfully labouring, and doing all in his power to become good? By no means. But why not? He had a bad heart. Yes, but he did as well as ever he could, notwithstanding that. No man could have done better, under his circumstances. And he was actually of a wicked *disposition*, no longer, than till he could possibly be otherways.

Thus people would be apt to judge in such cases.— And this shews what notions men have of inability *with respect to* the sinner's changing his heart; as also the reason why they say, the distinction of natural and moral inability signifies nothing. For by whatever *name* it is called, they will conceive of it as being of the same *nature*. If they own it lies in the wicked disposition of the sinner altogether, yet they do not conceive it lies in the disposition he *acts from*, but in a disposition he is *acting against*, but is unable to overcome. They suppose the inability he labours under is such, that he may be well disposed, and do well; yea, that he may be disposed to do the whole duty of one under his circumstances, and actually do it, and yet not be able to help being of an entirely depraved and wicked disposition. Nor could they find the least shadow of an excuse for him, did they not view his case in this absurd light;—did they not consider him as faithfully exerting himself with an honest and good intention, endeavouring to *become good*, but all in vain. Or at least, did they not suppose him willing enough to exert himself in this manner, only he knows it will signify nothing. In this way it is, that a perverse and stubborn will, a wicked and unwilling mind, comes to be thought as innocent a thing, and as good an excuse, as any in the world. It is viewed as a mere weakness; a thing not inconsistent with *trying* to be holy, but inconsistent with being so, let one try ever so heartily; which is the proper notion of *natural* inability. And to maintain this notion, they have a double meaning to every word, by which "the abominable thing" which men are to blame for, can possibly be expressed. They will affix such ideas to every word that can be made use of to express an evil disposition of mind, as to make an innocent thing of it;— a kind of dead weight, which, either they make themselves as easy as they can under, knowing they must bear it; or else are striving with all their might to shake off, but cannot effect it. Thus "deceitful above all things," is the heart of a sinner! Thus artful in hiding itself and keeping forever out of sight, and laying all blame somewhere else! The *heart*, the *disposition*, the *inclination*, the *will*, are readily allowed to be altogether wrong and sinful, while at the same time, what is properly meant by all those words, is still supposed to be good enough; and hence the sinner cannot see how he is to blame. Yea, the very thing for which alone any one *can* be to blame, is looked upon as his sufficient excuse and justification. Thus a deceived heart hath turned him aside, that he cannot deliver his soul, nor say, Is there not a lie in my right hand.

4. We may hence learn, what alone is sufficient to convince a man that his utter impotence does not lessen his obligation in any measure, or afford him the least cloke for his sins. It is only his being made sensible what his impotence really is, and wherein it consists. The apostle Paul says, Rom. vii. 8, 9. "Without the law sin was dead. For I was alive without the law once: but when the commandment came, sin revived and I died." The former of these situations of the Apostle, is that of every sinner who cannot see how it is possible he should be wholly helpless and yet altogether inexcusable, at the same time, and in the same respect. He has no just conviction of "the plague of his own heart." He is alive, and sin is dead. He sees neither his impotence, nor his sin, in a true light. If he saw *one*, he would necessarily see both. Let an unregenerate sinner only see his *real* heart, and he will see that he is helpless enough. And let him only see *this sort* of helplessness, and he will never have a thought of its being of the nature of an excuse. A man never finds himself utterly helpless

in this view, utterly unable to become good, by reason
of his actual wickedness, until he finds all the bottom
springs and principles of action within him, are entirely wrong.   That he does not so much as *intend* to
do his duty, as duty, and never did.   That he does not
mean well, in any thing he does.   This makes him see
that his plowing is sin, and that all his most painful religious duties must be an abomination to him who
looketh on the heart, and knows what they all spring
from. He sees he has no regard for God's glory, cares
nothing what becomes of it, if *he* could but be safe
and happy himself.   He sees *he is dead,* and all his
works are *dead works;* and that he must be created
anew, or he shall never do any thing as he ought.—
But does this view of his deadness make him loose
sight of his sinfulness and guilt? Does he now feel
himself excused and free from blame, because his
heart is so totally depraved, so opposite to God and all
that is good? No. Sin revives just as fast as he dies.
His deadness is seen to be nothing but the very life and
soul of sin. His *having* such a heart, his *being* of such
a temper, that he can do nothing, can delight in nothing but sin, he sees is the very thing that God's law
condemns him to everlasting burnings for, and that
most justly. If such a disposition as he finds himself
now to be of, would extenuate a creature's guilt, there
is not a devil in hell that could ever be damned.—
When a sinner once sees what he really is, his helplessness and his sin are seen to be quite consistent;
and one just as great as the other. For, indeed, they
are *one and the same thing.*

5. From what has been said, it may be easily seen,
that there is no want of *directions* proper to be given
to sinners, but that all the difficulty is, they are not in
a disposition to regard and follow them. People are

always ready to ask, " But after all, what shall sinners
do ? Can you give them any directions how to get out
of this helpless condition? Is there *any thing for them
to do*, or is there not ?" Now this, however common
it is, is certainly very impertinent. If it is a settled
point, that the case with sinners is, they have no heart
to do any thing that is good, people must strangely
forget themselves who ask, " Is there any thing for
them to do ?" As if all the difficulty lay in answering
this question, or in pointing out *duty* to them ! Surely
there is enough to be done, if they would but do it.—
It is easy to direct them to the course they *ought* to
take ; and it would be easy to put them in a way in
which they might have great reason to hope for salvation, if they thought. it a matter worth taking pains
about, and were of a teachable spirit and willing to follow good advice. It is much easier to say what they
should do, than it is to make them willing to do it.—
They *should* become serious and thoughtful about eternal things. They *should* " amend their ways and their
doings." which are not good. They *should* search
the scriptures, take every method, and improve every
opportunity in their power, to acquaint themselves
with God and Jesus Christ—the law—the gospel—and
with their own character and state. They should
" cry after knowledge, and lift up their voice for understanding." They should " seek it as *silver*, and
search for it as hid treasure." They should lie open
to conviction, be willing to know the truth, and to embrace it when discovered. They should not cover their
sins, but be sensible of, humbly confess, and heartily
forsake them. They *should* " return unto the Lord,"
their Maker and rightful Sovereign, submitting to his
authority, owning his justice, and accepting his grace

through the Mediator   Or, in other words, they
SHOULD repent and believe the gospel.

But if they will not follow these, nor any good directions that can be given them, who can help it? If
they will set at nought all the counsel of wisdom, what
good can the best counsel do them? If they do not
hearken to the calls of the gospel, will not come unto
Christ that they might have life, will do nothing proper to be done by persons in their circumstances,
there is, absolutely no help for them, unless God himself interpose, " and work in them to will and to do
of his own good pleasure."

6. According to what has been said, there can be no
reasonable objection against God's giving no encouragement of salvation on lower terms than an actual
compliance with the gospel.   Many are ready to say,
if there are no promises to any thing short of saving
faith, God is not in earnest in his proposals to sinners,
and does not treat them well, but rather trifles with
and mocks them in their misery; for he knows that
no unregenerate sinner can come up to such terms,
any more than he can make a world.   But according
to what has been said, if sinners were but in *earnest
themselves* about their salvation; if they were disposed to *treat God well*, and not to *mock* and *trifle with
him*, there would be no difficulty in the case.   There
were indeed infinitely great difficulties in the way of
our obtaining salvation.   By sin, we had cast such dishonour upon the holy law and government of God, as
it was not in the power of creatures to wipe off.   And
until this was done, it seems not to have been consistent with the honour of God's character and the rights
of his government to show favour to the sinner.   But
Christ has removed every difficulty of this kind.   By
his all-sufficient sacrifice he has made full atonement

for sin, and opened a way for the honourable exercise
of grace. By his obedience unto death he has wrought
out an all-perfect righteousness, for the sake of which
God is well pleased, and stands ready to justify every
sinner who is willing to submit to this righteousness,
and consents to forsake his sins and be saved in this
way. And now he can say, and has actually said, " All
things are ready:" " Ask, and it shall be given you:
seek, and ye shall find; knock, and it shall be opened
unto you. For every one that asketh, receiveth; and
he that seeketh, findeth; and to him that knocketh, it
shall be opened." Past sins are no bar in the way;
for there is " a fountain set open," not only " for Judah
and Jerusalem," but for all the world " to wash in,
from sin and from uncleanness." The greatest unworthiness is no objection; for the invitation is, " Ho
every one that thirsteth, come ye to the waters, and he
that hath no money; come buy and eat, yea, come buy
wine and milk, without money and without price.
Whosoever will, let him come, and take the water of
life freely." Sinners, you have really as fair an opportunity for life, according to the gospel, as probationers
can possibly have; as full a price in your hands, as
your hearts can possibly desire. There is nothing on
earth; there is nothing in all the decrees of heaven;
there is nothing in all the malice and power of hell,
that can hinder your salvation, if you do not hinder it
yourselves. Nor need you be discouraged by reason
of any bad disposition brought upon you by Adam,
which you are heartily sorry for, and would be glad to
get rid of, but cannot. For the *second* Adam is able to
help you in this as well as in other respects; and will
do it in a moment if you in the least degree really desire it. The very thing he came for was to save from

sin, the power as well as the guilt* of it ; and to save whoever desires to be thus saved.   Nor need you imagine, that you must lay out all your own strength first, and do all that can reasonably be required of one under your circumstances; and then may have just an *encouragement* of being saved by *grace* after a life of such perfection.   This is the most reproachful idea of the God of all grace, that you can possibly entertain.   No: If you do so well that it would be hard for God to refuse you salvation, he will consider himself as under *obligation* to save you, and will never desire you should *pretend* to think there is any grace in it.   But he will receive you *graciously* and love you freely, if you desire it, though you have not done so very well.   He means to exercise as much grace, as he would have the honour of, and not to be eternally praised for what is not his real due.   He is willing to save you in as gracious a manner as ever you thought of, or can wish for. Only weigh the matter, and say whether you choose to be saved.   Enter into the nature of gospel-salvation ; attend to the character and laws of Christ.   And then say, whether you will have *him* and be *his ;* whether you are willing and would really choose to exchange the servitude of satan, for that liberty wherewith Christ makes his followers free ; or whether you must plainly say, you love your old master and your lusts, and choose rather, to have your ear bored, and be a servant for ever. But however, " be sure of this, that the kingdom of God is come nigh unto you ;" and if you refuse to have any part or lot in it, be assured, that when the wicked are turned into hell, with all the nations that forget

* The word " guilt" is used by the author as synonymous with *punishment,* as many respectable divines have done before him, but we think not happily.

                                    N. Y. Publisher.

God, it will be more tolerable for *Sodom* than for you. But I must not enlarge farther, by way of particular inference.

On the whole; I am not able to conceive how any one who enters into the matter, can question the propriety of making the distinction insisted on in these discourses; or with what appearance of reason, any can pretend it is an useless distinction. As to the importance of it; it may easily be observed, in how many instances, upon the most leading points, and in the most material respects, by the help of this distinction, common sense will cross the common notions of sinners exactly where the Bible crosses them. It sets reason, and scripture, divine justice, and divine grace, in a quite consistent view; whereas without it, I apprehend they must for ever appear irreconcileable.— It leads good men to see that human infirmities and imperfections, are not such comfortable extenuations of guilt, as they are sometimes ready to make them. That all their *moral* infirmity, all their want of *perfect holiness*, is entirely their own fault; and what they ought to be deeply humbled for, and go mourning under all their days.—It shows sinners, that their perdition is really altogether of themselves : that all ground of discouragement in their case, is their own wickedness. And not their unworthiness neither, but merely their *unwillingness* to be made clean. That this indeed makes their case desperate from every other quarter but the uncovenanted grace of God. In *themselves*, or from any thing that man can say or do, "there is no hope. No, for they have loved strangers, and after them they will go." And as to changing the hearts of such, God has reserved it as the sovereign prerogative of the throne of his grace, to " have mer-

G

cy on whom he will have mercy, and compassion
on whom he will have compassion."—It administers
not so much comfort, indeed, to sinners in their impenitence and unbelief, as they would be glad to have.
But in this awful condition, they have generally comfort enough, such as it is, and too much in all reason.
To kill their self-righteous hopes, and let them see
their guilt and danger, their utter helplessness, and
yet entire inexcusableness, is the kindest thing that
can be done for them.*

* This, however, is the grand objection; the grand reason why it is said, it does no good, it comes to the same
thing when all is done and said. The sinner is as helpless,
and as absolutely dependent on sovereign grace, if his inability lies in his disposition, as if any thing else was the matter with him. For a wicked heart will as infallibly shut a
man out of heaven, if he is left to it, as any thing in the
world could.—Hence very ingenious writers, even though
they make the distinction now insisted on, and by their first
expressions one would think saw the difference, will yet suppose, after all, that the terms of salvation must be level to
the *hearts* of men ; or that *something* must be done, whereby sinners *may* be saved, notwithstanding their *moral* impotence. That things must not be left so, that even " his own
iniquities shall take the wicked himself, and he shall be *holden*
in the cords of his sins."—To say, that " if salvation is offered to all who heartily desire and choose it, and so truly
ask for it, it is offered on the lowest terms," is therefore
treated with contempt ; and it is replied, 'then we may well
say, woe to the sinner whose confidence in his own sincerity
fails him. If a man has not this hearty desire and cannot
create it in himself, he is in a deplorable condition.' Accordingly the scriptures are ransacked for encouragement, if
not promises, to something lower than asking for salvation
or being willing to have it. And the totally depraved heart,
is carefully sounded, to find ground for doings that are not
unlawful, though altogether *unholy*. That upon these better
sort of unholy doings, on one side, and those encourage-

As to the foundation there is for the distinction ;

1. We have seen the *bible* is as express and full in making the difference supposed, as it is in any one thing whatever. We have seen that all the heart, soul, mind and strength ; that is, a perfectly willing and faithful exertion of all our faculties, however enfeebled they are, is all that God requires of us in his perfect law. Nor is there a single instance of natural impossibilities being required of any man, in all the sacred records. Nor is it once intimated, that *natural* impossibilities *might* justly be required of us, because our natural powers were impaired by the fall. But, on the other hand, we have seen that the most absolute *moral* impossibilities are required of all men, without the least scruple, as if there was no kind of difficulty in them. That a perfect heart and a perfect life, are as much required of men now, as if they were not fallen creatures; and required of the greatest sinner, as much as of the best saint. No peculiar provisos are made, in favour of even the most abandoned. Nor is it once intimated, any where in scripture, that the reason why men may be required to do that which is lawful and right, though it is contrary to their inclination, is because Adam did that which was unlawful and wrong, contrary to *his* inclination. Or that all the reason why a wicked heart is not entirely innocent, and a good excuse, is because man brought it upon himself, by his own folly and wickedness, before he had any thing of it. We have seen, that the way our Saviour took to convince men, that their rejection

---

ments on the other, a bridge may be built over all impossibilities of every kind, so that no sinner shall be in a deplorable condition, by reason of his moral depravity. But every one *may* get to heaven *in spite of his heart.* This is making distinctions that are something to the purpose !

of him and his gospel was their sin, was by shewing them, that it could proceed from nothing but the badness of their hearts; and not by leading them to believe it was primarily owing to a mere weakness or disorder in their *understandings* occasioned by the original fall. He readily admitted, that if men were blind, or if they had not sufficient means of information and conviction, their unbelief would be no sin.— Nor does it appear that any unbelievers in those times, had refined so far as to reply in their own vindication, that they could not help hating the light, because their hearts were evil. This seems to be a cloke for unbelief, of a more modern invention.

2. We have seen that *common sense*, most readily and fully gives into such a difference as this, in all common cases; in every supposable case in which the vindication of our own character is not concerned.— Yea, in cases where men are most interested, and most straitened for a plea in their own justification, they rarely think of pleading a bad intention and a very wicked heart. If a man, when questioned for a supposed faulty action, can shew that it was an oversight, and not owing to any ill design; or if he can make it appear, that he had not opportunity or capacity, to do better than he did; these are always allowed to be things to his purpose. But it is rare that any one undertakes to excuse himself, as to any injurious conduct, or omission of duty with respect to his fellowmen, by shewing that he is, and always was, of an exceeding wicked and unrighteous disposition, and that his *heart* was quite as bad as his *conduct*. No one, unless he was out of his wits, would ever think of making such a plea as this before a human court. It is only in matters of religion, and before the divine tribunal on their last decisive trial, that criminals them-

selves think of making this plea, or that it would avail any thing unless to their greater condemnation.

And we have seen that the reason why sinners are ready to look upon a wicked heart as a good excuse in matters of religion, is because they *mean* no such thing by it, nor do they think they *have* any such thing as a heart at all wicked. When they talk of moral depravity, deadness in sin, want of a disposition to that which is good, &c. they really mean by such expressions—they know not what. Something that is consistent with their *sincerely* wishing, desiring, and *endeavouring* to the utmost of their natural power, to do their whole duty. And this is all the reason they think a bad heart is an excuse with respect to these things, any more than in other cases. This is the reason why, in their view, " sin is dead," and looks like such a kind of thing as must necessarily always be dead ; it not being possible in the nature of things that it should be alive, longer than just to bring itself into existence.

It may therefore, notwithstanding this seeming exception, well be considered as a quite universal dictate of common sense, that the want of a heart, and the want of natural capacity, in regard to excusing men, are entirely different things.

3. We have seen that *reason* discovers a just foundation for this decision of the moral sense, and of the scriptures, as clearly as it discovers any thing of a moral nature. We have seen that an ability to act otherwise than agreeably to our own hearts, would only be an ability to act unfreely and by constraint : that actions which are done contrary to, or without our wills, are actions for which *we* cannot in reason be accountable : that only taking away moral necessity the necessity of men's acting or not acting accord-

ing to their own disposition and choice, unavoidably subjects them to a fatal necessity, a necessity of acting otherwise than they would choose, or whether they will or no. Reason plainly teaches, that things done under that necessity which arises from our own hearts, and that which is against them, are just as different, as things in which we are the agents, and things in which we are not :—just as different as Peter's girding himself when he was young, and going whither he would, and his being girded afterwards, and being carried whither he would not :—just as different as a man's wilfully murdering himself, and being murdered by another, in spite of all he could do in his own defence. We have seen, that if want of holiness excuses a person in being unholy, and if a disposition to sin excuses a person in sinning, then every unholy creature, every sinner in the universe, is perfectly excusable.

Thus if *scripture, reason,* and *common sense,* all concurring in the fullest manner, can confirm any thing, an essential difference betwixt natural and moral inability, the inability which arises from our own hearts, and that arising from any other quarter, is most fully confirmed. Nor can any one say, that these two kinds of *cannot,* come to the same thing, as to excusing men, without contradicting the *highest degree* of *every kind* of evidence we can have, of any moral truth.—He that hath an ear, let him hear.

The Perfection of the Divine Law, and its Usefulness for the Conversion of Souls.

A SERMON,

Delivered in the College-Chapel, in New-Haven, on the Morning after the Commencement, 1787.

By JOHN SMALLEY, *D. D.*

PSALM xix. 7.

The Law of the Lord is perfect, converting the soul.

SOME are said to teach such doctrine concerning regeneration, as supposes that *no means* can be of any efficacy or use, in the case of the unregenerate. Many, undoubtedly, have no opinion of *legal preaching*, as adapted to promote the salvation of men. It will, however, very universally be agreed, that means are to be used for the conversion of sinners, as well as for the perfecting of the saints. And I believe there are few who will not admit that the law ought to be preached, for both these purposes, as well as the gospel.

Good men may dispute about words ; and they may have different ideas, in many matters of nice speculation : But all good men delight to meditate in the law of the Lord ; and all good gospel ministers desire, by all lawful means, to be instrumental of the conversion of souls. For these reasons it is presumed that the words now read, if properly opened and illustrated, will not be uninteresting, or unentertaining to the present audience.

The general subject of this psalm, is the glorious manifestation which God had given of himself, by the light of nature, and by the light of revelation. In the first six verses are set forth, in lofty language, the illustrious displays of the divine perfections, in the works of creation and of common providence. *The Heavens*, it is said, *declare the glory of* God ; *and the firmament sheweth his handy work. Day unto day uttereth speech*, &c. At this seventh verse, the psalmist passes from the works, to celebrate the *word* of God, as discovering yet greater glories, and as being productive of still more wonderful effects. *The law of the* Lord *is perfect*, says he, *converting the soul : the testimony of the* Lord *is sure, making wise the simple. The statutes of the* Lord *are right, rejoicing the heart : The commandment of the* Lord *is pure, enlightening the eyes.*

By the law of the Lord may be meant, the whole revelation of God's mind and will, which had then been given to mankind. But what is here said of it is especially applicable to the *moral* law ; and to this only, particular attention will be paid in the present discourse. Two things are asserted in the text concerning the divine law. In regard to its intrinsic excellence, it it said to be perfect : respecting its use, in the present fallen state, it is spoken of as converting the soul. Accordingly it is proposed,

1st. To consider the perfection of the law of God ; and

2d. Its subserviency to the conversion of the souls of men.

The perfection of the divine law first claims our careful attention.

If it be asked in *what respects* the law of the Lord is perfect; the general answer is, in *all* respects. Like its glorious author, it is *light*, and in it *is no darkness at all*. But since an apostle hath said, *the law is holy, and the commandment is* holy, *and* just, *and* good; it may be proper to illustrate these three perfections of the moral law. more particularly.

First then, the law of God is *perfectly holy*. This appears in its prohibitions, in its requirements, and in its sanctions. *I have seen an end of all perfection,* says the psalmist, *but thy commandment is exceeding broad.*

· So extensive is the divine law that it forbids *all sin;* even in the very inclination of the mind, as well as in all manner of conversation. Human expositions, of old time, had indeed given it a more limited construction; as though, like the laws of man, it respected only overt acts, and the grosser instances of iniquity. But our divine teacher, who was in the bosom of the father, hath expounded it in a latitude becoming the law of the most holy God, who looketh on the heart. In his exposition it forbids not only actual murder, gross adultery, and bearing false witness; but every idle word, every lascivious look, and every first emotion of unreasonable resentment.

Nor hath he explained the law only to forbid all *po- sitively* evil volitions and exercises; as if no positive duty, on the contrary, were required. As if, *to him that knoweth to do good,* only *not* to do it, were no sin. As if bare *omissions* and *neglects*, were no more criminal in a rational creature, than in stocks and stones. According to our Saviour, and indeed, according to the letter of Moses, the law saith, not merely, thou shalt not *hate ;* but thou shalt *love.* Being benevolent and doing good, to the utmost of our capacity, is plainly enjoined ; as well as every thing that is positively evil totally forbidden.

The law is likewise glorious in holiness, in its awful sanctions. It requires sinless perfection, as now explained, on no less severe a penalty than everlasting indignation and wrath, tribulation and anguish. It says, *The soul that sinneth, it shall die. The wages of sin,* without exception, according to law, *is death.* The *soul's* death ; its eternal perdition.

Secondly, I am to show that this law is *just, perfectly just ;* in all the strictness of its *precepts,* and in all the severity of its *curse.* These will require a distinct consideration. Both are disputed by the carnal mind.

To the justice of the preceptive part of the divine law, indeed, what can human reason object ? May we not justly be required not to sin ? Not to sin at all, in omission or commission ?—The only objection is grounded on imbecility. " Were we able, doubtless we ought to keep ourselves from *all sin,* and might justly be so required. But this is by no means possible for the best of men. *There is not a just man upon earth, that doth good, and sinneth not.* And certainly to require that of us which is not in our power, is palpably unjust."

The objection seems strong, though built upon weakness. It is plausible ; but it is not unanswerable. If the meaning be, that more is required of us than would be in our power were we of a perfect heart ; I deny that, in this sense, any thing in the commandments is above our capacity. *If there be first a willing mind. it is accepted,* in all cases ; God's perfect law always accepts it, *according to that a man hath.* Where much is given, much is required; and where little, so much the less. Whether we have five talents, or two, or one, the perfect improvement of the talents we have, is all that is exacted. However weak our minds, or little our strength, to love the Lord our God with all our hearts—with all our *weak* minds, and *little* strength, is the whole of the first commandment of the law. There is none other greater than this, or more difficult to obey. Did we thus love God, we should keep all his commandments; and none of them would be grievous.

But if it be meant, that we have not a *perfect heart and willing mind*, and therefore sinless perfection cannot justly be required of us; what is this more or less than saying, We have not a disposition to do our whole duty, and therefore our whole duty cannot in justice be enjoined? What is it but saying, We have a great inclination to do iniquity, and therefore we ought to be allowed to do some iniquity, in all reason and righteousness? *Is the law sin*, because we are sinners! Is that to be condemned because we are disposed to transgress; when it would be altogether reasonable, had we only an inclination to obey! If the divine law, in order to its being just, ought to be lowered at all, on account of the depravity of the hearts of men; for the same reason it must be brought down entirely to every man's heart, however depraved, or it will not be just. Let this objection be carried as far as it will necessarily go, if there be really any thing in it, and it will come to this, that no law can be just, which requires any man to be or do, more or better, than exactly as he is disposed.

I am sensible that it is one of the hardest things in the world, to beat this objection out of the heads and hearts of men ; notwithstanding the stupidity of it is so exceedingly obvious.   And no wonder ; for as long as any man can wink hard enough not to see the absurdity of such a way of reasoning, from the painful reproaches of his own conscience, he is so far entirely free, and feels completely self-justified ; whether an imperfect saint, or a most profligate abandoned sinner. But I believe it will be found at last that there is the same law, as a rule of duty, for the one and for the other.   A law which alters not as men alter in degrees of moral depravity.   And that according to this law, which requires the wickedest of all mankind to be perfectly righteous, every mouth will be stopped, and all the world, notwithstanding the present boasted plea of being sinful fallen creatures, be found guilty before God.   The only question is, which ought to be condemned, an imperfect creature, or a perfect law ! The creature, because his heart is set in him to do that which is perfectly wrong ; or the law, because it insists upon that which is perfectly right !

We are next to consider the justice of the penalty of God's holy law ; and to show, that as he doth not lay upon man more than is right in its perfect requirements, so neither will he in the infliction of its awful threatenings.

Eternal death for every transgression and disobedience, is a dreadful punishment, indeed, and undoubtedly it seems to many, when they seriously think of it, excessively severe.   " Can every idle word, every evil thought, every unlawful wish, every deviation, in the smallest punctilio, from perfect righteousness, really deserve everlasting destruction ! Can even any crimes, of a finite creature, committed in a momentary life, justly merit endless misery !"

To this it may be replied. The sins we commit, however little many of them may appear in other respects, are transgressions of the law of the great eternal God. In this the evil, even of the grossest immoralities, as it were, wholly consists. Hence David, when he had been guilty of the atrocious crimes of adultery and murder, says, in his penitential confession to God, *Against thee, thee only have I sinned.* And hence St. Paul speaks of sin as becoming, by *the commandment*, *exceeding sinful.* If all the evil of sin consisted in the present injury done to creatures like ourselves, temporal death would be a punishment too great by far for most offences. Were there no God, or had God given us no law in any way whatever, and had our iniquities no respect to him, many of them would be truly very trivial. But *Disobedience is as the sin of witchcraft.* And the criminality of disobedience is ever supposed to be enhanced, in some proportion to the authority commanding, and the obligation we are under to obey. Now the authority of God our Maker, and the obligations we are under to be obedient in all things to Him, are absolutely infinite. Infinite, therefore, must be the sin of breaking His laws, and dishonouring Him.

This is the common way of vindicating the justice of endless punishments. And certainly, known transgression of an express command of the infinitely great and glorious God, must be sinful beyond conception. But that every moral evil, in the most ignorant rational creature, so far partakes of this aggravation as to be a crime absolutely infinite, is a thing which cannot perhaps easily be *made manifest to all men.*

I therefore desire that it may be seriously considered, whether the ill desert of sin, whatever may be its aggravations, be not of such a permanent nature, that it may justly be punished with the fire which never shall

H

be quenched. It may be a question worthy of consideration, whether any crime, be it greater or less, will not deserve the same punishment forever, that it deserves at first. Perhaps suffering pain can never take away blame-worthiness on account of sin : and perhaps as long as blame-worthiness remains, just desert of punishment must remain. Both these I believe, are real truths, and that they would be felt as such by every man's conscience, could all misapprehensions be prevented.

That suffering doth not, in any measure, take away the blame-worthiness of one who hath committed sin, may easily be perceived to be a plain dictate of common sense. After any criminal hath been punished as much as the laws of men require, is he ever thought to be at all less blame-worthy than he was before? The *damage* which his crime has done, or had a tendency to do, to the public, or to individuals, may be compensated or prevented by his punishment; but does any one suppose he is for that reason *blameless*, just as if he had never offended? Is he ever thought to be any freer from actual guilt, than if he had been permitted to escape with impunity? Has he less sin to repent of, or less reason to judge and condemn himself, because he has been imprisoned or scourged, or branded, according to law? The lash may change the Ethiopian's skin, or the leopard's spots; but it can never make a criminal innocent. Nothing is more evident than this, that crimes are not to be obliterated, and innocence restored, by involuntary sufferings. Sin is ever so written with a pen of iron, and the point of a diamond, as never to be effaced in regard to the ill desert, or blame-worthiness of the sinner.

That as long as blame-worthiness remains, just desert of punishment must remain, is what I apprehend

would also appear a plain dictate of common sense,
were it not for some confusion of thought arising from
inadequate comparisons; or from confounding ideas
which are really different. I know we are apt to think
that when a culprit hath suffered a certain number of
stripes for a crime, for that particular offence he deserves no more. But I suppose the only reasons why
we think thus are, either because in that case we measure desert by the law of the land, which is the judge's
rule, beyond which he has no right to go: or else, because we measure desert by the supposed need there
is of punishment. To punish beyond *law*, is wrong in
a *judge*; it is illegal. To punish beyond *necessity*, is
wrong in a *legislator*; it is *unmerciful*. But deserving punishment according to human laws, and deserving it in justice, are two things. Whether it would be
necessary to punish, and whether it would be just, are
also two things. In point of strict justice, abstractly
from mercy, and from all idea of a limiting law, I
think it must be a clear case, that blame-worthiness
and punishment-worthiness, are ever exactly commen-
surate. That just as much, and just as long, as blame
is deserved, punishment is deserved. Until therefore
the sinner can stand up before his eternal Judge, and
truly say, I have suffered so much, or so long, that I
am become *perfectly innocent*, and deserve not to be
faulted at all; he cannot plead releasement from prison,
and from all further pains and penalties, as a matter of
absolute justice. But I believe a sinner may suffer to
all eternity, before he will be able truly to say this, of
whatever magnitude his sins may have been.

This way of accounting for endless punishments, is
far from supposing that all sins are of equal demerit.
It does not go upon the supposition that they all, nor
any of them, deserve infinite punishment. It only sup-

poses that the ill desert of every sin, is durable, unalterable, and everlasting. The degree of punishment, which men deserve, is in proportion to the numbers and aggravations of their iniquities : but that degree of punishment, whatever it may be, they will deserve forever. Little things may be as lasting as things that are great. The soul of man is not infinite, yet we suppose it will exist without end.

If neither of the foregoing solutions should satisfy ; there is yet another way of vindicating the sentence of eternal condemnation, as perfectly just. It may be considered as a sentence of reprobation to endless sin, and to endless misery as the necessary consequence. Certainly it is a righteous thing in God to say, whenever he sees fit, *He that is unjust, let him be unjust still ; and he that is filthy, let him be filthy still.* The most High is not under obligation in justice, to keep his creatures from falling into a state of sin and misery ; surely then we cannot suppose him under any such obligation to recover fallen creatures to holiness and happiness. Those finally left to themselves will forever sin ; and for this they will deserve to be forever vessels of wrath. Sin can never be innocent, or undeserving of punishment, by reason of the peculiar circumstances in which the sinner is placed. Being in a state of probation, and in a world of hope, is not certainly the only thing which renders impenitence, blasphemy, malice, or any kind of iniquity, culpable, and worthy of divine indignation. It is true we read that in the other world, every one shall receive according to the deeds done *in the body,* whether good or bad. But this needs not to be understood as implying, that nothing shall ever be received for things done after this life is ended. It may only mean that all, by the sentence of the Supreme Judge, will commence their fixed future existence in a degree of happiness or misery, proportioned to their good or evil conduct in the present probationary state. There are ways, undoubtedly, in which the perfect justice of God's holy law in its penalty, as well as in its precepts, may be fairly and fully vindicated.

We proceed to the vindication of its perfect goodness. A good law, is one that is necessary and well adapted to answer good ends. However pure or equitable a law may be, yet if it be needless, and will do no good, it cannot well be called a good law. A law perfectly good, lays no duty on the subject, nor any penalty on the transgressor, however justly it might be laid, but what is requisite for some important or beneficient purpose.

That the divine law, in the preceptive part of it, is thus perfectly good, may very easily be evinced. We may be sure that the commandments of God are perfectly good, because they require perfect goodness, and nothing but goodness. From those summaries of the moral law, which are given both in the Old Testament and in the New; and indeed from an attentive perusal of the whole book of the law, it is easy to see that the *law of kindness*, comprehends the whole law of God; or that every duty enjoined in the law and the prophets will readily and necessarily flow from love of God and our neighbour. *Love is the fulfilling of the law;* and such a law must certainly be dictated by love. No laboured proof will be required to convince any man that a law is good which obliges all others to be perfectly benevolent and good to him; and will any one be so inconsistent as not to acknowledge that it must be likewise a good law, which commands *him* to be perfectly benevolent and good to *all others.*

Besides, it is easy to show, that all the duties enjoined upon us are necessary for our own good, as well as for the glory of God and the good of our fellow creatures. We may truly say as Moses did, Deut. vi. 24. *The Lord commanded us to do all these statutes, for our good always.*

Is not this evidently the case in regard to the personal duties of sobriety and temperance ? Certainly it would not have consisted with a perfect attention to our private temporal happiness, for God to have given us a law allowing us to live in luxury and excess, in gluttony and drunkenness. It is requisite for our worldly interest, for our bodily health, and for our best enjoyment even of the pleasures of sense, that we should deny ourselves those inordinate, sensual gratifications which are made unlawful in the word of God. Fleshly lusts war against the soul, and against the body too. To abstain from them as we are commanded, is necessary for the comfort of the life that now is, as well as in order to the happiness of that which is to come.

Is not this evidently the case in regard to the commands of righteousness and charity towards our neighbour ? It is generally found to be most for the security and advancement of a man's wealth and outward estate, and is always most for his real happiness, to do justly and love mercy ; to provide things honest in the sight of all men, and to be as liberal as the divine law requires. All the commanded social affections, are delightful affections ; and all the forbidden unfriendly passions, are painful passions. Had nothing been in view but only our own felicity, the feelings and duties of humanity could not have been enjoined otherwise than they are.

Is not this also evidently the case in regard to the duties of religion ? The tempers and exercises commanded immediately toward God? Can any thing be more essential to our highest happiness, than to remember our Creator, and trust in him? to fear and love the greatest and best of beings, and to worship him in spirit and in truth?

Every one who rightly understands the statutes of the Lord, and knows what it is to obey them in sincerity, can testify with David in the context; *more to be desir; d are they than gold, yea, than much fine gold ; sweeter also than honey, and the honey-comb. Moreover, by them is thy servant warned: and in keeping of them there is great reward.* The ways of God's commandments are all ways of our truest wisdom.— Not only will they be infinitely profitable in the end, but for the present, they are ways of pleasantness, and paths of peace. How much more would good men find them to be so, if they observed them wholly, and with a perfect heart.

But perhaps it will be supposed, that the perfect goodness of the *curse* of the law, cannot so easily be made evident. I think, however, it may be shewn beyond contradiction, that we have no reason to believe the contrary. Not only the threatning, but the actual infliction of eternal death, for transgression and disobedience, for any thing that we can tell, may be dictated by perfect goodness. Not goodness to the individuals who are made to suffer this awful penalty, to be sure. Their good is given up. But goodness to the universe. We know not what severity against sin is necessary, for all the important purposes of perfect government, in the vast dominion of God. That other ends are proposed by penal laws, and the execution of them, in all communities, besides the good of the punished, we well know. A regard to the safety of society, to the support of government, and to the sup-

port of his own character, will influence a good earth-
ly judge, to condemn criminals of certain descriptions, to perpetual imprisonment, or to death; notwithstanding the tenderest feelings of humanity towards the unhappy sufferers. The same reasons will
influence a good legislator to enforce his salutary
laws with such terrible sanctions, when he supposes
nothing less severe would be sufficient. In like manner, it must unquestionably seem good in the sight of
the Supreme Ruler, who is perfectly benevolent, to
punish the transgressions of his infinitely important
statutes with eternal death, if the support and display
of his own holy character, and the greatest good of
the creation, so require. And why should it be thought
a thing incredible, that this should be the case? The
characters of law-givers and judges among men, are important characters; and it is incumbent on those who
sustain these characters, carefully to support them,
by enacting just laws, and by judging righteous judgment. How much more important the character of
the *Supreme Legislator and Judge of all worlds?* And
how much greater the necessity of its being perfectly
supported?

The declarative glory of God, as it concerns himself, is an end of inconceivable weight. It is the
highest end that can possibly be promoted. It is also
a matter of the utmost consequence to all the good part
of the intellectual creation; to holy angels and just
men. In his light they see light. In the light of His
countenance—in the knowledge and contemplation of
His perfections, is their supreme felicity. By the declarative glory of God is meant, the manifestation of
His essential glory; the giving rational creatures true
ideas of His real attributes. In order to this, it seems
necessary that He should make himself known by His

works and ways. This therefore is the method He hath taken, and which it is to be supposed, He will forever pursue. By works of *power*, He shows that He is *omnipotent :* By *doing good*, He shows that He *is good ;* and by *awful judgments* on the workers of iniquity, He shows that He is, beyond comparison, *glorious in holiness.* It may reasonably be presumed, that, for the sake of His declarative glory, in which He so much delights, and which is so essential to the good of created intelligences, it is necessary that these, His several perfections, should be thus eternally displayed.—This seems to be the account which we have in the scriptures, of the wise and good ends both of temporal and eternal punishments.

When Pharoah was drowned in the red sea, there was this good end to be answered by it, that God's name might be declared throughout all the earth.— And the Apostle says, *What if God, willing to shew His wrath, and to make His power known, endured with much long-suffering the vessels of wrath, fitted to destruction: and that He might make known the riches of His glory on the vessels of mercy, which He had afore prepared unto glory ?* We are sufficiently let into the reasons and ends of the wrath to come, to have rational grounds to believe that the law which punishes sin with eternal death, on the larger and universal scale, is perfectly good. Certainly it must argue great arrogance, rather than superior penetration, in any man to be confident of the contrary. Who but one who knows how to govern the universe, in the wisest and best manner, can safely pretend to say, that endless punishments, though just, cannot be necessary, nor answer any sufficiently important purposes? But it is time we proceed to consider as was proposed :

II. The subserviency of the perfect law of God, to the conversion of the souls of men.

There is such a thing as giving a new heart, or renewing a sinner in the spirit of his mind, which I conceive is by the supernatural power of the Holy Ghost; and in which the power of means can do nothing, more than in other supernatural works. But by converting the soul, I suppose, is here meant, correcting the errors of the understanding, and causing the heart actively to turn from evil and false ways; to the ways of truth and righteousness. This is by moral suasion, or by the moral power of the word; not indeed, independently of divine power, for thus no ordinary effects are produced. In this active conversion, this turning men from darkness to light, and from the power of satan unto God, I conceive the divine law has an essential instrumentality from first to last; and that it is as necessary for thus converting souls under the present dispensation of grace, as it was in the days of David.

It is by the law, that a sensible man will most likely be converted from *infidelity*. As long as men are ignorant of the law of perfection, or do not believe that they are under any such law, they will naturally, if rational and free thinkers, reject the grace of God which bringeth salvation. They see no need of it, and are therefore ready to look upon it as a cunningly, or rather, perhaps, a foolishly devised fable. But let them once be convinced, by sound reasoning, that they are bound by the law of nature, to sinless perfection; let them once see themselves shut up under perfect law, to the faith of Christ, as the only certain door of hope, and they will no longer make light of the Christian revelation, and discard it as a needless, trifling affair.

It is by the law, that man must be converted from any gross *heresy.* All essential errors, respecting the doctrines and design of the gospel, begin in loose notions of the law; and the most effectual way to correct them, is by bringing men back to this original standard of right, between God and man. Here the ideas are most plain and simple. Here the truth most readily commends itself, to every man's conscience. And the law, rightly understood, is the only easy, the only possible key, to all the grace and truth which come by Jesus Christ. Had no learned doctors in divinity been without law, some other elaborate and very curious keys to the apostolic writings, would probably never have been invented. Viewing the law, as not requiring us to be any other than imperfect creatures, just such depraved creatures as we actually are, it is really necessary to have recourse to very subtle criticisms, and to dig deep for unknown Greek and Hebrew roots, in order to make the Gospel at all consistent with our natural notions of *bare justice.* Whereas let the law be understood, as requiring sinless perfection, and that most justly, and the New Testament, in its obvious plain English, immediately opens to view, as full of *glorious grace.*

It is by the law, that *orthodox* unbelievers are converted from *stupidity* and *self-righteousness.* How many are there in all our congregations who make light of a preached gospel, and pay little attention to it, though in speculative sentiments they are not infidels, nor gross heretics? They do not believe enough to make them tremble. They have no sense of their sins. However much they may hear of the wrath of God, yet they inwardly say, *Because we are innocent, surely his anger shall turn from us!* *Every way of a man is right in his own eyes.* The reason is, men have loose notions of the rule of right. They conceive nothing but imperfection can be expected or required of fallen creatures. Hence the man who has ever been, what the world calls moral, supposes he hath kept all the commandments from his youth up, and is ready to say, *What lack I yet ?* Such were the apprehensions of St. Paul before his conversion. *I was alive*, says he, *without the law once.* Without the knowledge of the law, and supposing all it did or could require, was only such obedience as is consistent with the moral depravity of fallen men, he imagined he had kept it very perfectly, and that he was justified by it, and in no danger of its curse. *But when the commandment came*, says he, *sin revived, and I died.* When he found that the law was as perfect as if we were not at all depraved; when he saw that it required him to be perfectly holy in heart and life, and most justly so required; *sin revived.* It appeared alive in him, and in every thing that he did. All his supposed religious affections, and all his most specious moral duties, were seen to be full of sin. *And he died.* He felt himself not only condemned, but spiritually dead ; utterly unable to do any thing but dead works, till quickened by renewing grace. Such knowledge of sin, and of ourselves, is by the law ; and such knowledge of sin and of ourselves is necessary in order to a sound conversion. I may add,

It is by the law, that the soul is actually converted, as well as brought to those convictions which are prerequisite. Saving conversion consists in repentance toward God, and in faith toward our Lord Jesus Christ : and in effecting both these, the law of perfect righteousness is of great and necessary use.

Repentance toward God, is from a sight of the glorious holiness, justice and goodness of the divine law ;

and can never be produced by all the grace of the gospel, while the law is not thus seen. I am sensible it hath been common, and is still, to distinguish two kinds of repentance, by the names of *legal* and *evangelical* repentance: and to consider the former as hypocritical and false: the latter only as repentance unto salvation. But perhaps, what might properly enough be called by either of these names may be true repentance; though as they have often been explained, I apprehend both are false. According to some, the former is the effect of fear; the latter the effect of hope; but neither of them the fruit of love, except self-love. The legal penitent is supposed to repent, because he is afraid he shall go to hell; the evangelical penitent, because he hopes he shall go to heaven; but neither the one nor the other because he hates sin, or has any concern for the glory of God, ultimately considered. All antinomians make their legal, and their evangelical repentance, equally selfish, and equally void of virtue; unless it be more virtuous to be actuated by mercenary hopes, than by slavish fears.— Many, it is true, who, in conformity to long established custom, make use of these distinguishing epithets, explain them in a manner that does not imply antinomianism. By evangelical repentance they mean, that which implies sorrow for sin, and a hearty turning from it, because it is against God: by legal repentance, only being sorry for our sins, and purposing to forsake them, because they are seen to be of dangerous consequence to ourselves. I have no objection to this as a just account of *true* and *false* repentance; but the propriety of calling one *legal*, and the other *evangelical*, I do not readily comprehend. The difference in repentance, as being selfish or ingenuous, hypo-

I

critical or sincere, I conceive, is not owing to the different representations of God and sin, in law and gospel; but to the different-dispositions of the men to whose minds these representations are made. The man who has the pious feeling heart of the psalmist David, will repent truly, when he sees his sins in the light of God's holy law. The man who has the hard selfish heart of the traitor Judas, will not repent truly, when he sees his sins in all the additional light reflected on them by the cross of Christ, and the grace of the gospel. Before genuine repentance can be produced, by any means, the heart must be changed by the renewing of the Holy Ghost. When the law finds a soul thus prepared, it will work in it godly sorrow, and repentance not to be repented of. When the commandment comes, and is seen to be perfectly good, holy, and just, unless we have perfect hearts of stone, we shall abhor ourselves, and repent in dust and ashes. When we think on our ways, and see how contrary they have been to the reasonable requisitions of our most rightful sovereign, if we have the least spark of godly sensibility, we shall mourn and be in bitterness for the dishonour we have done to Him; and not merely on account of the evils to which we have exposed ourselves. Apprehensions of the mercy of God in Christ, will quicken and increase true repentance; but can never begin it, without a previous true discovery and cordial approbation of the divine law.

The other part of a sound and saving conversion, namely, faith towards Jesus Christ, is also in consequence of right views of the divine law; and cannot take place without them. *The law was our schoolmaster*, says the Apostle, *to bring us unto Christ, that we might be justified by faith.* The humiliating lessons concerning God's righteousness, and our own unrighte-

ousness, which are taught in the school of the law
must be thoroughly learned and have their effect of
the *heart*, in the first place ; and then a sinner will b
easily reconciled to the way of life and peace. T
think of persuading men to embrace the gospel, be
fore ever they have understood and submitted to th
law, is absurd and impossible. It is reading the boo
wrong end upward. It is beginning at the last end of
the line.

Lastly ; it is by the law of perfection that good me
are made better. They are hereby turned still mor
and more from darkness to light, and from sin to h
liness : by being converted, is not always meant i
scripture, the first conversion of a sinner. Our S
viour said to Peter, *When thou art converted, strengt*
en thy brethren. The godly, when they have falle
into great sins, are recovered again by repentance
and in order to this, a new law-work is necessary.-
Such a law-work David repeatedly experienced, lon
after he had been eminently pious, as appears by mar
passages in his psalms. In the xxxii. he says, *Whe*
I kept silence, my bones waxed old through my roarin
all the day long. For day and night thy hand was hea
vy upon me : my moisture is turned into the drought
summer. And in the xxxviii. *For thine arrows stic*
fast in me, and thy hand presseth me sore. There is
soundness in my flesh, because of thine anger : neith
is there any rest in my bones, because of my sin. N
is it only after grievous back-slidings that good me
feel the powerful influence of the holy law, convertin
their souls. They experience its humbling and san
tifying efficacy, turning them from the errors of the
ways, in a gradual progression, all their lives. Throug
God's precepts they get understanding ; therefore the
hate every false way. *The commandment is a lam*

and the law is light.—Hence, *The path of the just is
as the shining light, that shineth more and more unto the
perfect day.*

All that remains is the improvement, and in this
there is time only for one or two particulars. We may
hence infer,

First. The exceeding unreasonableness of imagining that the divine law is abated; or that Christ hath
redeemed us, in any measure, from the moral law, as
a rule of duty. What has been said, both of the perfection, and of the salutary use of this law, shows the
extreme absurdity of such an imagination.

Can it be supposed that an all-perfect Being should,
on any consideration, disannul a law which was and
always will be, holy, just, and good, in perfection;
and, enact another, not *so holy*, not *so just*, nor *so
good?* Can it be supposed that the Son of God, the
brightness of the Father's glory, and express image
of his person, should come down from heaven, and
bleed and die, to procure an alteration in an *all-perfect,
law?* an alteration which could not be for the better,
but must be for the worse! It is true, Christ hath opened a glorious way for the gracious pardon and acceptance of penitent believers, though *very* imperfect.—
But certainly he hath not liberated, either believers or
unbelievers, from the obligation they were under to
observe and obey the original perfect law of his heavenly Father. At his first entrance on the execution of
his prophetic mission, he gave a solemn caveat to the
great congregation in which he preached righteousness, not to think that inculcating such licentious doctrine, or opening a door for it, was any part of his design. He assured the multitude, in his sermon on the
mount, that to alter *one tittle* of the moral law, was

as far from his intention, as it was a thing in itself utterly impossible.

Nor would sullying the lustre, or lessening the purity and perfection of the divine law, at all have comported with the benevolent office he came to perform in favour of mankind. He came to convert souls.— He came to *save his people from their sins.* He *gave himself for us that he might redeem us from all iniquity.* He *loved the Church, and gave himself for it, that he might sanctify and cleanse it, with the washing of water by the word ; that he might present it to himself a glorious church, not having spot or wrinkle, or any such thing ; but that it might be holy and without blemish.*— But in order to all this, it was surely necessary that the law of perfect holiness, should remain stedfast and unaltered. How could sinners be converted by a flexible law ? a law which was itself converted to their depraved hearts and crooked ways ! How could men be saved from their sins, or even have the knowledge of sin, by such a law ? What end could be answered by giving to imperfect creatures an imperfect law, unless to keep them imperfect and to justify their imperfections ? The notion of a fallen law for fallen men, must certainly be, not from the Saviour, but from the *adversary* of souls. It is one of the most capital devices of the god of this world, who was a murderer from the beginning. As long as he can blind the minds of them that believe not, with the imagination of such a divine law, he is sure of their souls. They will never be converted. The light of the glorious gospel of Christ, who is the image of God, cannot shine unto them.

Secondly. We hence infer, that *legal preaching,* truly so called, ought not to be censured, and must by

no means be omitted. Some would have the constant
strain of the preacher what they call purely *evangelical.*
All faith, and no works. To hear moral duties explained and inculcated, they do not like. It is not ex-
perimental. They are not fed. But such are as ill
affected to the real gospel of our Lord Jesus Christ, as
to the holy law of God. Ministers may keep back nothing that is profitable ; they must not shun to declare
all the divine counsel, and surely they must not shun
to declare the divine law, whether men will hear or
whether they will forbear. *This is a faithful saying,*
says the Apostle to Titus, *and these things I will that
thou affirm constantly, that they which have believed in*
God *might be careful to maintain good works : these
things are good and profitable unto men.* They are profitable to the doers of them, as well as to their neighbours. They are profitable not only in regard to the
life that now is, but likewise in relation to that which
is to come. The more good works men do on earth,
the greater will be their reward in heaven : nor can
they get to heaven at all without good works. *Know
ye not,* says St. Paul, *that the unrighteous shall not inherit the kingdom of* God? *Be not deceived.* Preaching the law is certainly necessary, *for the perfecting of
the Saints,* and for the detection of false professors.
But it is also necessary for the conviction and conversion of sinners. Accordingly we find, that the inspired
preachers and writers of the New Testament, insisted
much on the law, in order to awaken attention to the
gospel. John the Baptist did so, we may be sure ; and
he had wonderful success. Jerusalem and all Judea,
and all the region round about Jordan, went out to him
to be baptized, confessing their sins. James and John,
who were sir-named Boanerges, that is, the sons of
thunder, were doubtless, great preachers of the law ;

and not merely loud and noisy preachers. Paul reasoned of righteousness, temperance and judgment to come; that is, he preached law rationally when Felix trembled. This was the common apostolic method. See 2 Cor. v. 11. *Knowing the terrors of the* Lord, *we persuade men.* And certainly, never was there a more perfect preacher of law, than the author and finisher of our faith.

It is true, there is a kind of *legal preaching*, so called, which is justly censurable; and which tends not to the conversion or edification, but to the destruction of souls. Should we represent that all the duty which God requires of the unregenerate, is only abstaining from external immoralities, and attending upon the outward and ordinary means of grace, from such principles, and with such hearts, as they at present have; and that if they do these things, they need not fear failing of divine mercy; we should heal the heart of awakened sinners slightly: We should only assist them in going about to establish their own righteousness. Or should we teach that good men are under an abated law, which requires only such imperfect goodness as God hath given them, our doctrine would tend to make them feel, as far as they believed it, altogether self-justified; instead of leading them to see their constant entire dependence on free grace, through the redemption that is in Jesus Christ.

But such preaching to sinners or to saints, is not proper *legal* preaching. It is not properly preaching the law of *the* Lord, but a law of *our own.* It is making *the commandment of* God *of none effect by our tradition.*

Preaching the divine law, as it really is, and as our Saviour and the apostles preached it, has no tendency to quiet the consciences of unbelievers, nor to make good men self-righteous, but quite the reverse. By this *the loftiness of man* is *bowed down, and the haughtiness of men* is *made low, and the* Lord *alone* is *exalted.* From the law of perfection, principally, are those *weapons of our warfare, which are mighty through* God *to the pulling down of strong holds : casting down imaginations, and every high thing which exalteth itself against the knowledge of* God, *and bringing into captivity every thought to the obedience of* Christ. Let the law be truly preached, and divinely impressed, and sinners will see the necessity of fleeing to a better refuge than their own graceless duties. The best of men will also see that they *stand by faith,* and will *not be high-minded, but fear.* They will see that they must be *justified by the faith of* Christ, *and not by the works of the law.* They will see that in point of justification, *all our righteousnesses are as filthy rags. Through the law* they will be *dead to the law,* though more than ever engaged to *live unto* God. The man of the greatest attainments in grace and holiness, will not feel as if he *had already attained, either were already perfect : but this one thing* he will *do, forgetting the things which are behind, and reaching forth unto those things which are before,* he will *press toward the mark, for the prize of the high calling of* God *in* Christ Jesus.

Eternal Salvation on no account a Matter of just Debt ; or, Full Redemption, not interfering with Free Grace.

———————

A SERMON,

DELIVERED AT WALLINGFORD, CONNECTICUT,

By JOHN SMALLEY, *D. D.*

———————

Justification through the Merits of Christ, an Act of the free Grace of God.

———

ROMANS iii. 24.

Being justified freely by his Grace, through the Redemption that is in Jesus Christ.

———

T H E point laboured in the preceding part of this epistle, is the impossibility of salvation for any of mankind, on the footing of mere law, or of personal righteousness. The apostle hath *proved that both Jews and Gentiles were all under sin ;* and hence he infers, as the necessary consequence, that " by the deeds of the law there shall no flesh be justified in the sight of God." This point being established, that the original way of life was now forever barred against the race of fallen man, the apostle proceeds, for the comfort of sinners, to open to view the gospel method of justification through a Redeemer. See the context, ver. 21, and onward. "But now the righteousness of God without the law is manifested, being witnessed by the law and the prophets ; even the righteousness of God which is by faith of Jesus Christ, unto all, and upon all them that believe ; for there is no difference. For all have sinned and come short of the glory of God. Being justified freely by his grace," &c.

It is of the last importance that this new way of access into the divine favour, and of obtaining eternal life, should be rightly explained. By many it has been so misunderstood as either to make void the law, or to frustrate the grace of the gospel, or both. Some speculative inaccuracies also, it appears to me, respecting justification through the atonement and righteousness of Christ, have been inadvertently adopted by many, if not most, of the orthodox, of which men of erroneous sentiments have availed themselves to very pernicious purposes.

The great difficulty respecting this subject, to which I have in view to pay particular attention at present, is, how to reconcile the full satisfaction of Christ, with the free grace of God in the pardon of sin and the justification of sinners. It is proposed, agreeably to the words before us,

1st. To explain gospel justification.

2d. To consider how this is through the redemption of Christ. And,

3d. To show that still it is of the free grace of God.

But on the last of these heads I mean mainly to insist.

I. I shall endeavour very briefly to explain what we are here to understand by being justified.

Justification literally signifies judging one to be just. A man is said to justify himself when he asserts his own innocence, or denies that he has been to blame in any instance. So one is said to justify another when he stands up for him, or undertakes his vindication. Among the Jews this was a law phrase, or was used in reference to their courts of judicature. See Deut. xxv. 1. " If there be a controversy between men, and they come into judgment, that the judges may judge them, then they shall justify the righteous, and condemn the wicked."

From this judicial use of the word, it came to be applied to the case of mankind, in regard to the sentence of the Supreme Judge. The legal justification of man, had he persevered in perfect rectitude, would have been the sentence of his Maker, pronouncing him righteous, and confirming him in immortal happiness. But gospel-justification—the justification of fallen men before a holy and just God, must be supposed to have something peculiar in it. The application of the word to this case, must be understood as borrowed and figurative ; yet the thing intended is sufficiently analogous to the primary meaning of the phrase to well warrant this metaphorical use. It bears a resemblance to the legal and literal justification of the righteous in the two most essential points. It implies an acquittance from sin as exposing to eternal death, and the grant of a sure title to everlasting life.

1st. Gospel justification implies an acquittance from all sin, as exposing to eternal death. To this purpose see Acts xiii. 38, 39. " Be it known unto you therefore, men and brethren, that through this man is preached unto you the forgiveness of sins ; and by him all that believe are justified from all things, from which ye could not be justified by the law of Moses." In the Mosaic law, provision was made for cleansing persons from ceremonial, but not from moral transgressions. Not from *sin*, the apostle to the Hebrews observes, *as pertaining to the conscience.* Hence David says, Psalm li. 16. " For thou desirest not sacrifice, else would I give it." That is; there were no sin-offerings instituted for such crimes as those of which he had been guilty. But through the atonement of Christ believers are justified from *all things*. His *blood cleanseth from all sin.* Accordingly we read, Rom. viii. 1. " There is therefore now no condemnation to them who are in Christ Jesus." That is, no condemnation to eternal death. Not that there is no kind of condemnation to those who are justified according to the new covenant. The best saints are liable to temporal punishments, notwithstanding their justification. Moses, and David, and Hezekiah were condemned for their sins, and sorely punished for them in this world, though good men, and interested in the covenant of grace.— And St. Paul, reproving the Corinthians for their unworthy attendance on the Lord's Supper, says, " For this cause many are weak and sickly among you, and many sleep. For if we would judge ourselves we should not be judged. But when we are judged, we are chastened of the Lord, that we should not be condemned with the world." Believers, by being justified, are not exempted from all expressions of the divine displeasure. The pardon implied in this gracious act of God, is only a discharge from the condemnation of the wicked; that is, from future and eternal punishment. But,

2d. Gospel justification implies the grant of a sure title to eternal life.

This is more than merely being delivered from the curse of the law. Adam, before his fall, was perfectly free from all condemnation; but he was not confirmed in the divine favour. He was placed in a state of probation with only a conditional promise of final happiness. If he obeyed he was to live ; if he disobeyed he was to die. And he had no assurance of effectual grace to preserve him from final apostacy and perdition. In this last respect, the case of those who are justified through the redemption that is in Jesus Christ, is essentially different. Indeed, some have supposed that believers in Christ, have, in this life, only conditional promises of final salvation. Nor can it be denied that persevering obedience to the gospel is made necessary in order to eternal life. It is written, " The just shall live by faith ; but if any man draw back, my soul shall have no pleasure in him. He that endureth to the end," says Christ, "the same shall be saved. To him that overcometh will I grant to sit with me in my throne, even as I also overcame, and am set down with my Father in his throne."

From such passages as these many have been led to suppose, that all the promises of the second covenant, like those of the first, are only conditional, and depend upon the mutable will of man for their ultimate accomplishment. But texts enough may be produced, which assert the absolute safety of all who are once justified by faith. Justification and glorification are spoken of as infallibly connected, Rom. viii. 30. " Whom he justifieth, them he also glorifieth." And our Saviour says, John v. 24. " Verily, verily, I say unto you, he that heareth my words, and believeth on him that sent me, hath everlasting life, and *shall not come into condemnation.*"

Nor are these at all inconsistent with those other texts, which imply that none shall be saved at last, but such as obey the gospel to the end of life. For perseverance in faith and holiness may be made absolutely

K

sure in the first justification. And that this is actually the case is most evident from scripture. Christ says of his sheep—of all who " hear *his* voice, and follow *him*, I give unto them eternal life ; and they shall never perish, neither shall any pluck them out of my hand." Those who truly believe, we are taught, are not of them that draw back unto perdition. They are said to be " kept by the power of God, through faith, unto salvation." We may be confident of this very thing, according to the apostle, that he who hath begun a good work in any one—a work of faith with power— he will perform it until the day of Jesus Christ. From these passages, and many more in the New Testament, it appears evident enough that those who have once obtained gospel justification, are not only put into a new state of trial upon a milder constitution, according to which it is possible they may be finally saved ; but that their salvation is made infallible, by this better covenant, established upon better promises ; this everlasting covenant, ordered in all things, and sure.

II. I proceed to speak of the redemption of Christ, the essential ground of gospel justification.

To redeem, signifies to deliver ; more strictly, and most commonly, to deliver by ransom. There were various laws in Israel concerning redemptions :—the redemption of lives, of lost inheritances, and of persons sold to slavery. Every first born male, according to law was the Lord's ; but the first born of man, and the firstlings of certain beasts might not be sacrificed ; provision was therefore made for their being redeemed by the substitution of others in their stead. See Exod. xiii 13. " Every firstling of an ass thou shalt redeem with a lamb ; and if thou wilt not redeem it, then thou shalt break his neck ; and all the first born of man *amongst thy* children shalt thou redeem." With re-

gard to the redemption of inheritances, see Lev. xxv.
25. " If thy brother be waxen poor, and hath sold
away of his possession, and if any of his kin come to
redeem it, then shall he redeem that which his brother had sold." Of the redemption of Israelites who
had sold themselves, see the same chapter, ver. 47—49.
" And if a sojourner or stranger wax rich by thee, and
thy brother by him wax poor, and sell himself unto the
stranger; after that he is sold he may be redeemed
again; one of his brethren may redeem him : either
his uncle, or his uncle's son may redeem him, or any
that is nigh of kin unto him of his family may redeem
him; or, if he be able he may redeem himself."

In allusion to these and such like redemptions in
Israel, Christ is called our Redeemer, and is said to be
made of God unto us redemption. Agreeably to these
different instances and ways of redeeming, the redemption that is in Jesus Christ may be understood as comprehending, both the merit of his obedience, and the
manifestation of divine justice made by his sufferings,
in our nature and stead. We were waxen poor; our
eternal inheritance was alienated; and such was the
grace of our Lord Jesus Christ, who " was rich, *that*
for our sakes he became poor, that we through his
poverty might be rich." He took upon him the form
of a servant—the nature and place of man, and, in that
nature and capacity, obeyed perfectly his Father's law
as man ought to have done, that " by his obedience
many might be made righteous," and obtain the inheritance of eternal life. We had sold ourselves; the
Son of Man therefore, our kinsman, came to seek and
to save—to ransom and redeem us. Hence we are
said to be bought with a price; and to be redeemed,
not with corruptible things as silver and gold, but with
the precious blood of Christ. We were devoted to ut-

ter destruction ; for it is said, " The soul that sinneth
it shall die ; and, cursed is every one that continueth
not in all things written in the book of the law to do
them. Christ therefore suffered for us, the just for
the unjust. He hath redeemed us from the curse of
the law, being made a curse for us. He was wounded
for our transgressions ; he was bruised for our iniquities ; the chastisement of our peace was upon him,
and with his stripes we are healed."

What rendered the vicarious obedience and sufferings of our Saviour necessary, was, that we might have
remission of sins and the rewards of the righteous, and
yet the honour of the divine law and government be
maintained. " To justify the wicked, is abomination
to the Lord. He will by no means clear the guilty."
This were to countenance iniquity, and to cast an indel-
ible slur on his own glorious character. It were to
bring the eternal law of righteousness, and the eternal
Law-giver of the universe into disregard and contempt.
God had given a law which was holy, and just, and
good. He had enforced this law with infinite sanctions, that it might be forever observed and had in re-
verence. This law had not been fulfilled by man, and
therefore the reward of righteousness could not be
given him. This law had been openly violated by man,
and therefore the penalty of transgression and disobedience must be inflicted upon him. " Shall not the
Judge of all the earth do right?" Better never to give
a law, than to let the violation of it pass with impunity.
But the holy law of God was not rashly given. His
own glory, and the good of the moral creation, required
that there should be such a law, and that the dignity of
it should be supported. A lawless, licentious universe
were infinitely worse than none. Hence heaven and
earth might sooner pass away, or be annihilated, than

the divine law be made void, or one tittle of it fail and not be fulfilled.

But the letter of a law may possibly be deviated from, and yet the spirit of it be supported, and the design of it fully obtained. We are told of a certain ancient king (Zaleuchus, king of the Locrians) who, that he might effectually suppress adultery, which exceedingly prevailed among his subjects, enacted a law that the adulterer should be punished with the loss of both his eyes. His own son was convicted of this crime. The royal father, whose bowels yearned for him, and who could not bear to have one so dear to him forever deprived of the light of day, devised an expedient to soften, in that one instance, the rigour of his own law, and yet not abate its force in future. The king in a most public manner, before all the people, had one of his own eyes plucked out, that so one of his son's eyes might be saved. By such a commutation as this, by redeeming one eye for his son, at so costly a price as the loss of one of his own, he conceived the law would appear as awful, and be as great a terror to evil doers, as if the letter of it had been executed. And it must, I think, be acknowledged that, by this means, the king's inflexible determination to maintain government and punish transgression, was even more strikingly evinced than if he had suffered the law to have its natural course, and neither of his son's eyes had been spared. For some fathers have been without natural affection, but no man ever yet hated his own flesh. The apple of one's own eye must certainly be dear to him.

In like manner, we are to conceive of the redemption of Christ, as an astonishing expedient of infinite wisdom and goodness, that we transgressors might be saved, and yet God be just, and his righteous law suf-

for no dishonour. This is the constant account we
have of the death of Christ in the holy scriptures.—
Thus immediately after my text, " Whom God hath
set forth to be a propitiation, through faith in his blood,
to declare his righteousness for the remission of sins,
&c.—To declare, I say, at this. time his righteousness, that he might be just. and the justifier of him
who believeth in Jesus." Thus Eph. i. 7. " In whom
we have redemption through his blood, the forgiveness of sins," &c.

But it was not enough that we should be redeemed
from death. In order to our being heirs of God, and
having an interest in the covenant of grace, it was
necessary that the law as a covenant of works should
be fulfilled; and so the forfeited inheritance of eternal
life be redeemed. This our Saviour did by his active
obedience. By his fulfilling all righteousness, a foundation was laid for God, to the eternal honour of his re-
munerating justice, to give grace and glory to all who
believe in Christ and belong to him. Thus it is written, " He is made unto us righteousness."

These two things are implied in the redemption
that is in Jesus Christ. The merit of his obedience,
and the manifestation of the inflexibility of divine vindictive justice, made by his sufferings and death. And
these two things were necessary in order to our being
justified, and yet the spirit of the law be maintained,
and God be just.

III. I proceed to shew, that notwithstanding this
plenteous redemption, we are dependent on the mere
mercy of God, and our justification is still freely by
his grace.

By grace is meant undeserved favour. This is the
common acceptation of the word. The bestowment
of any good which might justly not be bestowed, or

not inflicting any evil which might justly be inflicted, is a matter of free grace. Indeed, in the New
Testament grace may mean, doing good to those who
deserve ill; this being actually the case with respect
to all exercises of divine goodness towards fallen man.
However, if it can be shown that no man has any
claim to salvation upon the footing of justice, it will
be sufficient to my present purpose. The thing therefore I now undertake to prove, and clear up, is this:
That no man *deserves* eternal life. or even deliverance
from eternal death, on account of *any merit belonging
to him,* either *personal* or *imputed.*

The idea of *personal* merit is in general profe sedly
exploded. All will allow that the best man on earth, had
he no better righteousness than his own, could have no
other plea than that of the publican, " God be merciful
to me a sinner." But, on Christ's account, it has commonly been supposed, believers have a good plea even
before the tribunal of divine justice. *It hath been said
by them of old time,* and also by some modern writers
of very eminent note, that through the atonement of
our divine Redeemer, if we have an interest in him,
we *deserve* freedom from all condemnation ; and that,
through his all-perfect righteousness, we may *demand*
eternal glory as our *just due.* Very express to this
purpose is the following passage, in a late learned and
most excellent author.* " The justice of God that
required man's damnation, and seemed inconsistent
with his salvation, now does as much require the salvation of those that believe in Christ, as ever it required their damnation. Salvation is an absolute debt
to the believer from God, so that he may in justice demand and challenge it, not upon the account of what

* President Edwards. First set of Posthumous Sermons,
page 307.

he himself has done; but upon the account of what his surety has done. For Christ has satisfied justice fully for his sin; so that it is but a thing that may be challenged that God should now release the believer from punishment; it is but a piece of justice that the creditor should release the debtor, when he has fully paid the debt. And again, the believer may demand eternal life, because it has been merited by Christ, by a merit of condignity."

Another extract I will here give you from the writings of a more ancient pious divine, containing the same sentiment, and expressed in still bolder terms. His words are as follow: " He [Christ] fully merited, by way of purchase and complete payment made unto divine justice, the removal of all that evil we had deserved, and the enjoyment of all that good we needed, and could desire; and that by a valuable consideration tendered into the hand of divine justice in that behalf. However it is out of free mercy and rich grace that redemption is given to us; (for its out of mercy that Christ is given, that he gave his life, that both are bestowed upon us and not upon the world:) yet in regard to the Lord Jesus Christ himself, and the full payment he hath laid down, out of his own proper cost and charges. his own blood, it is justice it should be bestowed. and by justice it may be challenged, as that which he hath purchased in a righteous proceeding."

This he afterwards applies in a use of reproof to diffident believers, in the following words: " Why? have you laid down the purchase? Take possession then into your hand. Have you tendered the payment? Take the commodity It is your own; nay, your due.—He that knows at what the purchase will come, and hath the sum in sight, and under his hand,

can lay it down upon the nail ; pay it, take it ; here is
one and there's the other. Here's the blood of Jesus
which thou art well pleased with, hast accepted of,
therefore, Lord, give me my due : that comfort, that
peace, that wisdom, that assurance, which I stand in
need of."*

This notion of the atonement and imputed righteousness, it must be acknowledged, is frequently to be
met with in our most orthodox books, though it may
not be often improved just in the manner last quoted.
But we may *call no man master, or father*. We must
search the scriptures, whether those things be so.—
Where do we find our infallible teacher, instructing
his disciples to make such challenges from the Father,
even on his account, of deliverance from all evil, and the
bestowment of all good, as their just due ? Did he not
direct them humbly to *pray*, for even a competency
of outward comforts, as of God's free gift : and for
the *pardon* of their many offences, of his mere mercy ?
" Give us this day our daily bread, and forgive us our
debts as we forgive our debtors." He encouraged
them indeed to seek unto God for all needed good, in
his name, with an assurance of obtaining their re-
quests ; but he ever taught them to seek in the way of
petition, not of *demand*. " Ask, and it shall be given
you ; seek, and ye shall find ; knock, and it shall be
opened unto you. Verily, verily, I say unto you,
whatsoever ye shall ask the Father, in my name, he
will give it you." Did our Saviour, that we find, ever
insinuate an idea that the salvation of his redeemed
ones was of debt from the Father ? Did he not, in the
most explicit manner, acknowledge the contrary ? " I
thank thee, O Father, Lord of heaven and of earth,

---

* Mr. Thomas Hooker, first Minister in Hartford.

because thou hast hid these things from the wise and prudent, and hast revealed them unto babes. Even so, Father, *for so it seemed good in thy sight.*"

Do the inspired apostles, in any of their epistles or discourses, teach us that the salvation of believers, or any part of it, is of justice to the exclusion of grace? Do they not constantly express themselves most clearly in opposition to this sentiment? " By the righteousness of one, *the free gift* came upon all men unto justification of life. That as sin hath reigned unto death, even so might *grace reign*, through righteousness, unto eternal life, by Jesus Christ our Lord. He that spared not his own son, but delivered him up for us all, how shall he not with him also *freely give us all things ?*"

The doctrine that justification, and all subsequent, as well as antecedent blessings, are *free gifts*—matters of mere grace, is certainly a doctrine of scripture.— But still the great question remains ; how is this doctrine self-consistent? The redemption that is in Jesus Christ implies full satisfaction for sin, and the highest possible merit of eternal life ; how then can being justified through this redemption be of free grace?— What grace can there be in cancelling a debt when full payment hath been made? or in liberating a captive when an adequate ransom hath been received? or in reconveying an alienated inheritance after ample recompence? how is this difficulty to be removed?

I answer ; just as other difficulties are removed into which we are led by following the allusions and metaphors of scripture too closely. We are not to imagine a resemblance, in all points, between the redemption of Christ, and redemptions among mankind, any more than we are in other instances when divine things are spoken of after the manner of men : any more than we are to imagine that God is *angry* just as we are, or that he *repents* just as we do, or that he hath an *arm*, and *hands*, and *eyes* like ours, because these things are ascribed to him in a figurative manner.—— From the use of the words *ransom*, and *redemption*, we are no more obliged to suppose a literal purchase, or an obligatory satisfaction in what our Saviour did and suffered, than we are to suppose there was occasion for such kind of satisfaction, and for the same reasons as among men. We are selfish, and looking *for gain every one from his quarter :* but surely we ought not to form a like idea of the infinitely benevolent and ever blessed God. Certainly, " He who so loved the world *as* to give his only begotten Son, that whosoever believeth in him might not perish, but have everlasting life," would have pardoned and saved the world without any atonement or vicarious righteousness, had nothing but want of goodness prevented. The thing was, sin could not be pardoned, and sinners saved, consistently with just law and good government ; and therefore not consistently with the glory of God or the good of the universe. The removal of this just obstacle to the reign of grace, not the laying God under obligation, for value received, was what rendered the redemption of Christ necessary : and the former of these, not the latter, is the end effected by his obedience and death.

It hath indeed been said, in the present dispute, that a door could not be opened for the salvation of mankind, without making it necessary in justice that they should be saved. That justice requires whatever is consistent with justice. But this is a new and strange position. The perfection of justice no more requires that every thing which is just should be done, than the perfection of truth requires that every thing which is true should ᴗe spoken.   If justice required whatever is consistent with justice, no grace could be exercised— no free favour could ever be bestowed in any instance, either by God or man: nothing more than mere justice could ever be done.   That justice which excludes grace, which is the only proper notion of justice, at least the only one now under consideration, certainly doth not require many things which might be just. Justice did not require that God should give his only begotten Son, yet this was consistent with justice. Christ was not obliged in justice to consent to become incarnate and to pour out his soul unto death, yet there was nothing inconsistent with justice in his so doing. In like manner it is now consistent with justice for God to pardon sinners through the propitiation of Christ, yet this is not what justice requires.   Grace requires that the guilty should be forgiven, provided it may be done consistently with justice, and without doing hurt upon the whole ; but this doth make it no more grace.   Wisdom requires whatsoever things are for the best.   Goodness requires whatsoever things are for the greatest universal good.   But justice, as excluding grace, requires only whatsoever things are deserved.

Still, perhaps, it will be said, Were not the sufferings of Christ really adequate to all the punishment due to us for sin ? and did not his obedience actually merit eternal life by a merit of condignity ? and have not believers, at least, a just right and title to the atonement and merit of Christ ? Is not his righteousness imputed to them so as to become actually theirs ? And if these things be so, where can there be any grace in their justification ? In answer to all this, let me observe the following things.

1. I do not think that eternal life was merited, even by Christ, by a merit of condignity. A merit of condignity supposes something justly due for service done. But it is impossible, I apprehend, that God should receive any thing for which he is justly indebted. " For who hath first given to him, and it shall be recompensed unto him again ?" However ancient divines may have discoursed about merit of condignity and merit of congruity, the distinction, I conceive, is properly applicable only to merit at the hands of beings who may receive actual services to which they have no just claim. A merit of condignity can, I am persuaded, have no place in regard to God.

That *creatures* can merit no good at the hand of their Creator, in this high sense of merit, every one must be convinced, on a moment's reflection. *They* can render nothing to God, in a way of love or service, but what is his due from them. Adam would not have deserved any reward as a just debt, had he remained innocent, and fulfilled the law of perfection. He would only have done what it was his duty to do. The highest created intelligences can do no more. As they derive their all from God, so they can render nothing to him but what is of right his.

But, it will be said, Christ was not a mere creature. He thought it not robbery to be equal with God. Consequently his merit must be of a different kind from what Adam's would have been, and from that of the angels. The labour of a servant cannot bring his master in debt, because it was that to which he had a just right ; but if a neighbour, who is upon even terms with us, labour for us, we are indebted to him. He *deserves* wages, in the proper and strict sense of the word. And why must there not in reality be exactly this dif-

L

ference between the obedience of creatures, and the obedience of Christ.

To this I answer, though Christ was under no obligation to become incarnate, yet when he had assumed the form of a servant, it behoved him to fulfil all righteousness.   All he did was *obedience;*—obedience *justly due,* on our account at least, if not on his own. God hath not received, even in this way, that to which he had no right, and for which he is really indebted. Did the merit of Christ as properly belong to us as if it had been our personal merit, we should have no ground to challenge eternal life, nor any reward, as our just due.   Indeed, in that case, we should not deserve eternal death, nor any punishment.   Therefore, I must add,

2. I do not think the *merit* of Christ is actually *transferred* to believers; or, that his righteousness is so imputed to them as to become, to all intents and purposes, their own righteousness.   It is so far reckoned to them as to render it consistent and honourable for God, as above explained, to be reconciled to them; not imputing their trespasses by a rigorous, or an adequate personal punishment; but it is not *so their's* as to render them really *deserving* of good, or *undeserving* of evil.   The apostle states a distinction between justification by *works* and by *faith,* making the former in some sense of debt, but the latter of grace entirely.   Rom. iv. 2—5.   " For if Abraham were justified by works he hath whereof to glory, but not before God.   For what saith the scripture?   Abraham believed God and it was counted to him for righteousness. Now to him that worketh is the reward not reckoned of grace, but of debt.   But to him that worketh not, but believeth on him that justifieth the ungodly, his faith is counted for righteousness.   By this we are

plainly taught that justification by a righteousness
reckoned to us by faith, is of grace, in a manner different from justification by our own good works. That
the man justified by personal righteousness would have
ground for glorying as more deserving than other men,
though *not before* God, as having really merited eternal life, or any good, at his hand. Comparatively, the
justification of such an one would be of debt ; it would
indeed be in part of absolute justice to the exclusion of
grace : that is, as far as it implies only approbation,
and acquittance from the curse of the law. The righteous deserve not to be condemned ; and there is no
grace in not punishing them. But to him who is personally guilty, and is justified by faith, in the righteousness of another, and in him who justifieth the ungodly,
the whole is of grace. The apostle's reasoning evidently supposes that the righteousness of Christ doth
not become to all intents and purposes the believer's
own righteousness. For if it did, there could be no
difference, as to ground for glorying, between being
justified by faith and by works ; and one would be just
as much of debt as the other : nor could it be true, in
any sense, that God justified the ungodly. But that
there is not a strict and proper imputation of Christ's
righteousness to the believer—such an imputation as
implies an actual *transfer of merit*, is plain from the
whole tenor of the scriptures, as far as they have any
relation to this subject. It is evident from all that is
said of the chastisements of believers, of their confessions, and of the remission of their sins. Were they
as righteous as Christ was—had they, in any way, a
perfect righteousness, properly their own, they would
have no sins to confess ; they would deserve no punishment, and need no pardon. The truth is, our *ill
desert* is not taken away by the atonement of Christ.
That can never be taken away. Nor doth the obedi-

ence of Christ render us *deserving* of heaven, or *un-deserving* of hell. When God justifies believers on Christ's account, he considers them still as *ungodly :* as ungodly he *punishes* them still in this world; and as well might he punish them with everlasting destruction in the world to come, were it not for his gracious promise to the contrary. *Grace reigns* with unabated lustre in our justification, and in the whole of our salvation, notwithstanding its reigning *through righteousness,* because it is through a righteousness *not our own.*

Merit is ever personal. In the nature of things it cannot be otherwise. Another's having been righteous, doth not make me righteous, if I have not been so myself; nor can the sufferings of another make me faultless wherein I have been a sinner. Can a robber or murderer become innocent, because an innocent attorney or friend of his hath suffered the penalty he deserved? Certainly it is impossible. He must be, notwithstanding this, as vile, as great a criminal, as blame-worthy, as ever he was. And so are all mankind, notwithstanding the sufferings, and notwithstanding the obedience of Christ.

Debts may be discharged by an attorney. *Damages* of any kind may be repaired by a third person. But *moral turpitude* is not to be wiped away in this manner. *Ill desert* is never thus removed. *Merit,* and *demerit,* are things not to be acquired or lost by proxy. The *consequences* of the good or evil actions of one person may devolve upon another; not the *righteousness* or the *criminality* of them.

Our *crimes* were not transferred to Christ; only the *sufferings* for them. He suffered as a *lamb,* without blemish and without spot. So his *righteousness* is not transferred to us; only the *benefits* of it. He was numbered with transgressors, and treated as a sinner though innocent. We are numbered with the righteous, and treated as the friends and favourites of the Most High, though ungodly. He deserved the praises of heaven, when he was made a curse—when forsaken and expiring on the cross. We deserve the pains of hell, when delivered from the curse of the law, and received into the embraces of everlasting love. There is no transfer of merit, or of demerit, one way or the other, only of their fruits and consequences.

Justice admitted of laying on Christ the sufferings due for our sins, because it was by his own *free consent*, and because the *necessary ends* of punishing would thereby be answered; not because *he deserved* those sufferings. So, on the other hand, justice now admits of our being saved on his account, not because, on any account, *we deserve* salvation, but only because by giving us remission of sins and the happiness of the righteous, no injury will be done, no damage will accrue to the universe. There is nothing to oblige God to have mercy on any of mankind only his own wisdom and goodness. He can do it without any unrighteousness; and therefore *so it seemeth good in his sight.* Hence we are *pardoned*—we are *justified*—we shall be *glorified, freely by the grace of God,* notwithstanding the ample foundation laid for all in the plenteous *redemption which is in Jesus Christ.*

All that now remains, is to point out some of the doctrinal and practical *uses,* of this important subject.

In the first place; we may hence learn, that the argument for the certain salvation of all men, from the sufficiency of the satisfaction and purchase of Christ, is inconclusive. According to the common notion of a literal satisfaction and strict purchase in the atonement and obedience of our Saviour, similar exactly to satisfactions and purchases in matters of *meum* and

tuum (i. e. *mine* and *thine*) between man and man, this
argument of the Universalists, on which the greatest
stress is laid by some, would be exceedingly plausible: to me it appears, it would indeed be absolutely
unanswerable. The argument stands thus. God is
obliged in justice to save men as far as the merit of
Christ extends: but the merit of Christ is sufficient
for the salvation of all men; therefore God is obliged
in justice to save all. The minor proposition I dare
not deny. I question not the sufficiency of the merit
of Christ for the salvation of all mankind. I have no
doubt but that, in this sense, Christ " gave himself a
ransom *for all;* tasted death for *every man;* and is the
propitiation for the sins of the *whole world.*" The
only thing therefore which I have to dispute in this argument, is the *obligatoriness* of the Redeemer's merit,
on the Supreme Being: or, that it is of such a nature
as to afford any ground to *demand* salvation from God,
as of *just debt.* Had the believer any right to challenge pardon and eternal life, upon this footing, I see
not but that all mankind would have the same. If the
merit of Christ be such as obliges God, in point of
justice to save all believers; and if that merit be sufficient for the salvation of all men; why is not God
obliged in justice to save all men, whether believers or
not?—He may be under engagements to some and
not to others by *gracious promise,* predicated upon
faith; but if the obligation be in *absolute justice,* it
must be solely on account of the merit of Christ; and
is no greater after a man has faith than before. And if
there be merit enough in Christ for all, it obliges and
must obtain the salvation of all, though all men have
not faith. That alters not the case. Faith, or the want
of faith, alters nothing in point of justice; only in point
of promise: unless the obligatory merit be in faith

itself, not in the atonement and righteousness of Christ. If God cannot in justice *lay any thing to the charge of the elect*, nor inflict any punishment upon them, because Christ died for them : and if, in point of merit, Christ died for all men ; God cannot in justice lay any thing to the charge of *any man*, nor punish *any man*.

Thus the doctrine of certain universal salvation is established at once ; and established upon orthodox principles.

The argument, indeed, proves too much. More a great deal than any good man would wish : more, one would think than any man in his senses could believe. It turns the tables entirely respecting obligation and grace between God and man. According to it, all the obligation is now on God's part ; all the grace on ours ! He is holden and justly stands bound to us ; we are free from all obligation to him ! All the debts of all mankind, both of duty and suffering, are forever cancelled ! Christ hath done all their duty for them, as well as taken away all possible criminality from them ! If they now love or serve God it is of mere gratuity ! They are not at all obliged so to do ! If he bestow upon them all the good in his power, to all eternity, it is of *debt—absolute debt*, in the highest sense of the word ! He can do no more for them than by a merit of condignity hath been purchased for them, and is of absolute right due to them ! These admirable consequences will follow from this notion of the atonement and merit of Christ, as necessarily as the doctrine of universal salvation. An argument which thus overthrows every thing—*all law*, as well as *all grace*, must certainly be fallacious, whether we were able to discover the fallacy of it or not. Yet some, it is said, are not to be terrified by such frightful consequences.

They admit them, and plead for them. They allow, at least, and maintain, that *men are* not justly punishable by the Judge of all the earth, whatever iniquities they may commit ; and that, in fact, no man is punished of God at all, nor ever will be. So firmly are they established in the belief that the foregoing argument is demonstration, and can never be confuted.

But must not the weak place in this invincible argument, be made *manifest to all men ?* I cannot but flatter myself, the *attentive candid Universalist* must feel this firm ground give way under him. The hope of salvation built upon the idea that the holy sovereign of the universe is obliged in justice to pardon and save the vilest of sinners, is certainly a *very forlorn hope.*

That believers themselves do not deserve eternal life, nor even deliverance from eternal death ;—that God is under no kind of obligation, for value received, even to them, on any account whatever, seems plainly implied in our text, and hath been sufficiently illustrated, I conceive, in the preceding discourse. And if so, certainly he cannot be obliged in justice to save all men. Salvation is sincerely offered to all, if they will thankfully receive Christ as their Saviour, and penitently return, through him, to their Creator and their God. With regard to giving them a heart, or making them willing to do these things, God hath mercy on whom he will have mercy. Surely " by sending his Son into the world, that the world through him might be saved," he hath not brought himself so infinitely indebted to mankind as to be in justice obliged to save all the world, whether they will or not.

Secondly. Hence we may see, that the Socinians have no reason to object against the doctrine of atonement, as though it were irreconcilable with the doctrine of free grace, and represented God the Father as *unforgiving, implacable, unmerciful.**

As many have explained the doctrine of atonement, I cannot say that these reproaches cast upon it by its adversaries, are altogether unjust. Were it right to conceive of it under the literal, *low* notion of paying *debts,* or repairing damages, between man and man, it would indeed seem as if there were no proper *remission of sins* to believers, nor any mercy in granting them *deliverance from the curse of the law.* But if we consider God as acting in this great affair, in his own proper character, as Supreme Ruler of the world ; and requiring atonement in order to the salvation of

---

* Dr. Priestley, a celebrated modern writer on the side of *Socinianism,* has much to say upon this head. He says, " We read in the scriptures, that we are *justified freely by the grace of God.* But what free grace, or mercy, does there appear to have been in God, if Christ gave a full price for our justification, and bore the infinite weight of divine wrath on our account ? We are commanded to *forgive others, as we ourselves hope to be forgiven ;* and to be *merciful as our Father, who is in heaven is merciful.* But surely we are not thereby authorized to insist upon any atonement or satisfaction, before we give up our resentments towards an offending penitent brother. Indeed, how could it deserve the name of *forgiveness* if we did ?—It is impossible to reconcile the doctrine of satisfaction for sin by the death of Christ, with the doctrine of *free grace,* which, according to the uniform tenor of the scriptures, is so fully displayed in the pardon of sin, and the justification of sinners.—It is only from the literal interpretation of a few figurative expressions in the scriptures, that this doctrine of *atonement,* as well as that of *transubstantiation,* has been derived ; and it is certainly a doctrine highly injurious to God ; and if we, who are commanded to imitate God, should act upon the maxims of it, it would be subversive of the most amiable part of virtue in men. We should be implacable and unmerciful, insisting upon the uttermost farthing."

guilty men, only tor the support of *public* justice, and
that he might still be a *terror* to *evil doers*, at the same
time that he discovers himself *abundant in goodness and
ready to forgive.* If we consider, moreover, that the
demerit of sin is not at all taken away, nor the need
of pardoning mercy lessened by vicarious sufferings.
In a word, if the foregoing view of this subject be
scriptural and just, what shadow of ground can there
be for any such reproaches and objections?

Thirdly.   Hence we are furnished with an easy solution of a difficulty which some have imagined, respecting our being justified, at all, on account of the
active obedience of our Saviour.   The difficulty is this.
Christ, in his human nature, in which only he could
obey, owed obedience on his own account, and therefore could have no merit by that means to be placed
to the account of his followers as the ground of their
justification.   Hereupon some have supposed and
taught, that the *sufferings* of Christ, to which he was
under no personal obligation, are the only meritorious
ground of our acceptance unto eternal life.   Or, that
all further than deliverance from the curse of the law,
is from the grace of God, and the merit of our own
imperfect obedience.*

This imaginary difficulty, however, arises entirely
from the supposed necessity of merit strictly purchasing good at the hand of God ; and a merit properly *transferable.*   According to that conception of the
matter, it is certain *Adam's* obedience could have availed nothing in behalf of any but himself.   He, unques-

---

* The above difficulty was started, and the above doctrine
advanced, by a divine of some note in Germany the last cen-
tury ; who made a party considerable enough to be taken notice of by Dr. Mosheim, in his Ecclesiastical History. How
he was answered, I think the Docter hath not informed us.

tionably, was under personal obligation to yield the most perfect obedience to his Maker of which he was capable. Therefore had he remained innocent, and continued in all things given him in charge to do them, he could have had no merit of supererogation, to be reckoned to his posterity. Nor do I conceive that the *man Jesus Christ*, consistently with his personal duty to his heavenly Father, could have done less than to have fulfilled all righteousness. On supposition a *purchasing*, *transferable* merit had been necessary, I do not therefore see how this difficulty could be fairly obviated. But from the things which have been said, it is abundantly evident, I apprehend, that no such merit was necessary, is scriptural, or possible. God may do honour to himself, as one that loves righteousness, by making multitudes happy out of respect to the tried virtue and obedience of one, though that one have only done what it was his duty to do. All notions of supererogation, and of a fund of merit to be sold and bought, or any way communicated from one to another, proceed upon the maxims of *commercial*, not of *rectoral* justice. Every thing of this kind is going off entirely from the ideas of *sin* and *duty*, to those of *debt* and *credit*, *damages* and *reparations*.

Fourthly. From the foregoing view of the subject, we learn, that those who are justified in the gospel way, have nothing whereof to glory, but have all the reason in the world to be humble before God. They have merely a merit of congruity to plead in his presence ; and that merit, not at all their own.

Were " salvation an absolute debt to the believer from God, so that he might in justice demand and challenge it," to be clothed with humility, and to be a prostrate suppliant before the throne of grace, might, indeed, seem unbecoming, and quite out of character.

Had Christ " merited, by way of purchase and complete payment, the removal of all that evil we had deserved, and the enjoyment of all the good we needed
and could desire, and that by a valuable consideration
tendered into the hand of divine justice in that behalf ;"
and had we this " sum in sight, and under our hand,"
we might well assume a high tone, and say, " Here's
one and there's the other." Our beggary would be at
an end ; nor would it suit with our affluent circumstances, to be *so poor in spirit* as to *petition* and *pray.* We
might say to the Almighty, " We are lords, we will
come no more unto thee:" or, coming, might be so la-
conic as only to say, " Lord, give us our due."

But, my brethren, " you have not so learned Christ ;
if so be that ye have heard him, and have been taught
by him as the truth is in Jesus." Christians have not
these heaven-debasing, self-exalting sentiments, in the
bottom of their hearts, however they may speak un-
guardedly, or think inaccurately on some occasions. I
dare say the venerable divines above quoted, did not
mean so, neither *did their hearts think so.* They never
prayed as though those things were true ; they never
felt as if they believed them. Such speculative notions
of the atonement and imputed righteousness, owing
originally to the strong figures of holy scripture, literally understood, have been exceedingly common ; and
therefore have been received implicitly as unquestionable truths, by the learned as well as the illiterate ;
however inconsistent with innumerable other sentiments in which every true christian is most firmly established. Certainly, by the law of faith, boasting is
excluded. Certainly if our justification be freely by
divine grace, we have nothing whereof to glory. We
have as much reason to be humble—as much cause,
with deep abasement, to confess our daily sins, and to

implore the free remission of them—as much occasion to say, God be merciful to us sinners, as if we were not justified at all. The blood of atonement only gives us access to the mercy-seat. Let then all our feelings and all our thoughts, as well as our addresses to a holy God, be agreeable to this humiliating doctrine of our being justified freely by his grace, through the redemption that is in Jesus Christ. God thus established his covenant with us, that we may remember, and be confounded, and never open our mouths any more for our shame,·when, in this way, he is pacified towards us for all that we have done.

Fifthly. From what hath been said, we learn, nevertheless, that believers have as firm ground for hope and confidence in God, as if their justification were a matter of absolute debt. The new covenant is as *ever-lasting*, as well *ordered in all things*, and as *sure*, as if it were not at all a covenant of grace. The gospel plan of acceptance unto eternal life, is calculated, not in the least to mar our comfort, only to mortify our pride.

We have seen that there is no want of absolute promises to insure *grace* and *glory*, to all true believers in Jesus Christ. " All the promises in him are yea, and in him amen, unto the glory of God." And we know, says the same apostle, " that all things work together for good. to them that love God, to them who are the called according to his purpose. Who shall separate us from the love of Christ? Shall tribulation, or distress, or persecution, or famine, or nakedness, or peril, or sword? Nay, in all these things we are more than conquerors, through him that loved us. For I am persuaded, that neither death, nor life, nor angels, nor principalities, nor powers, nor things present, nor things to come, nor height, nor depth, nor any other creature, shall be able to separate us from the love of God which is in Christ Jesus our Lord. We have access, through Christ, by faith, into this grace wherein we stand, and rejoice in hope of the glory of God." Believers are as absolutely established in the divine favour and love, as if they were justified by the deeds of the law. Final remission of sins and eternal salvation, are as fully secured to them, as if their *ill-desert* were wholly done away, or as if they had even a merit of *condignity* and the Almighty were actually their infinite *debtor*. Hence another apostle *is very bold, and saith*, " If we confess our sins, he is faithful and just to forgive us our sins, and to cleanse us from all unrighteousness." Not that, on account of our confessions, or on any other account, we *justly deserve* to be forgiven *Deserved* forgiveness is *no forgiveness* at all. The meaning can only be, that God will infallibly be just and true to his word. A faithful and just man will fulfil his promises, however gratuitous the things promised: how much more He who " is not a man that he should lie, nor the son of man that he should repent ?" But, if his bare word were not enough, as the apostle observes, he hath added his *oath, that by two immutable things, in which it was impossible for God to lie, we might have a strong consolation, who have fled for refuge to lay hold upon the hope set before us.* We may, if we believe in God, and believe also in Christ, *come boldly* (though as humble beggars) *unto the throne of grace, that we may obtain mercy, and find grace to help in time of need.*

Sixthly, and lastly. Hence we should learn to *love mercy*, as well as to *walk humbly with our God*.

Had we the righteousness of Christ, as a perfect cloke for all our sins, so as to have no occasion for any *forgiveness*, it might more reasonably be expected that we should be *unforgiving*. Did *we need no mercy*, it would not be so very strange should we show none. But, my brethren, how far otherwise is the case with every one of us? Do we hope we are justified in the sight of a holy God? Be it so, it is *freely by his grace*, even *through the redemption that is in Jesus*. *If I justify myself*, says holy Job, *mine own mouth shall condemn me: if I say I am perfect, it shall also prove me perverse.* And indeed, as the same pious man demands, *How should man be just with God?* By *imputation* it hath been supposed he might; but we have now seen that even through the atonement and righteousness of Christ, we can have no plea of *not guilty*: And *personally* we cannot surely stand in judgment, should *he contend with* us, *nor answer him one of a thousand.*

Shall *we* then be strict to mark, and severe to revenge the trivial injuries or affronts we may receive from our fellow creatures. Read, Christians, the striking parable of the *ten thousand talents* and the *hundred pence*; read, and tremble at the awful application of that parable. Remember that most reasonable exhortation of the apostle, *which speaketh unto you as unto justified sinners*; Eph. iv. 23. " And be ye kind one to another, tender hearted, forgiving one another, even as God, for Christ's sake, hath forgiven you."

The Law in all respects satisfied by our Saviour, in regard to those only who belong to him ; or, None but Believers saved, thro' the all-sufficient Satisfaction of Christ.

A SERMON,

DELIVERED AT WALLINGFORD,

CONNECTICUT,

WITH A VIEW TO THE UNIVERSALISTS,

By JOHN SMALLEY, *D. D.*

None but Believers saved, through the all-sufficient Satisfaction of Christ.

ROMANS x. 4.

For Christ is the end of the law for righteousness, to every one that believeth.

THE capital argument of many who maintain that every one who believeth *not* shall be saved, we have particularly considered. That salvation is not a matter of just debt, on account of the redemption of Christ, hath been shown, it is presumed, beyond dispute.— This then being supposed a settled point, that God is at liberty to *have mercy on whom he will have mercy;* it remains that we must have recourse to the revelation of his sovereign will in his holy word, as the only way to determine, whether all, or only a part of mankind, shall be saved.

Nothing can be concluded from the universal benevolence of God, unless we knew, as he does, what would be for the greatest universal good. At first thought it may perhaps be imagined, that if it be only consistent with justice for God to give grace and salvation to all men, his infinite goodness must necessarily incline him to save all. But it ought to be remembered, that the operations of infinite goodness are ever under the direction of infinite wisdom. God will give eternal life to every rebel creature, however deserving of eternal death, if it be best; otherwise he will not. Its being at his sovereign option whether to do a thing or not, by no means make it certain what he will think proper to do. He was no more obliged in justice to permit any sin or misery ever to take place, than he is now to permit some to be forever sinful and miserable. From his goodness and power, we should have been ready to conclude he would have prevented the former, as we now are that he will prevent the latter. "His thoughts are not our thoughts. How unsearchable are his judgments," says the apostle, "and his ways past finding out! For who hath known the mind of the Lord? or who hath been his counsellor?" Were our understanding infinite, we might be able to judge, with great certainty, what he will think proper to do, on all occasions: but this not being quite the case, all conjectures respecting his determination, from what appears most desirable to us, must be very precarious. From his perfections we may be certain, in general, that he will ever do that which is wisest and best: but what is wisest and best, on the large scale of his universal administration, he alone can be supposed a competent judge.

Not leaning, then, to our own understanding, in a attep so evidently too high for us, let us, with unbiassed minds, attend to revelation as our only guide on the important question—Who of fallen creatures shall be saved?—Whether it seem good in the sight of God, to save mankind universally, without any conditions; or with certain limitations, and on certain terms.— This question is so abundantly resolved in the inspired scriptures, that to quote all the plain proofs that only particular characters in this world, shall have any part or lot in the salvation of the next, would be to quote, as it were, the whole bible. In the text now chosen, there is evidently implied, a restriction of deliverance from the law, to believers in the gospel; and in discoursing upon the words, among other things, occasion will naturally be given to adduce some part of the abundant scripture proof, limited in opposition to universal salvation.

The apostle having spoken, in the preceding chapter, of the rejection of the Jews for their unbelief, he begins this with expressing his sincere concern for them, and his most devout wishes that they might be recovered from their delusion, and not be lost. Ver. I. " Brethren, my heart's desire and prayer to God for Israel is, that they might be saved." However opposed any may be to us, we ought to feel entirely friendly towards them—to wish them no ill, but the greatest possible good. We ought also to entertain a charitable opinion concerning them, as far as the nature of the case will any way fairly admit. Such was the apostle's charity in regard to his deluded countrymen. He had no doubt that many of them acted conscientiously in their zealous opposition to the gospel, really believing it to be subversive of the divine law, and a system not according to godliness. He was once of the same way of thinking, as he confessed before king Agrippa. *I verily thought with myself,* says he, *that I ought to do many things contrary to the name of Jesus of Nazareth* From his own experience, therefore, as well as from much personal acquaintance, he could testify for them that their way was right in their own eyes, though really very erroneous and wrong. Ver. 2. "For I bear them record that they have a zeal of God, but not according to knowledge." He goes on to take notice whence their prejudices against the Christian revelation originated; namely, from wrong ideas of God. From not understanding his infinite and inflexible justice, the high demands of his holy law, and the absolute perfection required in order to legal justification in his sight.— Ver. 3. " For they, being ignorant of God's righteousness, and going about to establish their *own righteousness*, have not submitted themselves unto the righteousness of God." Then in the text he observes, that the cause of righteousness, for which the Pharisees were so full of anxiety, was in safe hands. That effectual care had been taken that the law should sustain no dishonour, but that the spirit of it should be supported, and its ultimate design be fully obtained. *For,* says he, *Christ is the end of the law for righteousness, to every one that believeth.* For the illustration of what is here asserted, I propose,

I. To show, in general, how *Christ is the end of the law for righteousness ;* and

II. In what respects he is so, in a particular manner, to believers in him.

I. I shall endeavour to show, in general, how Christ is the end of the law for righteousness.

He was the end of the ceremonial law of the Jews, as that was wholly typical of him, and was abolished by his death. But I cannot think the apostle here speaks merely, if at all, of the ceremonial law. That he has reference to the eternal law of righteousness, seems intimated by the manner of expression in the text; and it is evident from the words immediately following: Ver. 5...." For Moses describeth the righteousness which is of the law, that the man which doeth those things shall live by them." The ceremonial law was never able to give life, to those who trusted in the observance of it, however scrupulous and exact. It will therefore be incumbent on me to point out a sense, in which Christ is the end of the universal law of perfect righteousness; or of that law by the obedience of which innocent man might have obtained eternal life. He is not the end of this law in every sense which the carnal mind would wish, nor in several senses which many have supposed. More particularly,

1. It is certain Christ is not so, the end of the moral law, that it is no longer obligatory on mankind, as *a rule of duty.* That our Saviour had no such design as this, and that no such thing was possible, he was careful to inform the world in his first public discourse;—his sermon on the mount, " Think not," says he, " that I am come to destroy the law or the prophets: I am not come to destroy, but to fulfil. For, verily, I say unto you, Till heaven and earth pass, one jot or one tittle shall in no wise pass from the law, till all be fulfilled." Nor did he come to fulfil this holy law so as to make it lawful for us to live in the violation of it. We do not, surely, cease to be in duty bound to love God or our neighbour, because Christ hath loved both, as much as they deserve. It is not become right for us to practise all iniquity, because he hath fulfilled all righteousness. By his having been perfectly obedient in our stead, we are not freed from all the obligation we should have been under to obey the commands of our Maker; nor from any part of it. We have as

much duty which we ought to do, as if he had done nothing. He came to *save his people from their sins*, not from their *duty*.

2. Christ hath not so saved his people from their sins, that they cease to have *any guilt*, or *desert of punishment*. As our obligation to obey is not removed by his obedience, so neither is our criminality when we transgress, taken away by his sufferings. We are not to conceive God sees nothing amiss in us, and is not at all displeased with us, do what we will, because the blood of Jesus Christ his son, cleanseth from all sin. The eyes of the Omniscient are not so dazzled but that he can see our ways, and our hearts, as they truly are ; nor is the nature of things so altered by the atonement, that iniquity is become really blameless, and undeserving of divine wrath. I add once more on the negative side,

3. Christ is not so the end of the law, but that personal righteousness is still *necessary* in order to eternal life. Not only is perfect obedience as much our duty as ever, and all neglect or transgression as great an evil as ever ; but sincere conformity in heart and life to the moral law; is so required on the gospel plan, that without it we cannot be saved. Of this we are abundantly assured. " Repent and be converted," says the apostle Peter, " that your sins may be blotted out. Follow peace with all men," says the apostle Paul, " and holiness, without which no man shall see the Lord. Verily, verily," says our Saviour, " I say unto thee, except a man be born again, he cannot see the kingdom of God." And again, " I say unto you, that except your righteousness shall exceed the righteousness of the Scribes and Pharisees, ye shall in no case enter into the kingdom f heaven." To the same purpose, having explained 1e moral law in a much stricter sense than the most

rigid of the Jewish doctors, he concludes with saying, " Whosoever heareth these sayings of mine, and doth them, I will liken him unto a wise man, which built his house upon a rock. And every one that heareth these sayings of mine, and doth them not, shall be likened unto a foolish man, which built his house upon the sand."

But in what sense, then, it will be asked, is Christ the end of the law for righteousness? I answer, He is the end of the law as a covenant of life; or as the term of justification or condemnation. That is, the end for which probationary obedience was required of man, in order to his confirmation, is answered by the obedience of Christ; and the end for which death was threatened in case of any disobedience, is answered by the sufferings and death of Christ.

According to the original constitution, perfect obedience, through a certain space of trial, was made necessary in order to the justification of life There was some important end proposed by this, most certainly; otherwise the benevolent Creator would have confirmed our first parents, with all their posterity, in immortal happiness, without the hazard of a previous probation. The end which would have been answered by man's trial, had he persevered in innocence, may easily be conceived. Virtue would have been encouraged and had in eternal honour; and God, by crowning it with an eternal weight of glory, would have illustriously manifested his infinite love of righteousness. When man had sinned, he must, according to law, have been punished with everlasting destruction. Here again some good end, undoubtedly, was in view: God delighteth not *in the death of the wicked.* The misery of his creatures, however justly merited, cannot be an ultimate object to a Being whose name, and

whose nature is love. The end of the awful threatening and curse of the law, we are to suppose, was dis-
countenancing disobedience, and giving an eternal
manifestation of the glorious character of God, as one
who infinitely hateth all iniquity. Now, by the vicarious obedience and sufferings of his own incarnate
Son, the end of the law, in each of these views, is answered in the fullest manner.

. . The obedience of our Saviour answers every purpose, in regard to all who belong to him, which would
have been obtained by the sinless obedience of the first
federal head of mankind. Christ was *given for a covenant of the people.* He was constituted a public representative, as much as Adam was; and might, by his
own consent, as justly be so constituted. In this capacity he was *made under the law ;* and, *as it behoved him,
fulfilled all righteousness.* He was *holy, harmless, undefiled, and separate from sinners. He did no sin, neither was guile found in his mouth.* It was his *meat to
do the will of him that sent him, and finish his work.*
His obedience was tried to the uttermost. He had all
the temptations arising from poverty and the most dependent outward circumstances. *The foxes,* said he,
*have holes, and the birds of the air have nests, but the
Son of man hath not where to lay his head.* He had the
trial of cruel mockings, and of all the bitterest and most
injurious reproaches which the malice of man could
invent. *Consider him,* says the apostle, *who endured
such contradiction of sinners against himself.* He en-
countered the grand adversary that had been too hard
for our first parents, and under circumstances the most
disadvantageous He was led into the wilderness to
be tempted of the devil, that he might have the trial of
is utmost efforts in that solitary situation, without a
end—without a second to afford him any aid. Here

forty days he was without food ; and, thus enfeebled and distressed with hunger, he was attacked by the old serpent, the prince of the power of the air, who had permission to try every artifice—to carry him from pinacle to mountain, and exhibit all those scenes to his senses, which he judged most likely to seduce him into sin. But this second man was found invincible, and easily vanquished all temptations. Our Saviour's subjection was also tried by the last enemy—an enemy which Adam, in all his probation, had he kept his innocence, never would have seen. He was *obedient unto death, even the death of the cross.* In his agony, from the extremity of which we must conclude he had something far more dismaying in prospect than any other martyr ever endured, when he *kneeled down and prayed, saying, Father, if thou be willing, remove this cup from me ;* he added, *nevertheless, not my will, but thine be done.*

Now by such obedience, of so divine a person—by his *patient continuance in well doing,* amidst all possible provocations and temptations to the contrary, from earth and hell—by his perfect conformity and ready resignation to the holy will of his heavenly Father, through all the arduous work, and agonizing conflicts to which he was called—an opportunity was given for the Supreme Governor of the world, to encourage virtue, and to glorify himself as the lover and rewarder of righteousness, in the most illustrious manner possible. For here was an instance—a course of obedience and virtue, the most tried—the most perfect—the most exalted, that ever was, or could be exhibited, in the whole creation of God.

And no less fully answered was the end of the threatening and curse of the law, by our Saviour's sufferings. It was by the Father's appointment, though by his own most free consent, that he was made a curse in the room of guilty men. He was *stricken, smitten of God, and afflicted.* He was *delivered by the determinate counsel,* as well as *fore-knowledge of God,* when he was *taken, and by wicked hands, crucified and slain. Both Herod and Pontius Pilate,* with the rulers and people of the Jews, did against him, only what *God's hand and his counsels determined before to be done.* The hand of the Supreme Judge of all the earth, was particularly concerned in this surprising event. It was designed to be considered as an act of divine judgment, notwithstanding the wickedness of the instruments, and the innocence of the sufferer. For thus it was written, " Awake, O sword, against my Shepherd, and against the man, that is my fellow, saith the Lord of Hosts : Smite the Shepherd," &c.

Now by laying such amazing sufferings on his dearly beloved Son—by *its pleasing the Lord* thus *to bruise him,* and put him to grief, the divine vindictive justice was more awfully, as well as more amiably manifested, than ever it could have been by the punishment of sinners themselves, to all eternity.—It was more awfully manifested. The apostle, Romans i. 17, 18. having spoken of the gospel as the power of God unto salvation to every one that believeth, assigns the following reason : *For therein is the righteousness of God revealed from faith to faith :—For the wrath of God is revealed from heaven against all ungodliness and unrighteousness of men.* His meaning I conceive is this ; that there is a clearer discovery of the holiness and justice of God, to hate and punish all sin, in *Christ crucified,* than in any former revelation. And undoubtedly this is true. Not all the curses of the law, amidst the hunders and lightenings of mount Sinai—nor even the execution of those curses in the unquenchable flames of hell, gave, or can ever give, equal evidence of the righteousness or wrath of God, as the amazing scenes exhibted in Gethsemane, and on mount Calvary. Nothing could ever make the law appear so steadfast, or afford such full ground of faith that every transgression shall receive a just recompence of reward, as the bloody sweat—the deserted exclamation—the expiring agonies, of our Divine Saviour.

This exhibition of vindictive justice, it ought particularly to be observed, was finished and compleat. In this way *an end was made of sin ;* that is, of its adequate and threatened punishment. We may naturally understand this as a principal thing implied in those memorable words of Christ, when he bowed his head and gave up the ghost, *It is finished.*—Had only the letter of the law taken place, never could the execution of divine justice been compleat. *The wrath to come* would forever have remained. Nor could it ever have appeared by any thing actually done, that God determined to inflict sufferings for sin, in any respect, absolutely infinite. The death of Christ is the only *fact* which ascertains this, or could ever ascertain it.

And as the awfulness, so the amiableness of vindictive justice, is in this way most gloriously evinced.— That this attribute of the Supreme Being is at an infinite remove from malevolence—that he doth not punish from unkindness, or from any delight in tormenting, is what we are often taught, and what it is of great importance we should ever firmly believe. But in no instance is this so unquestionably manifest, as when the sufferings deserved by the iniquities of us all, were laid on Christ. Had only rebel creatures— the personal enemies of God, suffered the dreadful effects of his righteous displeasure, it would not have been so clear, that in his fierce wrath there was nothing cruel—nothing akin to the sweetness of human revenge. But when the same sword is commanded to awake against the man that is his fellow—when his only begotten Son is the victim of his holy indignation, against the ungodliness and unrighteousness of man, we must needs be convinced that want of benevolence can have no influence. Christ was certainly dear to to the Father—infinitely dear, even when he forsook him, and laid such insupportable sorrows upon him. *He was the brightness of his glory, and the express image of his person;* and he had done nothing to offend him, but was then doing that which infinitely engaged his most endeared affection. Yet when, out of obedience to the Father's will, and tenderest feelings for his injured honour, he had undertaken to be answerable for the offences of fallen man, not one drop of the necessary bitter cup was permitted to pass from him. *Judgment was laid to the line, and righteousness to the plummet,* in as rigorous and unrelenting a manner, as if he had actually been the most odious criminal in all the universe. By this it appears, with the highest possible evidence, not only that there is no respect of persons with God, but also that his inflicting the severest pains and penalties for sin, argues no want of infinite tenderness towards the sufferers. That it is owing only to a just regard to his own glory, and the general good.

Thus is Christ the end, and more than the end of the law for righteousness. The end of the probationary obedience required of man, is more than answered by his obedience; and the end of the curse denounced on fallen man, is more than answered by his being made a curse. We may now proceed,

II. To make some enquiry concerning the implied limitation in the text; or to consider why Christ is said to be the end of the law for righteousness, *to every one that believeth.* We are not to suppose, from this, that there is any want of sufficiency in what our Saviour hath done and suffered, to answer the original purposes of personal obedience and personal punishment in regard to all mankind, did they believe in him. Should all men come to the knowledge of the truth, and cordially embrace the gospel, they might be saved, and every end of the law be fully obtained. But still there are respects in which Christ is actually the end of the law to true believers only ; that is, to those who know him, and receive him, and trust in him as their Saviour. Particularly,

First, Christ is, in a peculiar manner, the end of the law for righteousness to believers, as, in their view and apprehension, the divine justice is established by his sufferings, as much as if law had been literally executed. By the everlasting destruction of every transgressor, God would not have appeared more glorious in holiness, than he now does by the sacrifice of his own Son, in the eyes of every one that believeth. *God, who commanded the light to shine out of darkness,* says the apostle, *hath shined in our hearts, to give the light of the knowledge of the glory of God, in the face of Jesus Christ.* The glory of God's justice undoubtedly, as well as the glory of his grace. But now to unbelievers, this glorious exhibition of the divine character is to no purpose. To them this *light,* if it shine at all, *shineth in darkness,* and is not comprehended. To those who never heard the gospel, or hearing understand it not, or do not believe it, this end of the law is not at all answered by it. Of old the preaching of *Christ crucified,*

The Law in all respects satisfied by our Saviour, in regard to those only who belong to him; or, None but Believers saved, thro' the all-sufficient Satisfaction of Christ.

A SERMON,

DELIVERED AT WALLINGFORD,

CONNECTICUT,

WITH A VIEW TO THE UNIVERSALISTS,

By JOHN SMALLEY, *D. D.*

None but Believers saved, through the all-sufficient Satisfaction of Christ.

ROMANS x. 4.

For Christ is the end of the law for righteousness, to every one that believeth.

THE capital argument of many who maintain that every one who believeth *not* shall be saved, we have particularly considered. That salvation is not a matter of just debt, on account of the redemption of Christ, hath been shown, it is presumed, beyond dispute.— This then being supposed a settled point, that God is at liberty to *have mercy on whom he will have mercy;* it remains that we must have recourse to the revelation of his sovereign will in his holy word, as the only way to determine, whether all, or only a part of mankind, shall be saved.

M 2

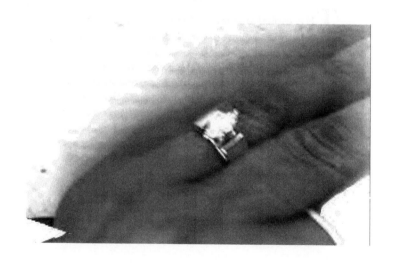

personal righteousness, or sanctification, is absolutely secured. But this is by no means the case with respect to unbelievers. In regard to those who have not the faith of God's elect, none of the foregoing things are true. Of them he is despised and rejected, or else altogether unknown. *When they see him, there is no beauty that they should desire him.* His doctrine they do not love, his cross they cannot bear, his commandments are always grievous to them. *They break his bands asunder, and cast away his cords from them.*—*They are dead in transgression and sin,* and walk *according to the course of this world, according to the prince of the power of the air, the spirit which now worketh in the children of disobedience.* Hence,

Fourthly, Christ is the end of the law to every one that believeth, as believers, and they only, are delivered from the curse, and entitled to eternal life, through his atonement and righteousness. This I know is disputed. But how it can be disputed, by any who admit the authority of the inspired scriptures, I am not able to conceive. All those texts which speak of our being justified by faith, plainly imply that believers only are in a state of justification. Nor can any thing less be implied in what St. Paul says was the constant tenor of his preaching, publicly and in private—" Testifying both to the Jews, and also to the Greeks, repentance towards God, and faith towards our Lord Jesus Christ." Undoubtedly he testified what was the way for every man, and the only way for any man, to obtain pardon and eternal life. And unless faith be infallibly connected with salvation, and absolutely necessary in order to it, what can be the meaning of that apostolic answer to the all-important question, *What shall I do to be saved ? Believe on the Lord Jesus Christ, and thou shalt be saved.* Unless unbelief will exclude from all part or lot in the salvation of the gospel, what can be meant by such solemn demands and assertions as the following? " How shall we escape if we neglect so great salvation? But if our gospel be hid, it is hid to them that are lost; in whom the God of this world hath blinded the minds of them that believe not, lest the light of the glorious gospel of Christ, who is the image of God, should shine into them. For as many as are of the works of the law are under the curse. Christ is become of none effect unto you, whosoever of you are justified by the law, ye are fallen from grace." The meaning of the two last mentioned texts plainly is, that those who expect justification by works, must stand or fall by the law of perfection; and that such dependance on any legal observance, as is inconsistent with trusting alone in the merits of Christ, cuts a person off from all interest in him, and from all benefit by the grace of the gospel.

But let us hear the great Teacher come from God— *the author of eternal salvation* himself, on this important question. " Verily, verily," he says, " I say unto you, He that heareth my word, and believeth on him that sent me, hath everlasting life, and shall not come into condemnation; but is passed from death unto life. For God so loved the world, that he gave his only begotten Son, that whosoever believeth in him, might not perish, but have everlasting life. He that believeth in him is not condemned : but he that believeth not is condemned already, because he hath not believed in the name of the only begotten Son of God. If ye believe not that I am he, ye shall die in your sins. He that believeth on the Son, hath everlasting life; and he that believeth not the Son, shall not see life; but the wrath of God abideth on him. Go ye into all the world, and preach the gospel to every creature. He that believeth and is baptized shall be saved ; and he that believeth not shall be damned."

It is needless to multiply scripture proofs of that to which all the scriptures bear witness. If we mean to build our system on the foundation of the apostles and prophets, or of Jesus Christ himself, the chief corner stone, we must, I think, make it one of the first and most fixed articles of our creed, that true believers, and they only, shall be saved. On no point is the New Testament more full and explicit, than on this.

What remains is by way of inference and application. From the view we have taken of the subject, we may learn,

1. That the gospel constitution, according to which a man is justified by, and not without, faith, is founded in the reason and fitness of things. If any will not be convinced of the fact that this is gospel, by the gospel itself, unless they can see the reason of it, a rational account of this matter may now easily be given. The three first particulars under the last head, are so many obvious and weighty reasons, why he that believeth shall be saved, and he that believeth not shall be damned.

It is reasonable and of importance that all men, by some means or other, should be made to know that God is a holy and righteous being ; one who infinitely hates, and will certainly punish sin. Believers are taught this by the gospel ; unbelievers must learn it by the law. To those in whom a proper impression is made of the vindictive justice of God by the death of Christ, there is no necessity that he should show his wrath in their own eternal sufferings. To those who get no reverential idea of God, as a consuming fire, by Christ crucified, it it necessary that he should make

himself known by terrible things in righteousness, personally inflicted. If men will not see, they must be
made to feel.   If the evangelical ministration of righteousness be hid, or will have no effect, the legal ministration of condemnation must have its course.   If by
God's not sparing his own Son, sinners, instead of seeing his wrath revealed against all ungodliness and unrighteousness of men, will be only led stupidly to conceive he is altogether such an one as themselves, some
other measures must be used.   He must reprove
them, and set things in order before their eyes, in another manner.   It may be necessary that he should
tear them in pieces, and that there should *be none to deliver.*

It is reasonable and of importance that all who are
saved, should be made sensible to whom the glory of
their salvation belongs, and not be left vainly to arro-
gate it to themselves.   For this, provision is made by
the law of faith.   Every one that believeth clearly sees
his own utter unworthiness, and that all his salvation is
owing to free grace, as the only moving cause, and to
the righteousness of Christ, as the alone meritorious
ground.   On the contrary, as hath been observed,
every one that believeth not, builds his hopes of the
peculiar favour of God on personal character;—on
works of righteousness which he hath done, or expects
to do; thus robbing Christ, as well as grace, of the
praise so infinitely deserved.   In a low degree indebted
to our great Redeemer, some unbelievers will indeed
acknowledge themselves.   Thus far only, that, by his
death, he hath procured an abatement of rigorous
law—a reasonable abatement; so that now, notwithstanding our enfeebled circumstances occasioned by
the fall, we may humbly hope for the gracious acceptance of heaven, if we only exert ourselves to the ut-

termost, and do the best we possibly can. This best they mean to endeavour to do, and doubt not God will be faithful and just to forgive unavoidable imperfections. They think already they have done more than others, and expect distinguishing mercy, since they have made themselves to differ. Now for God to justify those who view matters thus, would be giving up the whole controversy in favour of the carnal mind. It would be to justify sinners, just as they do themselves, on account of their moral depravity. It would be to concede to them that fallen creatures deserve pity, rather than blame, let them conduct how they will; and that really there is little grace, in all the great things done for their salvation. God cannot in justice to himself, or to his Son, be reconciled to sinners, while they are upon these terms;—while they only want justice, and to be treated in character, and they are not concerned. Wisdom, righteousness, grace—every divine perfection requires, either that these imaginations of men should be cast down, or else that they *should be treated in character*, and have ample justice done them. Hence, with highest reason, thus it is written: "Behold all ye that kindle a fire, that compass yourselves about with sparks; walk in the light of your fire, and in the sparks which ye have kindled. This shall ye have of mine hand, ye shall lie down in sorrow."

It is reasonable and of importance, that every rational creature, in some form or other, should be kept under the divine moral government. To discharge mankind from liableness to law, while they are in no subjection to the gospel, would be breaking all bands asunder. It would be letting sinners loose, without any *guide, overseer, or ruler;* and without any thing to control or make them afraid. Such anarchy can by

no means be tolerated, under the all-perfect divine administration. Against such lawless liberty, therefore,
the grace of God which bringeth salvation effectually
guards. This great evil, which else would arise from
remission of sins, is prevented by the gospel terms ;
repentance from dead works, and *believing with the
heart unto righteousness.* Every one is under the
curse, till he is under law to Christ. Nothing avails,
in order to an interest in the atonement, but faith
which worketh by love. On this plan, no sinner has
reason to consider himself safe from the wrath to
come, but in proportion to the evidence he has that
he is *created unto good works.* On this plan the restraints of *fear* are not at all taken off, but in proportion
as *love* prevails, and *casteth out fear*—that love which
is the fulfilling of the law. On this plan, the unrighteous shall not inherit the kingdom of God, because it
is certain they are not the disciples of Christ. For in
vain do any call him their Saviour, unless they keep
his commandments. He will be the author of eternal
salvation to all them that obey him ; but to them who
have not obeyed him, he will afford no shelter or pro-
tection. His enemies, who would not that he should
reign over them, shall be slain before him. That
such should be the constitution of the gospel, was
necessary, that Christ might not be a minister of sin,
but that righteousness and peace might be established,
as far as his kingdom should extend. This was neces- ·
sary that all restraints from iniquity might not be taken
off, but that, one way or other, every soul of man,
should be subject to the moral government of God.—
And to the fitness and propriety of these terms of the
dispensation of grace, unless we will be avowed advocates for the cause of unrighteousness, what can
we in reason object. For,

2. We infer from the things which have been said, that the requisition of faith, lessens not the glory of free grace, nor of the all-sufficiency of Christ; but quite the reverse. Some indeed have supposed a difficulty here. How faith, or any thing else in us, can be requisite, and available, in the affair of justification, without giving man whereof to glory; or without detracting from the fulness of Christ's merit, and the freeness of God's grace, many have been at a loss to comprehend. That some nice distinction is necessary in order fairly to get over this difficulty, the most who have attended at all accurately to the matter, seem to have been sensible. But what the proper distinction is, few have been able to satisfy others, if themselves. To say, as some have done, that faith is not a *condition*, but only the *instrument* of justification, it appears to me, rather darkens than clears up the subject. Faith is a conviction of the mind, and an act of the soul; and cannot with any propriety be called an instrument. Besides, it is plainly that on which our salvation is suspended—that without which we cannot be, and having which we certainly shall be saved; which is the proper idea of a condition, call it by what name we will. It is, however, of the last importance that this difficulty should be clearly obviated. Were it impossible for faith which worketh by love to avail any thing, without lessening our dependance on the righteousness of Christ, and obscuring the lustre of free grace, this would seem indeed a weighty objection against its being supposed necessary. But we need not invent *another gospel*, according to which a man is justified *without faith*, and may get to heaven *without holiness*, that boasting may be excluded, and that grace may abound. The only thing needful is to show, that nothing in us is required or

available, as in any sense meritorious. We may distinguish between *a condition*, and a *meritorious* condition; *a congruity*, and a *merit* of congruity. This distinction applies in a multitude of common instances. Something is often required to be known or done by a person, in order to his inheriting an interest, or being the proper subject of certain immunities and privileges, when it is not at all required under a notion of its rendering the person deserving, and is of no kind of avail in that view. That thus it is in the case before us, and how it is thus, may easily be perceived from the things now said upon this subject.

We have not only seen, under the first head, that what our Saviour hath done needs no addition, in point of atonement, or of merit: but, under the second, we have seen that Christ is the end of the law for actual justification, to believers rather than unbelievers, not because of any worthiness in the former, more than in the latter; but for other reasons altogether. What merit is there in being made to see the justice of God, as displayed in the sufferings of his own incarnate Son, the sinners substitute?—Yet this is necessary that the divine character may be vindicated, in the eyes of every one who is saved.—In the next thing implied in saving faith—being convinced of our infinite unworthiness, and of the all-sufficiency of Christ's righteousness, and the sovereign freeness of God's grace—certainly we can have no merit here, nor has this any tendency to self-exaltation. The very reason why a right understanding and belief of these things are required, is, that pride might be hid from man, and that he who is justified might glory only in the Lord. And what mighty merit is there in consenting to have such an one as Christ for our Saviour, when, *in the day of his power,* we are made *willing?* Can this be so great a thing in such creatures as we are, as to deserve the remission of all our former infinite offences, and to render it no more than suitable that we would be immediately received as the sons of God, and heirs of immortal glory!—No such thing surely can be supposed   The congruity here cannot, by any means, be a merit of congruity.   There is not even a *comparative* merit in the believer, in many cases.   Other things being equal, it is true he is a little more excellent than the unbeliever ; but very often the man who believes to the saving of his soul, in point of desert, all things considered, is ten times more a child of hell, than thousands who perish in their sins.   Notwithstanding he is so good, through divine grace, as to consent to be saved, yet, upon the whole, he is a much greater sinner than multitudes who do not thus consent ; which shows that worthiness is not the thing needed, nor regarded.—The congruity that every one who cordially embraces the gospel should be saved, does not consist in personal excellency, but is quite from another quarter. By this act he puts himself under the care of Christ, who thereupon becomes surety for his recovery from all iniquity, and that he shall be zealous of good works : hence he may safely be released from unpardoning law, and be interested in *a better covenant, established upon better promises, in the hand* of a mediator.   Christ is guarantee for as many as receive him ; therefore to all such the happy privilege is given, to become the sons of God.—In every view of the matter, *boasting is excluded by the law of faith ;* in every view, *therefore it is of faith, that it might be by grace.*   By a right understanding, a firm belief, and a cordial compliance with the gospel, the sinner is sunk down, in his own eyes, to his proper place ; while to the Father of mer-

cies, and the all-sufficient Saviour of them who were
utterly lost, is given the glory so infinitely deserved.
Christ and grace are more exalted, and man is more
abased, than if remission of sins and eternal life were
given to sinners, remaining in ignorance and unbelief.

3. The things which have been said may help us to
see, that there is really an universal door of mercy
opened to sinners, and a glorious hope set before all
without exception, for which they have infinite reason
to glorify God and to be thankful; the limitation in the
text notwithstanding. Had no sufficient provision been
made for the salvation of but only a remnant of mankind; or, were the terms of obtaining an interest in the
covenant of grace *naturally impossible* to men, without
that special divine influence which is given only to an
elect number, it would indeed seem, as some have objected, that the offers of mercy could not, with any
sincerity, be made to the non-elect; and that it could
not be their fault that they are not saved. But neither
of these is truly the case. *Christ hath tasted death for
every man,* so that no man need *taste the second death,*
because of any want of sufficiency in his atonement.
He is the propitiation for the sins of every one that believeth; and not for theirs only, *but also for the sins of
the whole world.* He hath rendered all that obedience,
and endured all that suffering which the law made necessary, in order to the eternal redemption of every
individual of the human race. By *his righteousness the
free gift* may come *upon all men unto justification,* unless it be because they *will not,* or do not, *come unto
him that they might have life. This is a faithful saying,
and worthy of all acceptation, that Christ Jesus came
into the world to save sinners; the chief of sinners.——*
and what doth the Lord our God require of us, in

order to an interest in Christ and in his salvation? Nothing naturally impossible, surely. Nothing which would be hard, were it not for an evil heart. It is but to understand what is most plainly revealed—to love that which is obviously most excellent—and to do that which is evidently most reasonable. As to knowing what we are to believe, as far as is necessary in order to eternal life, were men willing to come to the knowledge of the truth, there would be no difficulty. A very little serious attention to the bible would be sufficient. There is no necessity of ascending high, or diving deep, to find the infallible truth, the word is in all your hands, in which it is fully made known.—Nor would it be any harder to perceive the things of the spirit of God, as they are spiritually discerned, than to understand them in speculation, were it not for the blindness of men's hearts; their selfishness, pride and other corrupt passions. To see the hatefulness of sin, the desirableness of salvation, and the universal loveliness of the Lord Jesus Christ, would be the easiest things in the world, were it not for a totally vicious taste, whence wicked men *call evil good, and good evil; put bitter for sweet, and sweet for bitter.*—And as to doing what is required—being willing to be followers of Christ, denying ourselves and taking up the cross; nothing in this is impracticable, or arduous, provided we have any real inclination to be good. His *yoke is easy*—his *burden is light*—his *commandments are not grievous.* What God said to Cain, he may most justly say to every murmurer against the terms of the gospel, as hard and impossible; *Why art thou wroth? and why is thy countenance fallen? If thou dost well, shalt thou not be accepted? and if thou dost not well, sin lieth at the door.* If doing at all well be our duty, or if doing not well in any case be our sin, it must lie at our own door if we perish, or fail of eternal life. No unbeliever can dispute this, unless he will assert, that dispising and rejecting Christ, making light of the gospel, and neglecting so great salvation, is doing well.—A door of salvation is set open to all men. *Whosoever will,* is heartily bid welcome to *take of the water of life freely.* Yet,

4. From the limitation in the text, as explained in the foregoing discourse, have we not great reason to apprehend that many receive the grace of God in vain, and that, through their own fault, Christ will become of none effect to multitudes? Such apprehensions, however uncharitable, are abundantly suggested in the holy scriptures. When our Saviour was asked, *Lord, are there few that be saved?* he did not assert the contrary, but answered and said, "Strive to enter in at the strait gate: for many, I say unto you, will seek to enter in, and shall not be able." In another place he says, "Enter ye in at the strait gate; for wide is the gate, and broad is the way that leadeth to destruction, and many there be which go in thereat: because strait is the gate, and narrow is the way which leadeth unto life, and few there be that find it." And according to the account of the gate and the way of salvation now given, men must be exceedingly pressed, and very powerfully persuaded, before they will be disposed to enter in at that gate, and to walk in that way. How many are perfectly careless concerning the world to come, and scarce ever ask the question, what they shall do to be saved? When the gospel is preached to them, they make light of it, and pay little attention to it. Their farms, their merchandize, their luxuries, diversions and pleasures, engross their whole time: their bibles they rarely read, and God is not in all their

"ghts. How many have not faith, and take no pains

to know what they are to believe ? How many are left to strong delusions to believe lies, and stop their ears like the deaf adder, against all arguments to convince them of the errors they have imbibed ? How many *say to the seers, see not ; and to the prophets, prophesy not unto us right things, speak unto us smooth things, prophesy deceits ?* How many are *far from righteousness ?* far fom being *zealous of good works ?* How many are *disobedient, serving divers lusts and pleasures, living in malice and envy, hateful and hating one another ?* If *the curse which goeth forth over the face of the whole earth,* even under the gospel, be such, that *every one that is unrighteous shall be cut off on this side according to it,* and every one who is *self-righteous shall be cut off on that side according to it,* how few will be left ? Have we not reason to fear that the *blessed,* who shall *inherit the kingdom of God,* are, comparatively, but a *little flock ?*

Were saving faith only a belief, that, through the atonement, good men shall be saved on account of their own goodness ; and did this faith save men, only as it is a principle of moral virtue, or a motive to good works ;—personal morality being the alone real ground of distinction between one man and another, in regard to eternal life, as some have supposed ; we might, indeed, extend our charity very far. We might think, with men of liberal sentiments, that, whatever men's faith may be, or whether they have any faith at all, they will be saved, provided only their lives be good. For if the *only* end of believing the gospel were to make men moral, provided this end be obtained, no matter about the means. Yea, in that case, we might say to the christian, Because thou hast believed the future things revealed, thou hast been careful to maintain good works ; blessed are they that have not believed, and yet have maintained good works. Their virtue and reward must be greater, in proportion as their motives have been less.

On the other hand, were the faith by which a man is justified, only a belief that he is in a state of justification ; and this without any ground, from scripture, or sense, or reason, more than what every man has, all which others have taught, we might well extend our charity further still. We must conclude, on those principles, that all men are actually in a state of justification ; or else run into the palpable absurdity of supposing that a thing before not true, is made a truth by being believed.

But very different must be our apprehensions, concerning the safe and happy condition of mankind, according to the things which have now been advanced. The true evangelical faith implies, a right understanding and firm belief of the glorious revelation of God's righteous wrath against the ungodliness and unrighteousness of men, by the substituted voluntary sufferings of his own incarnate Son ; it implies an entire dependance on mere mercy, through the alone merit of Jesus Christ, for acceptance unto eternal life ; viewing ourselves as infinitely unworthy, and the chief of sinners :—it also implies a cordial willingness to be saved from our sins, and to be subject in all things to our divine Redeemer ; and its never-failing consequences are, remaining and increasing righteousness and true holiness, in heart and in all manner of conversation. Every one that hath this faith, shall be saved ; and every one that hath it not, shall be damned. If, by searching the scriptures, we be fully convinced that these things are so, our charity must necessarily be very narrow and contracted. Though we would fain hope all things, and believe all things, as far as the utmost bounds of rational probability; yet we cannot but fear, it is still the sad case, that many are in the way which leadeth to destruction; and that few find the gate, and are going in the way which leadeth unto everlasting life.

5. Hence you easily see we cannot approve the very extensive charity of those, who believe that all mankind are in a state of grace, and will certainly be saved, however much they may break the law of God, and make light of the gospel of Christ. Not but that a very small degree of universal benevolence, would undoubtedly lead any one most devoutly to wish that the bitter cup of never-ending misery, might pass from every soul of man, *if it were possible ;*—if it might be, consistently with the highest glory of God, and the greatest universal good. Not but that we ought undoubtedly to pray for the worst of men, and our bitterest enemies, that they may be saved; and to do all in our power to promote their salvation. Universal charity is good, if it be used charitably. But we must think the Universalists exercise and express their charity, to destruction and not to edification. We cannot think that the likeliest way to save those who are going on in their sins, is to tell them they are in no danger : Nor can we possibly believe, unless we had quite another gospel, that the careless neglecters of the great salvation—the abusers of the goodness, and forbearance, and long-suffering of God—the despisers and rejecters of a dying Saviour—and liars, and thieves, and murderers, are all in the sure way to immortal happiness. How any who believe the bible, can believe this, we cannot comprehend. Yet such, we hear, are the glad tidings of great joy, of late proclaimed by some, in the pulpits of Him who is the end of the law for righteousness : who, they suppose, hath so effectually put an

end to all divine law, that every lover of iniquity may give full scope to all his appetites and lusts, with certain impunity, and even without sin ! So they preach, and so some of you, my hearers, I understand, believe.

If this be *glory to God in the highest ;* if it be most conducive to *peace on earth,* and expressive of the greatest *good will towards men,* so would we gladly believe and preach likewise. But to convince us of this, we want much more substantial reasons than any we have yet heard. We are not satisfied that unbelievers are as safe as believers, excepting only their present anxiety, merely by the fine story of a weak old woman, thrown into a mighty panic at hearing cannon on an occasion of public rejoicing.* That a sinner may be saved without the faith of the Univerlsalists, as well as with, were that faith true, is too self-evident to require any great parade of candor in them to own, or of address in order to its illustration. But that men who *know not God, and obey not the gospel of our Lord Jesus Christ,* are really as safe as the soundest believers, and most virtuous christians ; not all the wit of man, nor all the subtilty of the old serpent, will be able to give full satisfaction to every one.

I have read several of the most celebrated pieces on the side of universal salvation; but have seen nothing in any of them that looks like more than the shadow of an argument in its support. Nothing that in any measure shakes the foundation upon which the contrary doctrine rests. *Every way of a man is right in his own eyes.* Theirs doubtles is so to some of

---

* A story told by the famous Mr. Murry, in a sermon preached just before in the same place, of an aged lady who was frightened out of her wits, by the firing in consequence of the capture of Lord Cornwallis; insisting that the enemy were coming, and refusing to be pacified.

them. They have naturally enough been led into it, it must be granted, by the errors of many others, who have not carried their inquiries so far, nor been so self-consistent. I am ready also to suppose, that the tender feelings of humanity may have had considerable influence with some, to induce them to believe this seemingly most benevolent doctrine. However, if any rational man who has been leaning that way, will candidly advert to the reasons and proofs in support of the opposite opinion, even only as now partially stated, I cannot but think he will be somewhat staggered. I imagine he must be convinced thus far, at least, that risking men's souls on the presumption that all will be saved, is going upon a very *forlorn hope.*

Let me intreat such an one, not to endanger himself, or others by presuming thus, *and teaching men so ;* be sure without weighing the matter well, and being very certain that he is not in an error. It is better not to have the honour of leading a party, and being of the foremost in singular discoveries, than to *go down to the grave with a lie in one's right hand ;* or to lead others upon ground which will not support them, and be the occasion of their falling into the pit, out of which there may be no redemption. It is better that men should not *laugh now,* than that they should *mourn and weep forever and ever.* If the doctrine of universal salvation be true, all the good that is done by its propagation, is only preventing a little present disquietude to sinners, who are generally pretty secure and easy already. If it be not true, the mischief done by thus encouraging them in carelessness and transgression, may be no less than being the means of their everlasting ruin. Not to mention the flood-gate to *confusion and every evil work*—to the destruction of all the tem-

P

poral happiness of society, which, whether true or false, is opened by this doctrine.

But *if the blind* will *lead the blind*, we must *let them alone.* Let me however intreat those who have eyes, to open them, before they *fall into the ditch. Search the scriptures*, my beloved hearers, *whether these things be so. Search the scriptures which testify of Christ,* and in which he hath *borne witness to the truth.* If any man teach another gospel than that which He hath taught, believe him not. He may be a very moral man; but his doctrine is not according to godliness, nor favourable to honesty. It subverts all moral obligation. He may be a man of fine sense; but *great men are not always wise.* Great men have often been great opposers of the saving truth. Great men, from the days of old, have sometimes said, *Peace, peace, when there was no peace.* Yea, the greatest of all fallen intelligences, has from the beginning said, " Disbelieve and transgress with safety;" *Ye shall not surely die.*— Believe not this though it be *not new divinity*, but a most ancient doctrine, and a doctrine of the great.— Think not that neither *the unbelieving*, nor *the abominable*, nor *murderers*, nor *whoremongers*, nor *sorcerers*, nor *idolators*, nor any *liars, shall have their part in the lake which burneth with fire and brimstone. Let no man deceive you with vain words. If the bible be true, because of these things cometh the wrath of God upon the children of disobedience.*

REDEMPTION AND ATONEMENT,

NOT THE SAME.

(From the Theological Magazine.)

BETWEEN atonement and redemption, divines, as yet, so far as I have been acquainted, have made no distinction. They have always considered those terms as conveying one and the same idea. It is thought to be evident, however, that redemption and atonement are, by no means, convertible terms. This evidence arises out of the holy scriptures. Atonement is *for* sin ; redemption is *from* sin. The word *redemption*, however, in the third chapter of Paul's epistle to the Romans, and in some other places, signifies the same as atonement. But, in those places it is used by a figure, the effect for the cause. Redemption, in its proper sense, and as the word is used in the holy scriptures, doth not mean, the *precious things*, by which captives are delivered from bondage, but it is deliverance itself. Sinners do not obtain redemption through redemption, but through the precious blood of Christ : his blood is not redemption itself ; it is the price of redemption. And it is through this precious blood, that believers have redemption, even the forgiveness of their sins ; through this blood they obtain *deliverance* from eternal death ; through this blood also, they obtain the salvation of their souls, even eternal life.

Redemption is deliverance from evil. And the Greek word, *Apolutrosis,* which signifies redemption, is used by the writer of the epistle to the Hebrews, for deliverance. " And others were tortured, not accepting *deliverance.*"* Redemption, in the holy scriptures sometimes means deliverance from natural, and sometimes from moral evil, and sometimes it implies exemption from both kinds of evil. In the book of Job it is said, " in famine he shall redeem thee from death : and in war from the power of the sword." The apostle Peter speaks of redemption from *sin ;*† the apostle Paul means the same by redemption as the *forgiveness* of sin :‡ and it is also spoken of as implying eternal life.§ These great blessings simply in atonement are not implied. This, however, will more abundantly appear from the following considerations :

1. "Christ died, not for a select number of men only, but for mankind universally, and without exception or limitation. The sacred writers are singularly emphatical in expressing this truth. They speak not only of Christ's dying for us—for our sins—for sinners—for the ungodly—for the unjust ; but affirm, in yet more extensive terms, that he died for the world—for the whole world ; that Christ gave himself a ransom for all ; yea, that he tasted death for every man."

The Greek word for ransom, is, *Antilutron,* which signifies the *price of redemption.* The price of redemption, therefore, is given for all men ; that is, atonement is made for the sins of the whole world. But, that *redemption itself* is not equally extensive with the price of redemption, will appear evident by attending to the holy scriptures. A few passages cited from St.

---

* Heb. xi. 35. † 1 Pet. i. 18.
‡ Col. i. 14.   § 1 Cor. i. 30. Heb. ix. 11.

John's Revelation only, will be sufficient for the present purpose. He, speaking of the saints, saith, " And they sung a new song, saying: Thou art worthy to take the book and open the seals thereof: for thou wast slain, and hast redeemed us to God by thy blood, out of every kindred, and tongue, and people, and nation." And in another place in the same revelation, referring to the saints, it is said, " These were redeemed from among men." Atonement, therefore, extends to every kindred, and tongue, and people, and nation; but the *redeemed* are gathered *out of* every kindred, and tongue, and people, and nation. Hence atonement extends to all men, but redemption will apply only to a number from among men.

2. Atonement doth not imply the forgiveness of sin. This is evident; for, when all things were made ready, through the blood of Christ, and sinners invited to the gospel feast, the language not only of some, but of every one was, " I pray thee have me excused." These were undoubtedly impenitent sinners; they were those, however, for whom Christ died; otherwise it never would have been said to them, " Come, for all things are now ready." Redemption implies, not only that there is a way opened for the forgiveness of sin, but it implies forgiveness itself. It implies deliverance from the dominion of sin; it implies also exemption from the wages of sin. This is evident from the reasoning of the apostle Peter, in his address to those to whom he wrote: " Ye know that ye were not redeemed with corruptible things as silver and gold, from your vain conversation, but with the precious blood of Christ, as a lamb, without blemish and without spot."* This is the blood of atonement, which speaketh better

* 1 Pet. i. 18, 19.

things than the blood of Abel. Through this blood, eternal redemption comes to sinners. Atonement therefore is the foundation of redemption, and not redemption itself. The latter is good enjoyed by men; the former, the channel through which good cometh. Atonement proclaims liberty to the captives, the opening of the prison to those who are bound; it opens the *way* to the chamber of the bridegroom; but to go in, and *partake* of the marriage supper of the Lamb, is reserved for the *redeemed only*. " These are they which were not defiled with women; for they are virgins : these are they which follow the Lamb whithersoever he goeth : these were redeemed from among men, being the first fruits unto God, and to the Lamb."* Whithersoever the Lamb goeth, him *all* the redeemed follow. But this is not the case with respect to all those for whom atonement is made : for there are some who " deny the Lord who bought them, and bring upon themselves swift destruction."

· 3. Between good men, and those who were redeemed from among men, the holy scriptures make no distinction. Redemption, therefore, implies regeneration. In atonement the new birth itself is not implied. It only renders it consistent for God to have mercy on whom he will have mercy. All the redeemed are cordial friends to the Lord Jesus Christ : but thousands for whom atonement is made, are his greatest enemies. Good men, and redeemed men, mean the same. This is evident. The prophet Isaiah, therefore, speaking of the way of holiness, saith, " No lion shall be there ; nor any ravenous beast shall go up thereon, it shall not be found there, but the redeemed shall walk there : And the ransomed of the Lord shall return and come to Zion with songs and everlasting

` * Rev. xiv. 4.

joy upon their heads; they shall obtain joy and gladness, and sorrow and sighing shall flee away." Every
excellency of character which belongs to good men, is
also ascribed to the redeemed from among men. Of
the redeemed, therefore, it is said, " In their mouth
there is found no guile; for they are without fault before the throne of God."

4. If there were no difference between atonement
and redemption, to *pray* for the *one* would be equally
improper as to pray for the *other*. But it was a common thing for saints of old to pray for redemption; yet
we find none of them ever praying for atonement. It
is true, however, that *Katallage*, the Greek word for
atonement, is the same which the inspired writers use
for reconciliation; and there is the greatest propriety
in praying that we may be subjects of reconciliation.
Hence said the apostle, " We pray you in Christ's
stead, be ye reconciled to God." It is evident, however, that for reconciliation, as made by Christ, for the
sins of the people, we ought not to pray. "Christ was
made like unto his brethren, that he might be a merciful and faithful high-priest in things pertaining to
God, to make reconciliation for the sins of the people."
Now, in this sense of reconciliation or atonement, the
work is already completed, even if reconciliation, as an
exercise of our heart, doth never take place.

Hence, atonement, in the sense of the word now under consideration, was completed when Christ rose
from the dead: for " he was delivered for our offences,
and was raised again for our justification." It would
not be proper, therefore, to pray that Christ would
make atonement for sin; because this he did while in
the days of his flesh, by his obedience unto death. To
pray for atonement, therefore, would be implicitly to
pray that Christ might die a second time. But of the

propriety in praying for *redemption*, we have examples from the best authority. The psalmist prays for mercy and redemption in the same sentence. "But as for me, I will walk in mine integrity: redeem me, and be merciful unto me."—"Draw nigh to my soul and redeem it."

The work of atonement being already finished, and the work of redemption implying a building, which God is now rearing up on the foundation of atonement, prove their difference.

We are informed by the apostle, that believers are sealed unto the day of redemption.* The day of judgment, with the righteous, will emphatically be the day of redemption. When, therefore, they shall see the Son of Man coming in a cloud, with power and great glory, they will look up, and lift up their heads; for their redemption draweth nigh.†

From the observations which have now been made, we infer the following remarks:—

1. Not to distinguish between atonement and salvation is an error.

2. Notwithstanding Christ has given himself a ransom for all, yet none will be profited thereby, except those, who, by a true and living faith, are united to the Lord Jesus Christ. Christ is the living bread, the bread of atonement, which, if a man eat, he shall live forever. But he who eateth not of this bread shall die, being destitute of wisdom, righteousness, sanctification and redemption.

3. "Christ has given himself a ransom for all." On this the Universalists pretend to build their scheme: but, if the above distinction be just, they cannot, with any propriety, infer universal redemption *(salvation)* from the universality of the ransom or price of re-

* Eph. iv. 30.   † Luke xxi. 8.

demption. Universal atonement therefore is consistent with particular redemption : it is also consistent with the doctrine of election.

Atonement is the price of redemption. Redemption itself is the actual exemption and escape from bondage. No one is redeemed therefore from the curse of the law, until he is united to the Lord Jesus Christ. Of man, nothing is required in order to atonement ; but, in order to redemption, or deliverance from the curse of the law, it is necessary that he be reconciled to God, or that he receive the atonement.

4. To distinguish between redemption and the *application* of redemption is improper. But between atonement and the application of *atonement*, there is the same propriety of distinction as between atonement and redemption.

The Lamb of God, the Great Atonement.

(Extracted from the Rev. John Newton's Messiah.)

THE extent of the atonement is frequently represented, as if a calculation had been made, how much suffering was necessary for the surety to endure, in order exactly to expiate, the aggregate number of all the sins of all the elect ; and that so much he suffered, precisely, and no more ; and that when this requisition was completely answered, he said, *It is finished, bowed his head, and gave up the ghost.* But this nicety of computation does not seem analogous to that unbounded magnificence and grandeur, which overwhelm the attentive mind, in the contemplation of the divine conduct in the natural world. When God waters the earth, he waters it *abundantly.* He does not restrain the rain to cultivated, or improveable spots, but, with a profusion of bounty worthy of himself, his clouds pour down water, with equal abundance. upon the barren mountain, the lonely desert, and the pathless ocean. Why may we not say with the scripture, that Christ died *to declare the righteousness of God*, to manifest that he is just in justifying the ungodly, who believe in Jesus! And for any thing we know to the contrary, the very same display of the evil and demerit of sin, by the Redeemer's agonies and death, might have been equally necessary, though the number of the elect were much smaller, than it will appear to be, when they shall all meet before the throne of glory. If God had formed this earth for the residence of one man only; had it been his pleasure to afford him the same *kind* and *degree* of light which we enjoy; the same glorious sun, which is now sufficient to enlighten and comfort the millions of mankind, would have been necessary for the accommodation of that one person. So, perhaps, had it been his pleasure to save but one sinner, in a way that should give the highest possible discovery of his justice, and of his mercy, this could have been done by no other method, than that which he has chosen for the salvation of the innumerable multitudes, who will, in the great day, unite in the song of praise, to the Lamb *who loved them, and washed them from their sins in his own blood.* As the sun has a sufficiency of light for eyes (if there were so many capable of beholding it) equal in number to the leaves upon the trees, and the blades of grass that grow upon the earth; so in Jesus, the Sun of Righteousness, *there is plenteous redemption,* he *is rich in mercy to all that call upon him;* and he invites sinners without exception, to whom the word of his salvation is sent, even to the ends of the earth, to *look unto him, that they may be saved.*

A DISCOURSE,

Designed to explain the Doctrine of Atonement : in Two Parts.—Delivered in the Chapel of Rhode-Island College, on the 11th and 25th of November, 1796.

By JONATHAN MAXCY, D. D.

PRESIDENT OF RHODE-ISLAND COLLEGE.

PART I.

HEBREWS ii. 10.

For it became him for whom are all things, and by whom are all things, in bringing many sons unto glory, to make the Captain of their salvation perfect through sufferings.

THE sufferings of Christ were essential to his character as a Saviour. Without them the pardon of sin would have subverted the authority of the divine law, and have prostrated the dignity of the divine government. For, if God should not execute the penalty incurred by the transgressor, if he should not manifest in his moral government the same abhorrence of sin that he does in the declarations of his law, his word and his conduct would be repugnant to each other, and he would afford no convincing evidence, that his law was a transcript of his will; that it ought to be considered as sacred, and respected as an universal invariable standard of obedience for all rational creatures. One great and chief design of the atonement made by the sufferings of Christ, was to impress a thorough conviction of God's displeasure against sin, though he should pardon the sinner. It was essential to a consistent exercise of pardon, that in some visible expression, God's real disposition towards sin should be manifested as clearly, fully and unequivocally; as it would be in the execution of the penalty of the law on the transgressor. This disposition, when brought into view in some sensible manifestation, vindicates God's character from all suspicion, and fully discovers his attachment to the dignity of his government, to the rights of his justice, and the truth of his law. The sufferings of Christ appear to have been available to the procurement of salvation, so far as they portrayed God's displeasure against sin, and evinced the infinite value he set upon his own character and law. Hence it is, that the scriptures so frequently bring into view a suffering, crucified Christ, as the only hope of salvation. His sufferings support the dignity of God, as the moral governor, while he extends mercy to the guilty; they present him in a glorious point of light, as the universal sovereign and proprietor, as the great source from which all things have proceeded, and in which all shall finally terminate. It is therefore with great reason and propriety that the text declares, that " it became him for whom are all things, and by whom are all things, in bringing many sons unto glory, to make the Captain of their salvation perfect through sufferings."

These words, by bringing into view the passion of Christ, as essential to a display of the divine character in the pardon of sin, present the doctrine of atonement in a light truly interesting and important. For surely no thing can be calculated more effectually to awaken the solicitude, and raise the desponding hopes of the guilty, than a prospect of forgiveness. Why God should require sufferings and the effusion of blood as a pre-requisite to the remission of sin, has been a subject of much inquiry, and to many " a stone of stumbling, and a rock of offence." They have supposed, that if God would not pass by sin without an atonement, without full satisfation to his justice, he must be naturally implacable ; that he has no mercy, because he punishes the innocent for the guilty, and bestows no good without an adequate compensation. Sufferings, it is true, can add nothing to the love of God to his creatures : but they may be, and it is hoped can be, proved to be necessary to a consistent exercise and display of that love. Atonement does not imply a purchase of God's mercy ; it does not imply satisfaction to justice, as a cancellation of debt ; nor does it infer any obligation on justice for the liberation of sinners ; for if it do, then sinners are not saved by forgiveness, since it is impossible for mercy to pardon, where justice cannot punish. Atonement implies the necessity of sufferings, merely as a medium through which God's real disposition towards sin should be seen in such a way, that an exercise of pardon should not interfere with the dignity of government, and the authority of law.

The sufferings of Christ for sin characterise the gospel scheme, and distinguish it from all others. The atonement made by them, adds to the christian religion its chief superiority, and lays the only foundation of hope for all who have just views of the divine law, and the moral state of man. All the doctrines of the gospel will derive their peculiar complexion from

Q

the manner in which the doctrine of atonement is explained. A mistake here will be peculiarly injurious, and will infallibly lead into error in every part of divinity. Atonement is the great sun in the centre of the system. Blot it out, and you are lost forever. Not a ray from any other quarter will dart through the gloomy prison of sin, to cheer its disconsolate inhabitants, to disenthral them from their chains, and enlighten their path to freedom and glory.

The design of revelation is to unfold the true God to men, acting according to the principles of his nature. This God is just and merciful. He is disposed to punish and to pardon. How then shall his justice and his mercy be displayed towards the transgressor, without infringing or destroying each other? God threatens punishment to sin. Sin is committed. God, instead of punishing, pardons. Where is his justice? Where is his truth? Where is the regard due to his law, his character and government? If he punish, where is his mercy? These difficulties will be obviated by a right understanding of the atonement which Christ made for sin. To exhaust this important subject, to comprehend all its connections and consequences, perhaps at present exceeds all human capacity. Enough of it, however, can be known and understood, to enable us to perceive its excellency, and to secure our present and future felicity. As the design of atonement was to save men from the curse of the law, in consistency with the perfections and designs of God, the atonement had immediate respect to the law of God, to the moral state of men, and to the ultimate and chief end of God in creation. Without a just and proper view of these three points, all inquiries respecting atonement will be extremely defective, if not totally erroneous. They will leave us, like an unpiloted ship, driven by the winds over the pathless ocean.

In the subsequent discourse, therefore, I shall

I. First explain the nature of the divine law, the moral state of man, and the design of God in creation.

II. Secondly, the matter, the necessity, and the nature of atonement.

A few inferences will then close the subject.

I. I shall begin the first division of this discourse, by

First—Explaining the nature of the divine law.

Under this denomination we are not to include all the laws given to the people of Israel. For though these may be termed divine with respect to their author, yet they are not all of a moral nature, and consequently not obligatory on all mankind. For this reason all the positive laws appertaining to the former dispensation, are not included in the phrases, " divine law," and " the law of God." These are used by way of eminence, to denote the moral law, as it is promulged and epitomized in the decalogue.

* The laws given unto the Israelites were of three kinds, moral, ceremonial and forensic. The first re-

---

* Leges autem iis latæ non unius generis fuerunt. Tres omnino theologis recensentur. Moralis sive decalogica, ceremonialis, et politica, sive forensis. Scilicet tripliciter considerari Israeliticus populus potuit. 1. Ut oreturæ rationales, a Deo, uti suprema ratione tam moraliter, quam naturaliter dependentes. Et sic data fuit ipsi lex decalogica, quæ quoad substantiam, cum lege naturæ, homines qua tales obligante, una eademque est. 2. Ut ecclesia veteris testamenti ; expectans Messiam promissum, et lætiora per ejus consummationem tempora. Atque eo respectu acceperunt legem ceremonialem, quæ ostendit quidem, nondum venisse Messiam, et satisfactione sua, omnia consummasse, fore tamen, ut veniat et omnia faciat nova. 3. Ut populus peculiaris, rempublicam, genio ac indoli suæ convenientem, habens in terra Canaan.—Witsii de Oecon. Fœd. lib. iv. cap. iv. p. 609.

spected them as rational, accountable creatures ; the second, as members of the ecclesiastical body ; the third, as members of the political body. The two last kinds of laws were peculiar to the Israelites. They alone had the promise of the Messiah. His death and sufferings for sin were prefigured by the various offerings and sacrifices enjoined in their ritual. Hence they received the ceremonial law, as an indication of the Messiah yet to come, who being the substance of all its shadows, was by the sacrifice of himself to abrogate its authority, and discontinue its observance. Hence Christ, in the sufferings by which he made atonement for sin, had no other respect to the ceremonial law, than as he corresponded to its typical prefigurations.

The forensic laws of the Israelites were accommodated to their peculiar genius as a people; to their peculiar circumstances in the land of Canaan ; and were designed to form the whole nation into a republican theocracy. Hence it appears, that the ceremonial and forensic or political laws of the Israelites, were of a temporary nature, and obligatory no longer than continued by the express injunction of the legislator. In this view, as they did not originate in the eternal fitness and propriety of things, they may be styled positive, in contradistinction to those which are moral ; which express the unchangeable will of God, respecting the obligation, the obedience and disobedience, the reward and punishment, of rational creatures. These laws primarily flow from the absolute perfection of God, and like his nature are sacred, immutable and eternal. These laws, summed up in one body, are styled *the law*, or *law of God*. To this law the whole of Christ's work, in making atonement for sin, had immediate respect. Without a just view of this law, therefore, the doctrine of atonement cannot be understood, nor its necessity and propriety perceived. Concerning the divine law, two things must be particularly noticed.

1. It contains a prescription of certain duties. These are contained in the decalogue, as it was delivered at Mount Sinai, and are all summarily comprehended in love, as the fountain from which all real acceptable obedience flows. Thus Christ explained the law : " Thou shalt love the Lord thy God with all thy heart, and with all thy soul, and with all thy mind. This is the first and great commandment; and the second is like unto it, Thou shalt love thy neighbour as thyself. On these two commandments hang all the law and the prophets." Matt. xxii. 37, &c. Paul viewed the law in the same light, when he said, " Love is the fulfilling of the law." Rom. xiii. 10. No action, therefore, either mental or external, which does not proceed from pure love to God, can come under the denomination of true virtue or obedience. This law is a delineation of perfect rectitude, and was designed to govern the whole man, by inspiring right motives, and producing an entire correspondence between them and external actions.

2. The second thing to be noticed concerning the law is, that it contains comminations of divine vengeance against transgression. Without these, it would not properly in its nature have the force and authority of a law. The language of the law, expressing the penal sanction, is, " Cursed is every one who confirmeth not all the words of the law, to do them." Deut. xxvii. 26. This curse most undoubtedly is the just and proper punishment of sin. For it is inconsistent with the perfection of God, to threaten a punishment greater or less than sin deserves. This is the

punishment from which Christ delivers. Thus Paul says to the Galatians, " God sent forth his Son, made under the law, to redeem them that were under the law." Gal. iv 4, 5. That is, to redeem them from its curse, as he explains it in another place. " Christ hath redeemed us from the curse of the law, being made a curse for us." Gal. iii. 13. Let it here be particularly noticed, that this commination annexed to the divine law, is the sum and foundation of all the others expressed in scripture, and denounced against transgressors. Various threatenings are found in the the New Testament, denounced against those who reject the gospel. These threatenings express the real penalty of the divine law. For no man can slight, neglect or refuse the gospel, without violating the law, and incurring its penalty. That this penalty, which will be executed on the impenitent, in a future state, is endless misery or destruction, appears from the following passages of scripture. In Dan. xii. 2, it is said, " And many of them which sleep in the dust of the earth shall awake, some to everlasting life, and some to everlasting shame and contempt." Matt. xviii. 8, " It is better for thee to enter into life halt or maimed, than having two hands or two feet, to be cast into everlasting fire." Matt. xxv. 41, Christ says to the wicked, " Depart from me, ye cursed, into everlasting fire." And in verse 46, " These shall go away into everlasting punishment." Mark iii. 29, Christ says of him who blasphemes the Holy Ghost, that he is " in danger of eternal damnation." Paul says of those who disobey the gospel, " Who shall be punished with everlasting destruction." The punishment spoken of in these words undoubtedly is the penalty of the law. For the law only can condemn and punish. Here perhaps it will be objected, that the punishment implied in these words is not strictly endless, since the word everlasting is sometimes appropriated to express things of a limited duration; that it is not the nature of punishment to be endless, and therefore the term everlasting, when used to express its duration, does not prove it to be strictly endless. To this it is replied, that because the term everlasting is in-some instances used to denote a limited duration, it does not follow that it is used so in all; not even when used to express the duration of things which would cease to exist if left to the laws of nature; for God can perpetuate whatever he pleases. For all our knowledge of the nature and duration of future punishment, we are wholly indebted to revelation. In this revelation God has explained the duration of punishment, and consequently the true penalty of his law; not only by the word everlasting, but by unequivocal determinate phrases, denoting it to be strictly endless. This is fully evident from the following passages, which positively determine the meaning of the word everlasting, when used to express the duration of future punishment. In Mark ix. 43, Christ says, " It is better for thee to enter into life maimed, than having two hands, to go into hell, into the fire that shall never be quenched; where their worm dieth not, and their fire is not quenched." In Matt. xii. 31, it is said, " The blasphemy against the Holy Ghost shall not be forgiven unto men." In John iii. 36, it is said, " He that believeth not on the Son, shall not see life, but the wrath of God abideth on him." Of the same import are all those passages which speak of those who are said to perish, to be rejected, to be cast away, to be lost and destroyed. To these testimonies of scripture, ascertaining the penalty of the divine law to be endless misery or destruction, let us add the testimony of reason.

- The law, whose essence is love, tends in its nature to secure the highest happiness of all rational creatures. For if all comply with its requirements, if all love God with all the heart, and their neighbour as themselves, what room is there left for sin or misery? These originate not in any deficiency in the divine government, but in deviation from the divine law. In this God has discovered as much goodness as he has in the gospel. For the first tends to secure the highest happiness without sin, and the last to secure it after the introduction of sin. Whatever therefore is opposed to God's law, is opposed to his gospel; and whatever is opposed to either, tends to introduce universal endless evil. If, therefore, endless punishment be not the penalty of the divine law, it does not appear that it has any penalty. For whatever penalty God annexes to his law, must be just; that is, it must be as great as the evil introduced by transgression, or as great as the glory of God, and the good of the rational universe, require. The greatness of this penalty must be estimated from the consequences that would ensue from an unrestrained indulgence of transgression, and the magnitude of the object against which the transgression is committed. The law of God tends to universal good. As sin opposes that law, it tends to universal evil. Did all rational creatures commit sin without any restraint from divine interposition, all would be involved in endless ruin and despair. The law of God, which is as near to him as his own nature, would be universally violated and contemned. For all these consequences, so dishonourary to God, so ruinous to creatures, each one concerned in transgression must feel himself accountable. Sin is atheism. It denies God. It strikes at his government and character, and consequently at all good and all happiness. As sin therefore tends to introduce endless evil, if punishments are to be proportioned to crimes, sin deserves endless punishment. Having explained the nature of the divine law, in considering its precepts and penalty, I now proceed to explain,

Secondly, The moral state of man. By the moral state of man, we are to understand, the state in which he is, considered as an accountable creature, capable of praise and blame, of reward and punishment. This state, as it respects all men in unregeneracy, appears from the scriptures to be characterised by the following things.

1. It is a state of entire alienation of affection from God. - That is, it is a state in which the moral temper is averse to divine and spiritual things, insensible of their excellency, and regardless of their importance. This truth is expressed in scripture, by " being dead in trespasses and sins," " being alienated from the life of God, desiring not the knowledge of his ways," " receiving not the things of the Spirit." The moral state of man in this view, does not imply, that he does not possess noble and exalted capacities of mind. These are not of a moral nature, and consequently not susceptible of depravity. Man, though destitute of all real holiness in the sight of God, though wholly sinful in all the exercises of his heart, still possesses natural affection, gratitude, sympathy, and sensibility; desire of pleasure, and aversion to pain; these are merely the affections and propensities of his constitution, and belong to other animals which are not moral agents.— Man's depravity does not imply that he is destitute of all the natural ability on which the propriety of the divine commands and injunctions rests. If he be not a moral agent, if he have not ability to obey, it does not appear that he can be capable of disobedience. Deity

will never censure a blind man for not seeing, nor an idiot for not being wise. He requires the exercise of nothing farther than the capacity he bestows. All the depravity of man consists in the wrong use of his natural powers, and in his unwillingness to use them as God requires. The preceding description of the state of man by nature, is fully confirmed by the following passages of scripture. Gen. vi. 5, "And God saw that the wickedness of man was great in the earth, and that every imagination of the thoughts of his heart was only evil continually." Gen. viii. 21, "The imagination of man's heart is evil from his youth." Eccl. ix. 3, "The heart of the sons of men is full of evil." Jer. xvii. 9, "The heart is deceitful above all things, and desperately wicked." Rom. iii. 10, &c. "There is none righteous, no not one; there is none that understandeth, there is none that seeketh after God; they are all gone out of the way; there is none that doeth good, no not one." Paul testifies concerning himself, "I know that in me, that is in my flesh, dwelleth no good thing." He declares, that "the carnal mind is enmity against God:" that "the natural man receiveth not the things of the Spirit of God, for they are foolishness unto him; neither can he know them, because they are spiritually discerned." The conduct of men, in all ages and nations, fully exemplifies and confirms these assertions.

2. Another thing which characterises the state of man is, that it is a state of guilt and condemnation.— This necessarily follows, from the consideration that man is in the disposition of his heart opposed to God and his law. " By the law is the knowledge of sin." By this knowledge come guilt and condemnation. All men are under obligation to obey God's law. The law therefore lays its injunctions upon them, demands obe-

dience, and denounces punishment to the transgressor. "Now we know," says Paul, "that whatsoever things the law saith, it saith to them who are under the law; that every mouth may be stopped, and the whole world may become guilty before God." Rom. iii. 19.

3. Another thing which characterises the state of man is, a state of total impotency, as to the attainment of salvation. The truth of this appears from two considerations.

1st. The law requires sinless obedience. It promises life to the performance of all its requirements, and to nothing else. Its language is, "The man that doth them shall live in them." But man has disqualified himself in a moral view to do these things, since he is "under sin," and continues to commit it while in an unrenewed state. As man, therefore, while a sinner, cannot render sinless perfect obedience, he cannot effect his own salvation.

2d. Besides, man has incurred the penalty of the divine law. It stands against him. "Cursed is every one that continueth not in all things, written in the book of the law, to do them." This penalty has been demonstrated to be endless suffering. How shall man free himself from it? He can do nothing which can render it consistent with God to pardon. He cannot keep the law by perfect obedience, and consequently cannot be saved on that ground. If he undertake to endure its penalty, he of consequence must give up all hope of salvation.

Having explained the moral state of man, I now proceed,

3. To explain the design of God in creation.

It is a mark of a wise and intelligent being, to have respect in all his actions to the accomplishment of some end. This circumstance principally distinguishes the actions of men from those of brutes. In all operations performed by rational beings, we expect design, and an exact adjustment of every part to the accomplishment of that design. When we look at the majestic works of God in creation and redemption, we are at once impressed with the absurdity of even imagining them to have been made without a view to some great end. In these works we behold order, connexion, regularity and harmony. How these should have existed without design, is impossible to conceive. It is equally impossible to conceive, how God should make such stupendous works, without a view to some end exceedingly great, glorious and important. For it is inconsistent with wisdom to make great preparations, and to perform great actions, for the accomplishment of small purposes. If God have one chief end in his works, we may be assured that these works are harmoniously adjusted to its accomplishment. All God's works then must be considered as means wisely arranged, and tending to one final issue. This issue must be brought into view before the means of its completion can be seen in their propriety and beauty. Let us then propose to ourselves this question ; Why did God create ? Surely he was under no necessity to do this. For if he was, that necessity must have been eternal, and the same reason must have been assigned for the existence of things, as for the existence of God. That reason God gave, when he said, " I am that I am." God, as he is eternal, involves in his own nature the cause of his existence ; but this cannot be the case with any thing created. Creation, then, as it did not proceed from necessity, must have proceeded from choice. The question then stands thus ; " Was God's end in creation himself, or the thing created ?" The following considerations perhaps will assist us in answering this question.

1st. Before creation nothing exterior to God existed. The reason then why any thing has existed, must be sought for in God. That reason must have been his own choice, and if so, then his own pleasure and not the thing to be created. Should it here be objected, that God made creatures on purpose to bestow happiness upon them, the objection proves this only, that God is pleased with bestowing happiness. If so, then God made creatures for his own pleasure, and not for theirs. If God made creatures merely for the sake of making them happy, why does he permit so many of them to be miserable? We learn what God means by what he does, as well as by what he says. God has created all things, and in these has exhibited a picture of himself. But it would be absurd to suppose all this was done without design.

2d. The next consideration I bring into view is, that it is inconsistent for infinite wisdom and goodness to prefer an inferior to a superior object. Such conduct would carry the most striking marks, and wear the most prominent features, of injustice and imperfection. All creatures are as nothing, in comparison of the immense GOD. Collect all the powers and principalities of heaven, all the perfection of angels and virtues of men, all the splendours scattered over creation; collect all these into one vast assemblage, and they are lost before God, like a mote in the full blaze of the sun. Creation has added nothing to the real sum of virtue and happiness; for these, wherever found, are only streams from the great exhaustless fountain. God therefore created with a view to diffuse and communicate in different forms that immense ful-

R

ness which dwelt in himself. God must love and regard the highest excellency most; but this is nowhere
but in himself. Nor is this supreme regard of God
to himself, as some have affirmed, an exercise of
selfishness, but of the highest benevolence; for this
consists in a supreme regard to the greatest good.——
But this greatest good is God himself.

3d. In the next place we may consider further, that
for God to act with a supreme regard to himself, or to
the display of his true character, is to act in such a
way as will secure the highest happiness of intelligent
beings. For all true happiness results from the knowledge and enjoyment of the greatest good. God is
the greatest and the only true good in the universe.——
It follows from this, that the more this true good is
displayed, the more it will be known and enjoyed.——
Consequently, more happiness is secured by a display
of God, than could be by any thing else. God then
must surely, in all his works, act with a supreme regard to his own glory, or to himself. This is the uniform language of scripture. God declares, " that he
made all things for himself;" that " of him, and to
him, and through him, are all things."

From these considerations it appears, that God's
ultimate and chief end in creation, was himself.

PART II.

HAVING explained the several things proposed
in the first part of this discourse, concerning the law
of God, the moral state of man, and the ultimate and
chief end of God in creation; I now proceed to explain the matter, necessity, and the nature of atonement.

Since it appears that the ultimate and chief end of God in creation was the display of his own nature, we may infer with certainty, that this end will be kept in view in the continuance and government of creation, For if it be not, then the arrangements in the divine administration are not calculated so as certainly to coincide with the ultimate intention of the divine will. But God "worketh all things after the counsel of his own will." Therefore, all parts of the great scheme of creation, providence and redemption, will ultimately exhibit a complete picture of the true character of God. He will then appear in reality to be the "beginning and the end," "the all in all." The obedience and sufferings of Christ, as they are the medium through which God's love of holiness and hatred of iniquity are seen, so they answer, as to the display of God's glory, all the purposes and more than would have been answered by the endless obedience or sufferings of all transgressors. Atonement, therefore, by the death of Christ, is to be viewed as a necessary part of God's great plan, and as possessing the propriety and fitness of means for the accomplishment of an end. If we consider atonement, in a general view, as that part of Christ's mediatorial work which rendered the forgiveness of sin consistent with God's character, it will comprise, as essential to its nature, more than suffering, though suffering appears to constitute its chief and most important part. If grace were to be manifested, it was proper and necessary that that grace should "reign through righteousness;" that is, in such a way as was consistent with the rectitude or justice of God. Whatever, therefore, would bring into view the character and law of God as effectually as the perfect obedience or suffering of men, must be considered as the atonement for sin. Though the punishment of the transgressor would have displayed God's truth, and his hatred of sin, yet it would not have displayed his love of mercy, and disposition to pardon. But all these are displayed in the salvation of the transgressor, by the obedience and death of Christ.

Having premised these things, I proceed to explain,

First, The matter of atonement, or that in which it consisted.

1. The divine law requires perfect obedience. God, in giving that law, virtually declared that it was good, and ought to be obeyed. The sinner, by transgressing it, virtually declared that it was not good, and ought not to be obeyed. Should God in this case pardon, without manifesting his regard to the law, so as to establish its authority as a rule of obedience, and to display his aversion to sin, his conduct would coincide with that of the sinner, and tend to the destruction of his own government. But if God, by a vicarious or substituted obedience and suffering, give in his moral government a full confirmation and conviction of the goodness of his law, and the justice of its requirements, his conduct, though he pardon, stands as directly opposed to the conduct of the sinner, as if he should condemn the sinner to endure the full penalty of the law. The obedience of Christ, on account of the superior dignity of his character, honoured the the law, declared and confirmed it to be good, more effectually than the obedience of all finite creatures could have done to eternity. In Christ "dwelt all the fulness of the Godhead." As he had all wisdom and goodness, his voluntary obedience must produce a conviction that the law was good: for he could not err in his judgment concerning it, and consequently, if it

had been a bad law, he would not have submitted to its precepts. The obedience of Christ, therefore, as it virtually condemned sin, and expressed his approbation of the law, so as to establish its authority as a rule of righteousness, appears to constitute an essential, though not the principal part of atonement. Christ, as a surety, engaged to fulfil all the righteousness of the law. To do this, it was as necessary that he should obey, as it was that he should suffer. The language of scripture is, "He humbled himself, and became obedient unto death, even the death of the cross."— Phil. ii. 8. The obedience and sufferings of Christ, in making atonement, were inseparably connected.— "Though he were a son," says Paul, "yet learned he obedience by the things which he suffered." Heb. v. 8. "For what the law could not do, in that it was weak through the flesh, God sending his own Son in the likeness of sinful flesh, and for sin, condemned sin in the flesh." Rom. viii. 3. But did not Christ's obedience bear testimony against sin, and in favour of the law, as really as his sufferings? Were not both essential to a display of justice and mercy? So far as the obedience of Christ rendered the forgiveness of sin consistent, so far it constituted a part of atonement.

2. The great and principal part of atonement, and which the scriptures most frequently bring into view, was Christ's sufferings. These were essential to his character as mediator and surety. It was necessary that he should be "made perfect through sufferings." It was essential that he should maintain the honour of the divine law, by fulfilling it in its penalty, as in its precepts. Hence he said, "Think not that I am come to destroy the law or the prophets; I am not come to destroy, but to fulfil." "For verily I say unto you, till

R 2

heaven and earth pass, one jot or one tittle shall in no wise pass from the law, till all be fulfilled." . Matt v. 17, 18. Hence the sufferings of Christ were so far from disrespecting or abrogating the law, that they " magnified it and made it honourable." One jot or one tittle did not pass till all was fulfilled. Hence it appears, that Christ endured the real penalty of the law in its full extent and meaning. Without a penalty, the law would have had no force. It would have been no more than advice. As the penalty therefore was essential to its nature, and as one tittle of the law did not pass till all was fulfilled, it follows that Christ endured the penalty of the law. This is fully evident from the descriptions given of his death and sufferings. Isai. liii. 6. " The Lord hath laid on him the iniquity of us all." " For the transgression of my people was he stricken." " My righteous servant shall justify many, for he shall bear their iniquities." To bear iniquity, to be stricken for transgression, signify to endure the evil which sin deserves. It is through Christ's sufferings only, that we can obtain redemption and remission of sin. Thus says Paul, Eph. i. 7, " In whom we have redemption through his blood, the forgiveness of sins." We are said to be redeemed by " the precious blood of Christ." When Christ's blood is spoken of, it is in allusion to the sacrifices under the law, which were typical of his death, and pointed to that as making atonement, " It is the blood that maketh atonement for the soul." Lev. xvii. 11. " Christ also hath once suffered for sins." Hence the sufferings of Christ appear to have constituted the most essential part, and some contend the whole, of atonement.

Secondly, I proceed to explain the necessity of atonement. Why could not God pardon without it? Why should he require sufferings before he would extend forgiveness to the guilty? Would not his mercy have appeared more conspicuous in remitting the offences of his creatures, on their repentance only, without exacting satisfaction? Is Deity so inexorable, that he will show no favour until the full penalty of the law be endured, and all his wrath exhausted? These difficulties will perhaps be obviated by the following train of thought.

1. The government which God exercises over his rational creatures, is not a government of force, but of law. Nothing therefore can take place under this government, that is arbitary, or inconsistent with the real meaning and authority of law. The obedience required of the subjects, is urged by the promise of reward to the performer, and the threatening of punishment to the transgressor. This promise and threatening are predictions of things to take place, on the concurrence of particular specified events. On one hand stands the great Legislator, promulging his law, and enforcing it with the penal sanction; on the other stands the whole system of rational beings, receiving that law as an unalterable rule of righteousness. These beings become transgressors. They incur that penalty, for the execution of which God's truth and faithfulness are pledged. How then shall God, without executing this penalty, maintain the dignity of his character, and the authority of his law? Not to execute the penalty, is to give up his government; to repeal, to annul his law, and to fail in the accomplishment of his prediction. Hence it appears, that punishments are necessary in God's moral government. They support his law, they deter transgressors, and manifest divine displeasure against sin. But why cannot God govern his creatures without punishments? This is the same thing as to ask why he

cannot govern them without laws ? He can. He can't govern them by force. But they will cease to be moral, accountable creatures. Laws then are essential to moral government. Punishments are equally essential to laws. A law which has no penalty, or, which is the same, a law that is not executed, ceases to be a law. It loses all its force, and becomes mere advice. Therefore, if sinners are to be forgiven, it must be done in consistency with the meaning and authority of law; for God cannot contradict himself. The legislative and excutive parts of his government must coincide. Hence, if sinners are to be forgiven, something equivalent to the punishment of sinners must be done in order to fulfil the real meaning of the law, and to support government. Hence, in order to a consistent exercise of mercy, atonement is necessary on the same principle, and for the same end, that punishments would be necessary without atonement. Viewed in this light, atonement is a substitute for punishments. It not only answers all the ends of these, but many more. If these were necessary without atonement, atonement without these was equally necessary. If then we maintain that God can exericse pardon merely on account of the sinner's repentance, we must maintain that laws can exist in full force without any penalties ; or that God can govern the moral system by laws, without carrying them into execution. A greater absurdity than this cannot be conceived.

2. Atonement will appear necessary, if we consider it in the propriety of means adapted to the accomplishment of an end. The great plan which God has adopted for the existence, government, and final state of rational creatures, is undoubtedly the best possible, and will ultimately terminate in the highest and most noble purpose. To suppose the contrary, is to

suppose imperfection in Deity. For the present plan has been brought into operation by infinite wisdom, which must discern and choose the best ; by infinite goodness, which must prompt the best ; by infinite power, which can execute the best. Of consequence, every part of this great plan must be so arranged, as directly to conduce to the highest ultimate end of the whole. This end has been shewn to be God himself, or the display of his glory. Atonement, considered in relation to the moral state of man, and the display of God's mercy, in saving him from that state, appears indispensably necessary. Unless God's mercy be displayed, his character will not appear to his creatures in its full glory ; and consequently the highest happiness of the system will not be secured. If the display of mercy be necessary, atonement is necessary. Mercy appears great in proportion to the greatness of the danger, misery or ruin, from which it delivers. The moral state of man has been shewn to be a state of the greatest danger, a state of condemnation and total ruin. Atonement implies an acknowledgment of that state as it really is, and of the perfect justice of God, should he leave man in it without any prospect of relief. Atonement, therefore, is the only thing which presents salvation as an act of real grace, and brings into view God, plenteous in mercy. All the glory that will ultimately redound to God, from the salvation of sinners, will arise through atonement, as the great means by which God will accomplish the high and ultimate end of creation. Atonement was necesary, therefore, to the perfection of God's great plan.

3. The necessity of atonement appears from the consideration, that atonement has been made, and from

the frequent mention of it in the scriptures as the only ground on which we can obtain salvation. It is very unreasonable to suppose that Christ would have died for sin, unless his death had been absolutely necessary. In a view of the amazing sufferings he was about to endure, he prayed to his Father, saying, " If thou be willing, remove this cup from me," Luke xxii. 42. Had not his death been necessary, this prayer would undoubtedly have been answered. But without his death, neither the salvation of men could have been effected, nor the glory of God displayed. Hence Christ said, " Ought not Christ to have suffered these things ?" " As Moses lifted up the serpent in the wilderness, so must the Son of Man be lifted up." Paul says, " Without shedding of blood is no remission." In Leviticus it is said, " It is the blood that maketh atonement for the soul," xvii. 11. Christ at the institution of the supper said, " This is my blood of the New Testament, which is shed for many for the remission of sins." Paul says, " We are justified by his blood." " In whom we have redemption through his blood, the forgiveness of sins." " Who his own self bare our sins in his own body on the tree." The redeemed are represented as saying, " Thou wast slain, and hast redeemed us to God by thy blood," Rev. v. 9. Yet we are assured that " there is no other name given under heaven among men whereby we must be saved." If these expressions do not point out the necessity of Christ's sufferings to make atonement for sin, it is impossible for language to point it out.

Thirdly. I now proceed to explain the nature of atonement.

The limits to which I am necessarily confined in this discourse, forbid me to enter into a full and extensive discussion of this part of the subject. I shall therefore confine myself to the solution of what appears most embarrassing, and difficult to be understood. The nature of atonement has in some degree, and unavoidably so, been brought into view in the preceding parts of this discourse. What I propose to illustrate under this head is comprised in the following propositions :— That the nature of atonement was such, that though it rendered full satisfaction to justice, yet it inferred no obligation on justice for the deliverance of sinners, but left their deliverance an act of pure grace. This will doubtless be considered by many as a great absurdity and positive contradiction. For how can full atonement for sin be consistent with forgiveness ? If Christ has paid the debt for sinners, if he has given himself a ransom, if he has purchased them, how can they be said to be pardoned, or delivered by grace ? If an equivalent price be paid for their redemption, may they not on the ground of justice demand salvation ? How can those be subjects of forgiveness who owe nothing ? If Christ has paid the debt, will it not be injustice to exact it again of the sinner ? A man is arrested for debt, and thrown into prison. Property is demanded for the discharge of his obligation. Property is advanced by a third person. The creditor receives it. Is not the debt paid ? Can the creditor in justice demand any thing farther of the debtor ? May not the debtor on the foot of justice demand deliverance from prison ? May he not demand his obligation, since it is cancelled by the property advanced ? Is not the creditor bound by justice to comply with these demands ? Would not a refusal to comply be deemed dishonesty, injustice and cruelty ? The creditor complies. But does he show any grace or favour to the debtor ? Does he treat the debtor more favourably than he ought to treat him ? Does he do any thing more than he ought to do, or more than the debtor has a right to demand? The creditor exclaims, "I have treated this man with so much mercy and favour, that I gave him up his obligation when he had paid the whole sum for which it was given." Who does not perceive the absurdity of this? Thus it may be objected, that full atonement for sin is inconsistent with forgiveness. But the scripture insists on full atonement, and yet every where holds up the deliverance of sinners as an act of pure grace. This is a gordian knot in divinity. Let us not by violence cut it asunder, but attempt fairly to untie it.

Before we proceed, it may not be improper to observe, that the greatest difficulty with which this part of the subject is embarrassed, appears to have originated in the want of an accurate definition of justice and grace. Theologians have said much about these, yet few have defined them with sufficient accuracy to render them intelligible, or make them appear consistent.

I shall therefore,

First, explain the meaning of the word grace.

Secondly, the meaning of the word justice.

Thirdly, apply these explanations to this part of the subject, with a view to solve the difficulty with which it is embarrassed.

First. What are we to understand by the word grace?

We are to understand by it the exercise of favour, and consequently the bestowment of good where evil is deserved, and may in justice be inflicted. Where there is no exposure to evil, there is no room for the exercise of grace. He who is not guilty is not a subject of pardon. He who does not deserve punishment cannot be said to be freed from it by an act of favour. Grace therefore always implies, that the subject of it is unworthy, and would have no reason to complain, if all the evil to which he is exposed were inflicted on him. Grace will appear great according to the view which the sinner has of his own ill desert, and the consciousness he possesses of the punishment or evil from which he is delivered. Grace and justice are opposite in their nature. Grace gives; justice demands. Their provinces are entirely separate. Though they are united, yet they are not blended in man's salvation. Hence that remarkable passage in Rom. xi. 6 ; "If by grace, then it is no more of works, otherwise grace is no more grace. But if it be of works, then it is no more grace, otherwise work is no more work."

Secondly. What are we to understand by the word justice? It assumes three denominations ;—commutative, distributive, and public.

1. Commutative justice respects property only.* "It consists in an equal exchange of benefits," or in restoring to every man his own.

2. Distributive justice respects the moral character of men. It respects them as accountable creatures, obedient or disobedient. It consists in ascertaining their virtue and sin, and in bestowing just rewards, or inflicting just punishments.

3. Public or general justice, respects what is fit or right, as to the character of God, and the good of the universe. In this sense, justice comprises all moral goodness, and properly means the righteousness or rectitude of God, by which all his actions are guided, with a supreme regard to the greatest good. Justice, considered in this view, forbids that any thing should take place in the great plan of God, which would tarnish his glory, or subvert the authority of his law.

* See Doddridge's Lectures, p. 190; and also Dr. Edwards' third sermon, preached at New-Haven, 1735.

S

Thirdly. Let us now apply these explanations to the solution of the difficulty under consideration.

1. Did Christ satisfy commutative justice? Certainly not. Commutative justice had no concern in his sufferings. Men had taken no property from God, and consequently were under no obligation to restore any. But do not the scriptures represent Christ as giving himself a ransom, and as buying his people with a price? They do. They also represent men, while under the influence of sin, as prisoners, slaves, captives. These expressions are all figurative, borrowed from sensible to express moral or spiritual things, and therefore are not to be explained as if literally true. If we say that Christ hath redeemed us, that he has bought us, that he has paid the debt and discharged us—if we have any consistent meaning, it must be this: That in consequence of what Christ has done, we are delivered from sin, in as great a consistency with justice, as a debtor is delivered from his obligation, or the demands of law, when his debt is paid. That is, God extends pardon in such a way, through Christ, that he does not injure the authority of his law, but supports it as effectually as if he inflicted punishment.

2. Did Christ satisfy distributive justice? Certainly not: Distributive justice respects personal character only. It condemns men because they are sinners, and rewards them because they are righteous. Their good or ill desert are the only ground on which distributive or moral justice respects them. But good and ill desert are personal. They imply consciousness of praise or blame, and cannot be transferred or altered so as to render the subjects of them more or less worthy. What Christ did, therefore, did not take ill desert from men, nor did it place them in such a situation that God would act unjustly to punish them according to their

deeds. If a man has sinned, it will always remain a truth that he has sinned, and that according to distributive justice he deserves punishment. In this sense justice admits the condemnation of Paul as much as it does of Judas. The salvation of the former is secured, and his condemnation rendered impossible by another consideration.

3. Did Christ satisfy public justice? Undoubtedly he did. This is evident from what has already been advanced respecting the necessity of atonement, in order to a consistent exercise of mercy. Christ's sufferings rendered it right and fit, with respect to God's character and the good of the universe, to forgive sin. The atonement made by Christ presented the law, the nature of sin, and the displeasure of God against it, in such a light, that no injury would accrue to the moral - system, no imputation would be against the righteousness of the great Legislator, though he should forgive the sinner, and instate him in eternal felicity. Perfect justice therefore is done to the universe, though all transgressors be not punished according to their personal demerit. The death of Christ therefore is to be considered as a great, important, and public transaction, respecting God and the whole system of rational beings. Public justice requires, that neither any of these be injured, nor the character and government of the great Legislator disrespected, by the pardon of any. In these respects public justice is perfectly satisfied by the death of Christ. This is evident from the following passages of scripture. Rom. iii. 21 ; " But now the righteousness (rectitude or justice) of God is manifested without the law, being witnessed by the law." Before the introduction of these words, the apostle had demonstrated, that the whole world, Jews and Gentiles, were all under sin and condemnation.

"Now," says he, "we know that whatsoever things
the law saith, it saith to them that are under the law,
that every mouth may be stopped, and the whole world
become guilty before God." All, if treated according
to distributive justice, must be found guilty and condemned. "Therefore," says Paul, "by the deeds of
the law shall no flesh be justified." How, then, it might
be inquired, can any be justified, and yet God not give
up his law, but appear perfectly righteous and just?
The answer follows. "By the righteousness of God,
which is manifested without the law, being witnessed
by the law." Rom. iii. 21. That is, the righteousness
or justice of God, with respect to himself and the universe, is clearly manifested, though he do not execute
the law, as to distributive justice, on transgressors, but
pardon and save them. This is so far from being contrary to the law, that it is witnessed by the law. For
the sufferings of Christ demonstrate, that God no more
gives up the penalty of the law, than if he should inflict it on the original transgressor. The righteousness
or justice manifested in this way is through Christ;
" whom," says Paul, " God hath set forth to be a propitiation, through faith in his blood." For what end?
" To declare his righteousness for the remission of
sins." " To declare at this time his righteousness
(for this purpose) that he might be just, and the justifier of him that believeth in Jesus," Rom. iii. 25, 26.
Hence it is said, " Christ is the end of the law for
righteousness to every one that believeth," Rom. x. 4.
That is, the end of the law is as fully answered in the
salvation of men by Christ, as it would have been if
they had never transgressed, but had obtained life by
perfect obedience. It is said, " If we confess our sins,
he is just to forgive us our sins," 1 John, i. 9. He is
ust to himself, to his law, to the universe. God styles

himself " a just God, and a Saviour." Is. xlv. 21.
Hence justice and mercy harmonize in man's salvation.

From the preceding statement of the nature of grace
and justice, it appears,

First, That atonement, and consequently the pardon of sin, have no respect to commutative justice.

Secondly, That the sufferings of Christ did not satisfy
distributive justice, since that respects personal character only; and therefore, with respect to distributive
justice, salvation is an act of perfect grace.

Thirdly, That Christ's sufferings satisfied public
justice; and therefore, with respect to public justice,
salvation is an act of perfect justice.

Thus the seeming inconsistency between full atonement for sin, and pure grace in salvation, vanishes and
disappears. The system of redemption rises into view
like a magnificent edifice, displaying the greatest order,
proportion and beauty.

Having advanced what I proposed, respecting the
matter, the necessity and the nature of atonement, I
shall conclude with a few inferences.

1. From the preceding discourse may be inferred,
the indissoluble connection between the doctrine of
atonement and the divinity of Christ. For it has been
demonstrated, that the penalty of the law is endless
misery, and that that penalty was, in its full extent and
meaning, endured by Christ, in order to a consistent
exercise of mercy. No finite created being could, in
a limited time, endure the full penalty of the law in
any respect. Yet we are assured, that Christ endured
it when " he was made a curse." As he comprised in
his divine nature an infinite quantity of existence, he
could in a limited time endure a punishment which
to a creature would be endless. This does not imply

that the divine nature suffered. This was impossible. In this nature consisted the personality of Christ. As he took into union with it the human nature, he possessed a perfect consciousness of the oneness of that nature with himself. Hence the sufferings of the human nature derive all their worth and value from the divine nature. The divinity of Christ, therefore, was essential to atonement, and was the only consideration that made his sufferings answer all the ends of moral government, so as to render the salvation of sinners consistent or possible. It is unreasonable to suppose, that the Son of God would have been sent to effect the work of redemption, if it could have been effected by a mere creature; yet we are assured, that the "word that was God" "was made flesh." Hence, those who entertain such an opinion of the law of God, and the moral state of man, as to see no need of atonement, reject the divinity of Christ. But so long as atonement shall appear necessary, so long the doctrine of Christ's divinity must be admitted, and so long it will appear essential to christianity.

2. From the preceding statement of the doctrine of atonement, we infer the erroneousness of that scheme of salvation which represents Christ suffering on the ground of distributive justice. If justice could demand his sufferings, he was treated according to his own personal character, and of consequence his sufferings had no more merit than the sufferings of a transgressor. If these were just, in the same sense that those of the sinner would be just, he endured no more than he ought to endure. His death, therefore, on this plan, made no atonement for sin. Besides, to represent Christ's sufferings to be the same as those of his people, is to destroy all grace in salvation. For in him they have endured all to which they were

exposed, from what are they delivered? In what respect are they forgiven?

3. If the preceding account of the law of God and
the doctrine of atonement be true, we infer the erroneousness and absurdity of that scheme, which represents the punishments of a future state to be disciplinary, and designed wholly for the good of the sufferers. According to the scriptures, there is an exact
distribution of punishments in the next world. Those
who suffer are represented "receiving according to
that they have done," "being rewarded according to
their deeds." If so, they are treated according to
law. For as this is the true measure of holiness and
sin, this alone ascertains the merit and demerit of all
actions, and dispenses proportionable rewards and
punishments. If those therefore in a future state who
suffer, suffer according to their deeds, they suffer according to law. If they suffer according to law, they
suffer according to justice, and consequently all they
deserve, and all to which they were ever exposed.—
How then are they saved? It is contended that they
are saved by grace. How can this be? If they suffer
according to their deeds, they suffer all that justice can
inflict upon them, and consequently are not pardoned.
If they suffer all they deserve, there is no grace in
their exemption from farther suffering; for justice forbids this. Therefore this scheme of disciplinary punishments, while it pretends to vindicate grace, destroys
it. If men are saved after they have suffered according to their deeds, as they are not forgiven, they are
not saved by Christ, any more than if he had never
died. Of consequence, the scheme of disciplinary
punishments virtually sets aside the necessity and importance of Christ's sufferings. But revelation as-
sures us, that "other foundation can no man lay than

that is laid, which is Jesus Christ," 1 Cor. iii. 11.—
"Neither is there salvation in any other, for there is
none other name under heaven given among men,
whereby we must be saved," Acts iv. 12.

4. From the nature of atonement, nothing can with
certainty be inferred as to the numbers who shall finally be saved. Had God given us no further light on
this subject than what we derive from the sufferings of
Christ, whether we consider them for a part or for all
of mankind, we should have been wholly in the dark
as to the final issue of those sufferings. As the nature and design of these were to render the pardon of
sin consistent, it appears that the atonement is as sufficient for the salvation of millions of worlds, as of an
individual. For whatever would render one act of pardon consistent, simply as to the exercise of mercy,
would render another consistent, and so on in infini-
tum. The number of instances in which atonement
will be applied, and pardon granted, will depend wholly on the sovereign will and determination of God.—
One thing is doubtless certain, salvation will be extended as far as is consistent with infinite perfect benevolence, or as far as the glory of God and the highest good of the universe require.

I now conclude this subject, by recommending it
to your most serious and careful attention. You will
find it to be the only ground on which you can hope for
future felicity. Atonement for sin is a peculiar and
distinguishing doctrine of the christian system. Viewed as the scriptures represent it, it appears as high
above all human thought and invention, as heaven is
above earth. Upon a thorough examination it will be
found consistent with the soundest reason, suited to
advance the happiness of man, and to display the glory
of GOD.

ON THE

ATONEMENT.

(From the Connecticut Evangelical Magazine.)

QUESTION.

How are the invitations and calls to sinners, with which the scriptures abound, and the solemn declarations, that God hath no pleasure in the death of sinners, but that they would turn and live, reconcilable with their being left of God to go on in sin and perish? Or, in other words, if God be as desirous of the return and salvation of sinners, as those strong expressions, particularly in Ezekiel, xxxiii. 11. intimate; what reasons are there assignable, why he, in whose hand all hearts are, and for whom nothing is too hard, with whom nothing is impossible, doth not convert them to himself, provided the atonement be infinitely full?

ANSWER.

THE enquiries here proposed, are in themselves interesting and important—are such as often arise in reflecting minds, and are nearly connected with some of the important and essential doctrines of the gospel—doctrines, which concern the glory of God, and eternal happiness of mankind. The subject therefore is worthy of a very serious and careful attention.

It is conceded in the statement of the question, that all hearts are in the hands of God, and that he is able to convert all sinners to himself, if he pleases. It will therefore be unnecessary to adduce any arguments in proof of this truth. But the question seems to intimate, that the want of a sufficient or infinitely full atonement is the reason, why all sinners are not renewed and saved. In answering the question, therefore, it is proposed to shew that the atonement is infinitely full—that God's leaving a number of mankind to go on in sin and perish, is not inconsistent with the gospel calls and invitations to all, or with his solemn declaration, that he hath no pleasure in the death of the wicked, but that they turn and live; and then to assign some reasons why God does not convert and save all the human race.

I. It is proposed to shew, that the atonement of Christ is infinitely full or sufficient for all mankind.— It may tend to elucidate the subject to make some previous observations upon the nature and design of the atonement. An atonement is some expiation or satisfaction for a crime or offence, made by the offender, or by some other person on his account. The atonement of Jesus Christ respects the sins of mankind, and was effected by his obedience, sufferings and death. Thus the scriptures declare, that he " bare our sins in his own body on the tree—was wounded for our transgressions—was bruised for our iniquities, and with his stripes we are healed. We have redemption through his blood." As many in the christian world have entertained erroneous ideas of the atonement, it may be useful to observe, that it was not designed to render God the Father more merciful, and benevolent, than he otherwise would have been. Some appear to have considered God the Father, as very implacable and vindictive; and God the Son, as very merciful and compassionate; and therefore they seem to have supposed, that the sufferings and death of the Son were designed to appease a vindictive temper in the Father, and to render him more mild, compassionate, and benevolent. Such ideas are not only very erroneous, but also very degrading to the divine character. God the Father, as the scriptures declare, is love or benevolence. He is as merciful and benevolent as the Son; yea, they are perfectly one in temper and affections. It is therefore declared, that *they are one*, and that the Son is " the brightness of the Father's glory and the express image of his person." The Father then was just as compassionate and benevolent, and as much disposed to shew mercy to sinners, as the Son; provided it could be done consistently with the divine glory, law and government, and the highest good of the moral world. And if sinners could not be pardoned and saved consistently with these, the Son would no more wish it to be done, than the Father; as they are perfectly one in their holy desires and wishes. To suppose then, that the atonement was designed to appease a vindictive, implacable temper in the Father, is indulging very unworthy and erroneous sentiments of the character of Jehovah.

Neither was the atonement designed to abate the requirements of the divine law, so that it does not now require perfect obedience or holiness, but will accept and justify persons on account of their sincere though imperfect obedience. Some seem to suppose, that the moral law, which requires perfect holiness, and curses for every sin, is very rigid and severe— that it was hard and almost unjust for depraved creatures to be placed under such a law—that the Saviour, therefore, pitying their hard case, took their part against this rigid law, and bore its penalties to abate or soften down its rigorous requirements, so that they are not now under obligations to be completely holy; but are in some degree excusable for their failures and imperfections in point of obedience. Such ideas of the atonement and of the divine law are exceedingly erroneous and dangerous, and an evidence of great ignorance of the essential truths of religion. The divine law is the eternal, immutable rule of right, or standard of moral perfection. As far as any rational beings fall short of that love to God and their fellow-creatures, or of that perfect holiness or benevolence, which is required in the moral law; so far they must in their temper, be wrong and criminal—yea, it is impossible, that any rational creature should be sinless or excusable in any neglect of, or deviation from what the divine moral law requires. This law, as the apostle declares, is holy, just and good; and is so viewed by all, as far as possessed of real piety. Like the apostle, they delight in the law of God after the inward man, and earnestly desire to be perfectly conformed to its requirements.

It is then manifest, that the atonement of Christ was not designed to abate or disannul, in any degree, the divine law, that perfect and unchangeable standard of right. The Saviour therefore said, "Think not that I am come to destroy the law. For verily I say unto you, till heaven and earth pass away, one jot or one tittle shall in no wise pass from the law, till all shall be fulfilled." He was so far from lowering down or abolishing the law of God, or taking the part of sinners against it as being too rigorous, that one important design of his atonement was to support and magnify the law, and make it honourable.

It may be further observed, respecting the atone-ment, that it is not supposed, that the Lord Jesus en-dured the same quantity of pain and misery, as would have been endured by all mankind, or all the elect through eternity; had they been lost. As it was the human nature only of the Saviour, which was capable of suffering; it is inconceivable that he could endure as much pain in a few hours, as innumerable millions of men would through eternity. Nor was it necessary that he should; since the infinite dignity of his divine nature, united in the same person with his human, gave an infinite value or efficacy to his sufferings.

The design of the atonement was to support the au-thority of God's holy law, the dignity and stability of his moral government, and to manifest his just abhor-rence and displeasure against sin. The divine law denounces against every sinner eternal death, as the just wages of sin, as a just expression of his displea-sure against it, and as a most powerful restraint against all wickedness. But had sinners been pardoned with-out an atonement, or any thing done to support the law of God; it would have tended greatly to weaken and destroy its authority, and to bring the divine govern-ment into contempt. The appearance of it would have been, that the Most High was not much displeased with sin, did not view it as very criminal, and was not in earnest in his threatenings against it. Thus it would have greatly encouraged sin and rebellion, and been exceedingly injurious to the happiness of the moral world. The atonement therefore was designed to pre-vent those dreadful consequences by answering the same important purposes, which would have been an-swered by the punishment of sinners themselves, and thus to open a way, in which God could, consistently

T

with the authority and honour of his law and government and the good of his kingdom, show mercy to whom he saw fit, and pardon the penitent and believing sinner. These important ends have been effected by the obedience, sufferings and death of the Lord Jesus, who was one with the Father, and thought it not robbery to be equal with God. By assuming our nature, submitting to the greatest abasement, sufferings and most painful death in the stead of sinners, and thus bearing their sins in his own body, he strikingly supported and magnified the law, and made it honourable. It showed, that the Father would inflict all these sufferings on his well beloved Son, and that the Son would voluntarily submit to them, rather than the divine law should be weakened and dishonoured in the pardon of sinners. In this way Jehovah has manifested the highest respect for his holy law, and his fixed determination to support the authority and dignity of his moral government. And by sparing not his own Son, when in the room of sinners, he has clearly evinced his inflexible, impartial justice and opposition against sin, and his determination to punish and discountenance it.

Having made these observations upon the nature and design of the atonement, we shall proceed to show, from various considerations, that this atonement is infinitely full or sufficient for all mankind.

1. This is evident from the infinite dignity and excellence of the Saviour, and from the nature of the atonement. The Saviour, as has been already observed, was in his divine nature God over all, one with the Father, and equal with him in all divine perfection. And being thus a person of infinite dignity and worth, it gave an infinite value or efficacy to his obedience, sufferings and death, and thus rendered his atonement

infinitely full. The obedience, sufferings and death, of such an infinite personage did more to magnify and support the law and government of God, and to manifest his abhorrence of sin, than would the eternal punishment of all the sinful race of man. It is therefore evident, that this atonement must be abundantly sufficient for the salvation of mankind, if they would but receive it. To deny its infinite fullness or efficacy, must be derogating from the infinite dignity and excellence of the Saviour. The atonement does not lay God under obligations to sinners to save any of them ; but it opens the way, so that he can, consistently with his law and government, dispense his grace, to whom he pleases, and can be just, and yet "the justifier of him which believeth in Jesus."

2. It appears from express declarations of scripture, that Christ has died for all mankind, or has made an atonement sufficient for all. Thus it is declared, " That he by the grace of God should taste death for every man, and that he is the Saviour of all men, especially of those that believe." These passages clearly teach, that the Saviour has died or made atonement for all mankind, and it seems, that the last of them cannot rationally be understood in any other sense. For it expressly declares, that he is the Saviour, not of those who believe only, but of all men in distinction from these. Therefore his atonement must have had respect to all the human race. Accordingly Christ is called " The Lamb of God which taketh away the sin of the world; and the Saviour of the world." The apostle John, addressing christians, says, " He is the propitiation for our sins, and not for ours only, but also for the sins of the whole world." Here also Jesus Christ is declared to be the propitiation for the sins of the whole world, in distinction from those of believers.

These, and other similar passages teach in the clearest manner, that Christ has made an atonement for all mankind, or for the whole world. It seems hardly possible for words to express this sentiment more clearly than it is expressed in these passages; and some of them will not admit of any other sense, without a very forced, unnatural construction.

Should it be said, that such expressions as *all men, the world*, &c. must sometimes be understood in a limited or restricted sense; it may be answered, that it is an established, invariable rule, that all phrases or passages of scripture are to be understood in their most plain, easy and literal import, unless the connection, the general analogy of faith, or some other necessary considerations require a different sense. But in the present case it does not appear, that any of these considerations require, that these passages should be understood in any other than their plain, natural meaning. On the contrary, there are many weighty, unanswerable reasons for understanding them in their most plain and literal import. And it is with great difficulty, that some of these passages can be understood in any other sense.

3. That the atonement is sufficient for all mankind, is evident from the consideration, that the calls, invitations and offers of the gospel are addressed to all, without exception, in the most extensive language. It is said, " Look unto me, and be ye saved, all the ends of the earth. Whosoever will, let him take the water of life freely. Ho, every one that thirsteth, come ye to the waters, and he that hath no money: come ye, buy and eat, yea, come, buy wine and milk without money, and without price. Go, and preach the gospel to every creature." The preachers of the gospel are directed tell their hearers, that all things are ready—that all

may come, who will, and are to invite and urge all, to come to the gospel feast and freely partake of the blessings of salvation. But how could the offer of salvation be consistently thus made to all without any limitation; if the atonement was sufficient but for a part or for the elect only? On this supposition it could not with truth and propriety be said to all, that all things are ready, plentiful provisions are made for all, and whosoever will, may come. Were a feast, sufficient but for fifty provided; could we consistently send invitations to a thousand, and tell them that a plentiful feast was prepared, and that all things were ready for their entertainment, if they would but come? Would not such an invitation appear like a deception? If so, then the offer and invitation of the gospel could not have been made to all without discrimination, as they are; if there was no atonement but for a part. As therefore the invitations of the gospel are thus addressed to all, it is a proof that Christ has made an atonement for all mankind.

Again, the scripture represents, that there is no difficulty in the way of the salvation of the impenitent, but what arises from their own opposition of heart or will. Thus the Lord Jesus says to the unbelieving Jews, "Ye will not come unto me, that ye may have life. O Jerusalem, Jerusalem, how often would I have gathered thy children—and ye would not." In the parable of the marriage supper, it is represented, that there was no difficulty in the way to prevent those who were invited, from partaking of the feast, but their own unwillingness to come. But if there was no atonement made but for those only who are saved; then there would be an insurmountable difficulty in the way of the salvation of all others, aside from the one

arising from their own opposition of heart. As therefore the scripture teaches, that there is no difficulty in
the way of the salvation of any under the gospel, but
what arises from their own unwillingness, or wicked
opposition of heart, it is manifest, that there is an atonement for all.

4. The word of God teaches, that it is the duty of
all, who are acquainted with the gospel, to believe in
the Lord Jesus, and trust in him as their Redeemer,
and that they are very criminal for neglecting to do
this. It is therefore declared in the sacred scriptures,
that it is the command of God, " that we should believe
on the name of his Son Jesus-Christ, and that those,
who believe not, are condemned already, because they
have not believed on the name of the only begotten
Son of God."

- But on the supposition, that Christ has made no
atonement for those, who perish; how can it be their
duty to believe on, and receive him as their Saviour ?
Or, how can they be justly condemned for not doing it,
when he has made no atonement for them ?

Further, if the atonement is made for the elect only,
how can a preacher be warranted to make the offers of
salvation to any, or to urge them to receive the Saviour ; unless he knows, that they are of that particular
number, for whom Christ died? Or how can any, unless they know, that they are of this number, be au-
thorised to trust in him for salvation ? The subject,
upon the supposition of a partial atonement, certainly
appears to be attended with some difficulties in these
respects. These considerations afford additional proof,
that the atonement was made for all mankind.

It is manifest from the various reasons which have
been suggested, that the atonement of Jesus Christ is
infinitely full, or sufficient for the salvation of all man-

kind, if they would but cordially receive it, and that the want of such an atonement, is not the reason, why all are not saved.

But it may be here remarked, that it will not follow, that because the atonement is sufficient for all, therefore all will be saved. The atonement does nothing more than merely open a way of salvation, so that God can consistently show mercy to whom he pleases, and justify all, who believe in Christ Jesus. But it does not ensure the salvation of any, unless they comply with the terms of the gospel. It will no more follow, that all will be saved, because the atonement is sufficient for all, than it would, that all would eat of the marriage supper in the parable, because it was sufficient for all, and all were invited. This parable was designed to represent the gospel and its invitations.—As those, who neglected the invitation, never tasted of the supper, although the provisions were plentiful for all; so the scriptures teach, that many will not comply with the terms and invitations of the gospel, and partake of its blessings, although the atonement is abundantly sufficient for all. For the Saviour declares, that "many are called, but few are chosen, and strait is the gate and narrow is the way which leadeth unto life, and few there be that find it."

Neither will it follow, that part of the atonement will be lost, if it is sufficient for all mankind, and yet but part are actually saved.

For it appears from the nature of sin, and of the atonement, and from the character of the Saviour, that the same infinite atonement, which is necessary for the pardon of one sinner, will answer for the salvation of the whole human race. It is certain from scripture, that sin is infinitely evil and criminal, because it is threatened with an everlasting or infinite punishment:

Not one sinner therefore could be pardoned without an atonement of infinite value and efficacy, or without the sufferings and death of the Lord Jesus, a person of infinite dignity. And his obedience, sufferings and death, have done more to magnify and support God's law—to establish his moral government, and to condemn and discountenance sin; than would the ever-lasting sufferings of all mankind. This same infinite atonement therefore, which was necessary, that God might consistently pardon one sinner, would also render it consistent for him to pardon and save all the numerous millions of Adam's race, if he saw fit. It cannot then be said, that some part of the atonement is lost, if all are not saved, since the same infinite atonement which will answer for all, is necessary for the salvation of but one.

Or even if this were not the case, yet it would not follow, that part of the atonement was lost or useless, because all were not saved. For the infinite fullness or sufficiency of the atonement may answer other important ends besides the salvation of sinners. It may tend to display the infinite riches of divine grace—to manifest the infinite dignity and worthiness of the Saviour—to render it consistent for the invitations of the gospel to be addresssed to all, and thus to show the exceeding evil and obstinate nature of sin, and the great depravity of the human heart, in rejecting the Saviour, and to render the impenitent wholly inexcusable, since there is now evidently nothing in the way of their salvation but their own wilful opposition of heart. And in this way it will tend to glorify the justice of God in the everlasting condemnation of the wicked, and to magnify his grace in the salvation of the elect. These and other important ends are answered by the infinite atonement of the Lord Jesus; and therefore it will not be lost or useless, though but part of mankind are saved.

In answering this question, it has been shewn, that the atonement of Christ is infinitely full or sufficient for the salvation of all mankind; that therefore the want of such an atonement cannot be the reason why all are not saved.

It is proposed then to shew,

II. That the calls and invitations of the gospel, and the solemn declaration, that God hath no pleasure in the death of the wicked, but that they would turn and live, are consistent with his leaving numbers to go on in sin and perish.

And in doing this it is necessary to consider the precise meaning of the declaration, that God hath no pleasure in the death of the wicked, but that they turn and live. This passage must mean, either that God, taking all things into view, does not upon the whole choose the death or punishment of any of the wicked, but actually chooses that they should all turn and live; or else it must mean, that he takes no direct pleasure in their death or misery, in itself considered, but that their turning and obtaining life is in itself more pleasing and desirable. But it is evident from various considerations, that the passage cannot be rationally understood in the sense first stated. For if the Most High, all things considered, did actually choose that none of the wicked should go on in sin and perish, but that all should turn and live; then he must be greatly disappointed in his real choice and desire. For the scriptures expressly declare, that "wide is the gate and broad is the way which leadeth to destruction, and many there be that go in thereat;" and it is allowed in the statement of the question, that a number do go on in sin and perish. And if Jehovah is thus disappointed in his actual choice and designs, it must certainly occasion him great sorrow and unhappiness.—None, therefore, who have any just ideas of the divine perfections and felicity, can for a moment indulge the supposition that the infinitely wise, powerful and perfect God is thus frustrated in his desires, and rendered unhappy by his creatures.

Further, if Jehovah, upon the whole, did actually choose that all the wicked should repent and be saved, he certainly would convert and save them; since he possesses almighty power, has all hearts in his hand, and can with the greatest ease turn and bring the most stubborn to repentance, if he pleases. As God does not in fact bring all sinners to repentance, it is therefore certain, that upon the whole he does not really choose to do it.

Again, how derogatory would it be to the divine perfections, to suppose that the Most High did upon the whole actually choose that all the wicked should be brought to repentance and salvation, and yet was not able to accomplish his choice?

These various considerations clearly shew, that the import of this passage must be, that God has no direct pleasure in the death or misery of the wicked, in itself considered, but that their repentance and salvation in themselves, or aside from other infinitely wise reasons, in the divine government would be much more pleasing to him than their destruction. And that this is the truth is manifest from the divine character, and from other declarations of scripture. For " God is love," or benevolence; and therefore it is certain, that he cannot take any pleasure directly from the punishment or misery of the wicked, and that he never punishes but when it is necessary to answer wise and benevolent purposes and promote the general good.

But on the contrary, it is evident, that their repentance and salvation would be in themselves delightful,
and afford direct pleasure to the holy, benevolent mind
of Jehovah, if consistent with the wisest scheme of
government. It is therefore declared, that God " doth
not afflict willingly, nor grieve the children of men,"
and that to punish is his strange or unpleasant work.
But it is said, that " there is joy in heaven over one
sinner that repenteth," teaching, that it is a pleasing,
joyful event to God and the heavenly world. These
considerations confirm the sense of the passage last
given; that God takes no pleasure in the misery of
the wicked, in itself considered. Thus what the Most
High expresses in this passage towards sinners, is
very similar to what kind, benevolent parents express
towards their disobedient children. They often address their children in expressions similar to what God
makes use of in this passage : *We take no pleasure
in your punishment or pain, but it is much more pleasing
to us to see you reform and be obedient*. Such language
in a parent would imply, not that he would never
choose to punish any of his children when they deserved it, and the good of the family required it, but that
their punishment was not in itself agreeable to him,
and that he took no direct pleasure in it. So the declaration, that God hath no pleasure in the death of
of the wicked, but that they turn and live, imports,
that the misery or punishment of the wicked is not
in itself pleasing to him ; but is by no means saying
that he will send his Holy Spirit to renew and bring
all mankind to repentance and salvation. It is therefore very far from engaging or implying, that he will
never leave any to go on in sin and finally suffer that
everlasting punishment which they have justly deserved ; when he sees it best in order to display his

justice and perfections, promote the good of his kingdom, and answer other wise and benevolent purposes. Neither are the calls and invitations of the gospel at all inconsistent with God's leaving numbers to go on in sin and perish. The divine offers and invitations, such as " Look unto me, and be ye saved, all the ends of the earth—Turn ye, turn ye ; for why will ye die ? Whosoever will, let him take the water of life freely," are no promises that the Holy Spirit shall be sent to renew and make all who are favoured with these calls and offers willing to comply with them. God, in giving mankind these gracious calls and invitations, no more promises to bring them to a cordial compliance, by the efficacious influences of his Holy Spirit, than the king who in the parable sent his servants to call those that were bidden to the marriage supper, did by this invitation promise to compel all to come in by force, who neglected the call. No one ever supposed, that his offering a peculiar favour to another upon a most reasonable condition, was promising that he would oblige the other, if unwilling, to accept or comply with the proposed condition. Certainly then the Most High, by his kind calls and invitations to sinners, has made them no promise that he will renew and influence them to a compliance.

Neither do these invitations lay God under any obligations to do this for the impenitent. Can any pretend to say, that because God is so kind and merciful as freely to offer pardon and salvation to unworthy, hell-deserving sinners upon the most reasonable terms; therefore he is under obligation to dispose them to a cordial compliance by the efficacious influences of his spirit, upon their refusing these offers ? Or in other words, does their ungratefully neglecting one favour, oblige God in point of justice to do them another ?

Should a kind, generous benefactor provide a plentiful entertainment, and invite a number of unworthy beggars, and should they ungratefully refuse his kind invitation, surely no one could say, that he was under obligations to send his servants and compel them to come.

Since, therefore, the calls and invitations of the gospel are no promise, that God will send his spirit, and make sinners willing to comply with these, and do not lay him under any obligation to do this; how are they at all inconsistent with his leaving numbers to go on in sin and perish? Where is the least appearance of inconsistency for God to call, warn, and invite sinners to repent and be saved—to set motives of infinite weight before them, and yet leave them to follow their own choice, by going on in the ways of sin to destruction? Jehovah, in thus leaving the impenitent to perish in their sins, when he sees it best for the general good, violates no promise, no obligation of justice or benevolence. Neither does he injure the wicked or give them any just ground of complaint. For if they will ungratefully refuse or neglect the infinitely gracious and important calls and invitations of the gospel, they are certainly exceedingly criminal, and wholly inexcusable.

The invitations and offers of the gospel cannot be rationally understood as importing any thing more, than that God is willing and ready to pardon and save all, who repent and comply with the terms of salvation; and that their repentance is in itself pleasing to him. But this, as already shewn, does not imply, that God will not leave any to go on in sin and perish; when he sees it best to answer wise purposes. Should the Most High refuse to pardon and save, repenting, returning sinners, he might be justly accused of a want of consistency and sincerity in his calls, offers and invitations. But to accuse him of this, because he does not renew and dispose all mankind, by the efficacious influence of his spirit, to a cordial compliance with the gospel invitations, is most unreasonable and groundless.

Further, that God is sincere in his calls and invitations, and in the representations of scripture, that the return and salvation of sinners is in itself more pleasing to him, than their destruction, is manifest from his conduct, as well as from the declarations of his word. For he has given his well beloved Son to endure the severest pains and sufferings, that he might open for mankind a way of life and salvation, and rescue numbers from everlasting destruction. He has given them his holy word to teach them the paths of duty and way of salvation, and has set before them motives of infinite importance to influence them to receive the Saviour. He has directed his ministers to preach the gospel to every creature—to warn and persuade sinners, by the most important and endearing considerations, to secure their eternal concerns, and to pray them in Christ's stead to become reconciled unto God.

He strives with them by his spirit, by the convictions of their own consciences, and by the warning voice of his providence. In addition to all these powerful means, which are calculated to bring sinners to repentance, God does, by the special efficacious influences of his spirit, overcome the inveterate opposition of the human heart, and dispose thousands in every age to a cordial compliance with the terms of the gospel. And he kindly welcomes all penitent, returning sinners, however vile and unworthy—adopts them into his family, and makes them children and heirs of

God, and joint heirs with Jesus Christ to all the joys
and honours of that glorious inheritance, which is in-
corruptible, undefiled, and fadeth not away. Thus it is
manifest, from the conduct and dealings of God, as
well as from the declarations of his word, that he is
sincere in the calls and invitations of the gospel.

In the case of the impenitent, these invitations are
no promise of special, renewing grace, but import
the two following things, first, a declaration that all
difficulties, in the way of the sinner's salvation, except what arise from his own heart, are removed; and
secondly, an expression of the sinner's duty. Therefore it is easy to see that God is ready to receive every
returning sinner, and that he takes no pleasure in the
death or everlasting punishment of the wicked in itself considered, but is more pleased with their repentance and salvation. For were not this the case,
and did he not take pleasure in the return and salvation of sinners; he certainly would not use so many
means to effect and promote their salvation—would
not thus bring so many to repentance, by the efficacious influences of his spirit, and kindly receive and
welcome every true penitent however vile and criminal. And God's leaving some to go on in sin and
perish, when he in infinite wisdom sees it best, no
more contradicts the declaration, that he takes no
pleasure in the death of the wicked, but that they
would turn and live, or proves, that their punishment
or misery is in itself pleasing to him; than a kind parent's punishing a vicious disobedient child, when the
good of the family requires it, proves, that he is pleased with the pain of his child. In both these cases
the pain or punishment is by the supposition inflicted
to answer wise purposes, and to promote a greater
good, and therefore is a dictate of benevolence.

Some reasons will now be assigned, why God does not convert and save all the human race.

The question supposes, that some men will be left of God to go on in sin and perish. This is confirmed by the holy scriptures. Our Lord hath said, "Wide is the gate, and broad is the way, that leadeth to destruction, and many there be which go in thereat: because strait is the gate, and narrow is the way, which leadeth unto life, and few there be that find it." "They that have done good, shall come forth unto the resurrection of life, and they that have done evil, unto the resurrection of damnation." He will say unto some, "Depart ye cursed, into everlasting fire, prepared for the devil and his angels—and these shall go away into everlasting punishment."

It is not from any inability in God to renew and save all, that any are left to perish in their sins, for all hearts are in his hands, and nothing is impossible with him. "He hath mercy on whom he will have mercy, and whom he will he hardeneth." Nor are any left to perish, through a defect in his benevolence. "God is love." His benevolence is rendered unquestionable by the gift of his Son, the provision of an infinite atonement, and his direction that the offers of salvation should be made through all the world, unto every creature, without limitation, and by such an administration of government as produces the highest possible happiness in the universe. There can be no want of goodness in God. "There is none good but one, that is God." It surely can be no reasonable objection to his goodness, that when mankind reject Christ, and his great salvation, freely offered, and affectionately urged upon them, God does not in every instance subdue their obstinacy, and make them willing in the day of is grace. And it should be kept in mind, that this is the real state of men. They all begin to make excuse, when called upon by the messages of grace. Christ saith, "Ye will not come unto me that ye might have life." We ought rather to admire the wonderful benevolence of God, in reclaiming and saving any, after such abuse, and such a discovery of the extreme depravity of the human heart, than to harbour any jealousies of his goodness because he does not compel all to come in. There is a wide difference between offering salvation to sinners; and by an almighty act disposing them to receive it, after they have deliberately and ungratefully rejected the offer. It would have been a glorious expression of benevolence in God to have done the former, though he had not seen fit to have done the latter.

But if we were unable to assign any reasons why God leaves some to perish, it would still be arrogance in us to conclude that there were not sufficient reasons. It would rather become us to acquiese in the language of our Lord. "I thank thee, O Father, Lord of heaven and earth, because thou hast hid these things from the wise and prudent, and hast revealed them unto babes, even so, Father, for so it hath seemed good in thy sight." Though we can by no means fathom the counsels of God, nor pretend to know all the particular reasons of this instance of his administration, yet some valuable ends, which are answered by it, may be clearly seen. A few will be here mentioned.

1. By leaving some to perish in their sins, God makes a most full and impressive manifestation of his justice, greater than could have otherwise been effected. It is true, that the abhorrence of God towards all sin, and his regard to the divine law, have been so manifested by the atonement of Christ, that the justice of

God would not have suffered, though all had been saved ;
but then it would not have been manifested in God's
dealings with this sinful world, for it cannot be truly
said, that the sufferings of Christ were due to him, or
that they were a manifestation of distributive justice.
There is no room to question the right which God has,
even after an atonement, to leave some to perish ; and
in such circumstances, a display of justice is peculiarly
striking, and expressive of God's holiness. Thus God
is willing to shew his wrath, and make his power
known, on the vessels of wrath, fitted to destruction :
and all the inhabitants of heaven will say, true and
righteous are thy judgments, and will cry Alleluia,
when the smoke of their torment ascendeth forever and
ever.

2. God, by leaving some to perish, teaches his creatures that he will have his grace respected by them.
Mankind have placed themselves, by rejecting Christ,
in very different circumstances from those they were
in before grace was offered and refused. They are
now guilty of sin, not only against the law of God, but
also against the dispensation of his wonderful grace.—
This renders it suitable that they should be viewed in
a very different light, and be treated accordingly. Their
sins against the transcendant glory of divine grace, are
not only an infinite aggravation of their guilt, but they
form *a new species of wickedness*, distinct from their
disobedience to the law of God, and of a nature more
base, ungrateful and malignant. It is such a kind of
wickedness as the fallen angels never committed, and
as never before appeared in the universe ; for none
ever before sinned against redeeming mercy, and the
offers of a gracious pardon for rebellion against God.
It is therefore a species of sin, which never had been
punished, so as to manifest God's peculiar abhorrence

of it. Disobedience and rebellion against the law and authority of God, had been punished in the fallen angels. Their sufferings declare the wrath of God for that description of sin, but not for sins committed against redeeming love. For the same reasons for which it was necessary and suitable, that the fallen angels should suffer for their rebellion, that the law of God might be respected; it seems proper, that there should be examples of God's peculiar displeasure at unbelief, that the grace of God might be respected by his creatures. It was suitable in the eyes of infinite wisdom and rectitude, that this should take place.— This serves to exhibit the dignified nature of the dispensation of grace, and shows that though God is gracious and merciful, he is not regardless of himself, nor of his mercy; but will be respected, and will have his grace respected by his creatures.

3. The unyielding nature of a sinful spirit had never before been ascertained, by actual experiment, and clearly exhibited to creatures. The fallen angels never had the offers of mercy, and it was not known to creatures, that they were so utterly depraved, but that the offers of grace and motives of infinite importance, might have prevailed on them to have returned to God; and so the justice of God in their punishment could not be seen in its full strength and lustre. But the offer has been made to man, and motives of infinite weight have been presented, and it is now ascertained by actual experiment, in the case of those under the instruction of the gospel, who are left of God to go on in sin, that a sinful spirit is too obstinate to be reduced by any motives, or offers of pardon and acceptance. The implacable nature of sin is made clearly manifest. It is no longer questionable whether the carnal heart is so inimical to God, that it can never be subject to his law.—

As this shows the extreme malignity of a sinful spirit, and its irreconcilable aversion to any proposals, which a holy God can make, it very greatly illustrates the justice of God, in dooming evil angels, as well as men, to never ending misery. It becomes evident, that their hearts are such that they never could be reclaimed, but by the all-conquering and irresistible power of God, and that they are fit only to be consigned to hopeless misery.

4. God in leaving some sinners to go on in their wickedness and perish, makes a most glorious display of the prerogative of divine sovereignty, beyond any thing of the kind which had ever before been set in the view of his creatures. He exercises, before the eyes of all intelligences, his sovereign right to dispose of sinners as he pleases, for the purpose of his own glory, either as vessels of mercy, or of wrath. This had never before been exhibited by example. This is a striking manifestation, that God considers the sinner as having forfeited all good—as being in the hands of a righteous Judge, and that he himself is under no kind of obligations to spare him. He may therefore use him in any way that shall be most for his own glory and the good of his kingdom, either as an example of justice or of grace. This sovereignty is also further manifested, in giving some the offers of mercy, while a knowledge of the gospel is withheld from others. In all this the language of his proceedings is, " Hath not the potter power over the clay, of the same lump, to make one vessel to honour and another unto dishonour ?" If God renewed all, this glorious display of divine sovereignty would not have been made.

5. Another valuable end which is obtained by God, leaving some to go on in sin and perish, is the peculiar display which this makes of the riches of his grace

to those whom he renews, and chooses to be the vessels of his mercy. If God had renewed and saved the whole of mankind, it might never have been so strongly felt by creatures, that there was no kind of obligation on God to the sinner, to convert him; and that he was at perfect liberty, even after an adequate redemption had been provided, either to apply it or not apply it, to the salvation of the sinner, as should appear good in his sight.

Nor could this grace have appeared to such advantage, had all been saved, for want of the striking contrast exhibited in the different treatment which the vessels of wrath, and of mercy, respectively receive from the hand of God. This idea appears to have deeply impressed the mind of the apostle Paul, when he said, " What if God, willing to show his wrath and make his power known, endured with much long suffering the vessels of wrath fitted to destruction, and that he might make known the riches of his glory on the vessels of his mercy which he had afore prepared unto glory." Isaiah also gives us the same idea from the mouth of God. " And it shall come to pass, that from one new moon to another, and from one Sabbath to another, shall all flesh come to worship before me, saith the Lord. And they shall go forth, and look upon the carcases of the men which have transgressed against me; for their worm shall not die, neither shall their fire be quenched, and they shall be an abhorring unto all flesh." Thus the distinguishing exercise of grace makes a peculiar display of the riches of divine mercy, towards those who are saved.

From the whole it is conceived, that it is made plain, that the atonement is infinitely full—that God in his invitations to sinners, and in his solemn declaration, that he hath no pleasure in the death of the wicked, but

that the wicked turn from his way and live, is consistent with his leaving some to go on in sin and perish.
And that there are reasons which may be assigned
why God does not convert and save all the human race :
Particularly, that the punishment of unbelief, which is
a *new and peculiar* species of wickedness, might be ex-
emplified—the justice of God be more fully manifested—that by the exhibition of the unyielding nature of
sin, the justice of God in the endless punishment of
evil men and angels might be seen in its true glory—
that the sovereignty of God, and the dignified manner
in which he exercises his grace might be known—and
that the exceeding riches of his grace towards the redeemed, might appear as they are.—In all these respects, God illustrates his own glorious perfections, in
the view of his creatures, and enriches them with the
knowledge of himself, by leaving some to go on in sin
and perish ; and in proportion as he brings himself into
view, he adds to the everlasting blessedness of his
whole kingdom. The wisdom and goodness of God
are also displayed, in adopting a measure calculated to
produce so many valuable ends, and creatures are effectually taught the firmness and stability, with which
the Most High proceeds in his administrations of government.—These are great and valuable ends, which
we see are answered by the sovereign dispensations of
grace and justice among men. So many reasons for
this way of proceeding are made known to us ; perhaps more may be seen by a sufficient attention to the
subject, and probably many more will be discovered by
the people of God, in the world to come. But how
many reasons God has for these proceedings, no finite
creature can determine. " Canst thou by searching
find out God, canst thou find out the Almighty to perfection ?" Finally ; the things which have been noticed,

in attending to this important question, are calculated
to impress our minds with the infinite mercy of God,
in producing an all-sufficient atonement, and freely offering salvation to us all—with our infinite obligations
to Jesus Christ, for the things he has done and said to
purchase mercy for sinners—with the awful wickedness and inexcusableness of the impenitent and unbelieving, whose blood must be upon their own heads—
with the mercy of God, in reclaiming any from their
obstinate perverseness to himself—with the indispen-
sible duty of all who hear the gospel, to repent and believe without delay—with the reasons which sinners
have to tremble at their guilt and danger—and with
the peculiar obligations of those whom God has renewed, and adopted into his family, to admire distinguishing grace, and be constant and zealous in his service. And let the world admire the compassion, and
obey the gracious exhortations of God, who says, " As
I live, saith the Lord, I have no pleasure in the death
of the wicked; but that the wicked turn from his way
and live. Turn ye, turn ye from your evil ways; for
why will ye die, O house of Israel ?"

The Sufferings of Christ, a Gain to the Universe.

(From the Theological Magazine.)

IF the sufferings of Christ, a person of infinite dignity, were an evil equal to that which the sufferings
of all mankind would have been, had Christ never
died for sinners; what benefit, on the whole, it is asked,
accrues to the universe from his sufferings?

To this it may be replied, that, if the purposes of divine goodness and love are answered in the happiness and good which are actually produced and enjoyed in the system, we are, of course, to estimate this good by the quantity of happiness which is to be enjoyed. Consequently, the *evil,* which is considered as lessening the good, is also, on the other hand, to be estimated by *its* quantity. And, according to this rule of estimation, the sufferings of Christ are followed by an overbalancing and far greater good. For, in whatever other respects the sufferings of Christ are to be considered as an infinite evil, it may safely be concluded they were not infinite in quantity; but will be, in this respect, much exceeded by the happiness and enjoyment of those who are redeemed by the blood of Christ. The happiness and good, which will be the fruit of the sufferings of Christ, as they will be continually increasing in degree, and endless in duration, may be strictly said to be infinite; and therefore, the *evil* of Christ's sufferings will be overbalanced by the *good* which will be enjoyed by those who are saved by him.

The sufferings of Christ, considering his infinite dignity and excellence, may properly be said to be an infinite evil. They manifested a displeasure, in the divine mind, sufficient to produce the *eternal torments* of sinners, had it fallen upon them. Nevertheless, the divine displeasure, which appeared in these sufferings, is not to be estimated merely by their quantity: there are other considerations, of still greater weight, to be taken into the account. The merit, or value, of the sufferings of Christ, as a testimony of hatred of iniquity, arose more from the dignity of his person, and the exellence of his character, than from the degree of pain which is endured. These sufferings, considered in respect of their measure and quantity, may, therefore, be overbalanced by the happiness and enjoyment of those whom Christ has redeemed from death. So that, in this respect, it may appear that the sufferings of Christ have occasioned a great accession of good to the system.

But this is not all. Christ enjoys, in his own person, a full reward for all the sufferings he endured.—So that, aside from the happiness of the redeemed, considered as their own personal felicity, the sufferings of the Son of God are completely compensated in his own felicity.

Christ is as susceptible of *reward*, as of *sufferings*. However great his sufferings were, he is capable of a reward, which will fully balance them. Were he capable of going through *infinite sufferings*, he is equally capable of enjoying an *infinite* reward. If his sufferings were to be considered as an *infinite evil*, because of the superlative excellence of his person, the reward, which he, himself, reaps and enjoys, is, for the same reason, to be considered as an *infinite good*.

In whatever point of light the subject be viewed, it will appear, that the sufferings of Christ, though awfully great and extreme, though infinite indignity was offered to his person and character, were, nevertheless, no loss of good in the system; but so far from it, that all the good which the redeemed will enjoy to eternity, all that weight of glory which will be conferred upon them, is so much gain to the universe, and overplus of good, accruing from the work and sufferings of Christ.

X

IT is said by the opposers of the doctrine of atonement, that it is unjust, that an innocent person should suffer in the stead of a guilty one. Yet these same gentlemen hold, that our Lord Jesus Christ did suffer for the benefit of guilty sinners, by setting them an example of patience and persevering obedience under the greatest trials; by dying a martyr to the purest morality, and by teaching a future state of rewards and punishments by his own resurrection; thus laying a foundation for preaching the gospel, and leading sinners to repentance, that in consequence of this they might be pardoned and and saved. Now, why is not this as inconsistent with justice, as that Christ should die to make atonement for sinners, in order to their pardon and salvation? In either case, the innocent suffers for the guilty, the death suffered is the same, and the end is the same, the salvation of sinners.— Suppose my neighbour is a murderer, and he must die on the gallows, unless he repent; or unless satisfaction be made for his crime, by the hanging of another person. Now, would it not be as really unjust to hang me, in order to lead him to repentance, that his life may be spared, as it would be to hang me as a substitute for him, that the same end might be obtained?—Let the candid decide.

O.

On the Nature of the Satisfaction, rendered in the Atonement.

(From the Connecticut Evangelical Magazine.)

Question.—How doth Christ execute the office of a Priest?

Answer.—Christ executeth the office of a priest, in his once offering up of himself, a sacrifice *to satisfy divine justice.*

Ass. CATECHISM.

THE method of salvation, through the atonement of Christ, displays the infinite wisdom and goodness of God. It is suitable that we should endeavour to gain a right view of this atonement. For it is a fundamental docrine in the christian scheme, and a misconception here, may lead to consequences of a dangerous and destructive tendency.

We may believe that Christ, by his sufferings, hath endured the penalty of the law, in such a manner, as in this respect fully to satisfy divine justice. But the nature of this satisfaction, becomes a subject of inquiry. And it will be found that it does not necessarily terminate in the happiness of all the human race, but is rather an encouragement to the sinner, to set about the work of his salvation.

I. Concerning the nature of divine justice.

This is a formidable attribute; in it, God appears clothed in terrible majesty, making himself known in the judgment which he executeth. But it breathes the same spirit with benevolence, and has the same moral excellence. One individual principle actuates the divine mind. God is love. This affection, in its different modifications, gains the name of the several moral attributes. Justice may be considered, that attribute which fixes the sanctions of the moral law, and looks to the well ordering of the divine government.

One of these sanctions consists in death, or endless suffering, as the wages of sin. This penalty is of great extent, and involves the offender in remediless ruin. According to the tenor of the law, sin is an evil of infinite magnitude, and exposes to interminable misery, as the just consequence. This penalty, however, does not originate in a vindictive, revengeful spirit. And justice would lay aside its claims, if there were no other end to be answered, but the gratification which arises from the misery of the offender. The infliction of penal evil, must have something to justify it besides the satisfaction which the misery of the creature can give to the divine lawgiver. It will not do to vindicate the penalty of the law, by saying, " It is no more than the vile transgressor highly deserves." There must be some further reason why such treatment of the sinner is just, or which constitutes his ill-desert. And if no reason, of a public nature, can be found for inflicting the penalty of the law, it ought in justice to be laid aside ; for in such a condition as this, to exact punishment, would rather be the injustice and unfeelingness of a tyrant, than the tenderness of a wise and good sovereign. Hence we ay inquire,

II. Why justice required satisfaction.

And here we may bring into view the public and general good, as the great object which renders such a satisfaction necessary. It was not surely required for the sake of rendering God abundant in goodness, and ready to forgive. His moral nature is immutable, and can admit of no alteration. There is no want of compassion in him. Had nothing required the sufferings of Christ in the atonement, but a want of pity in the divine mind, they might have been spared. We must take heed, that we do not conceive of God as being unpropitious, malevolent, and revengeful. We must not find the ground of the atonement to lie in any such spirit of animosity.

But, it seems, that the best good of the intellectual and moral world, requires that God should appear to be a terror to evil doers. And this is to be seen, by his requiring the expiatory sufferings of Christ. The wise moral Governor, that he may be just, has an immense system of creation to watch over and protect. He has to guard and defend the rights and privileges of his moral government. This benevolent justice, which looks over creation with a watchful eye, is that kind of justice which rendered the atonement necessary. To maintain the interests of this kingdom it is requisite, that the divine law should be seen in its dignity, loveliness, and spirituality. And to this purpose, it must be supported; which is done by the atoning sufferings of Christ. Thus the law is magnified and made honourable. The divine authority of this law, is made to be respected through the holy part of creation.

Likewise, it is needful that there be an expression of the evil of sin. The good of the whole requires

X 2

this manifestation. For thereby, holy beings are deterred from transgression, and preserved in a state of rectitude. Also, a discovery of the turpitude of sin enhances the value of holiness, and renders it a greater good. In the satisfaction which is made by Christ, sin appears to be sin. The matchless sufferings of the divine Saviour, show that sin is an evil of infinite extent, and tends directly to mar the moral beauty of creation, and introduce confusion, and every evil work. Thus by this view of sin, holiness becomes more desirable, more lovely, and the happiness of the intellectual system is advanced.

We must further add, that God may appear amiable, and infinitely the best good, it must be seen that he has a detestation and abhorrence of sin. It is from the display of himself that his creatures are made happy. And that he may make the fullest discovery of himself, he must manifest his feelings with regard to the extreme vileness of sin. This is done in the atonement. These are some of the important truths which the satisfaction of Christ has served to elucidate, and confirm ; and for which it became requisite.

III. The satisfaction rendered in the atonement, is not to be viewed strictly as the payment of a debt.

Salvation is, indeed, blood-bought. The blood of Christ is represented as the price, which was laid down for redemption. But this must be viewed as a metaphorical expression, meaning that Christ's sufferings, and obedience, have made it consistent to forgive the sinner.

Placing the atonement precisely upon the footing of a pecuniary transaction, it is conceived, alters the nature of justice. In the payment of a debt, one equivalent good is rendered for another. And thus the damage is repaired, and entire satisfaction made.—

But suffering can be no good, upon any principle. It can, in itself, be no gratification or benefit to the pure and perfect justice of God. He hath no pleasure in the death of him that dieth. He is a tender, compassionate God. And misery can be no adequate compensation for his goods which sinners have received and wasted.

The atonement, then, is not to be viewed as the payment of a debt, after our manner of negociation, but is rather to be considered as an expedient which infinite wisdom has devised, rendering it consistent to forgive transgressors. The mere sufferings of Christ could have had no avail, to save, were it not for the great and extensive ends which they brought to pass. And, as far as these ends can be secured in a consistency with the salvation of guilty men, God will extend mercy. He will save to the uttermost; for his mercy endureth forever.

We will now add a few reflections.

1. We learn the sufficiency of the atonement.

Christ hath made full satisfaction to divine justice. The atonement is of infinite value. There is no deficiency in the merit of the Redeemer. He hath taken upon himself the penalty of the law, and submitted to its condemning sentence. His amazing sufferings have displayed its purity, justice and holiness, not less, and even far more, than the creature's sufferings could have done. When God spares not his own Son, but freely gives him up to the agonies of the cross, then sin appears to be sin; the law appears holy, just and good; the divine authority is clothed with dignity, and God is exhibited in his transcendent purity, viewing sin as odious, and delighting in holiness. These truths are not less clear in the atonement, than they would have been in the final destruction of the human race. Indeed, they are set forth in a vastly stronger light, on account of the matchless dignity of the divine Saviour.

So that we are not to suppose, that God's compassions can fail, by reason of any limitation in the atonement which Christ has made.

2. The sufficiency of the atonement does not imply that all are to be saved.

The satisfaction which Christ has rendered, is not such as to release the obligation of the sinner, and extinguish the claims of justice upon him. His character remains the same as before. His ill-desert is not diminished; and he is entitled to nothing but the wages of sin. The satisfaction is not so set to his account, as necessarily to discharge him from the condemning power of the righteous law. Christ has not so cancelled the debt of justice, as that the guilty offender must be set free. He is not substituted in the place of the sinner, in such manner, that his sufferings must, in equity, be taken in exchange for those which are the sinner's due.

The atonement does not necessarily terminate in the salvation of all men, any more than in the recovery of apostate angels, who kept not their first estate. God may have mercy on whom he will have mercy. He is still left free to dispense his mercies, as he pleases. If he sees wise ends to be answered, by leaving a portion of the human race to perish in unbelief, he has a right so to do. Notwithstanding the rich atonement, the renovation of the creature still rests as an independent favour, to be bestowed according to his wise and sovereign pleasure. And we may be assured that God will save to the extent of his goodness. He will confer grace and glory upon lost sinners, as far as he can do it consistently with his own perfections, and the general good.

3. The sufficiency of the atonement is our encouragement, to set about the work of our salvation.

No one need despair, on account of any defect in Christ's satisfaction. The chief of sinners may come, and find ample provision. Christ hath given himself a ransom for all. He hath made such display of the excellence of the divine law, that this does not lie as an obstruction in the way to salvation. Whosoever will may come. The invitations of the gospel are free and large. A great and effectual door is opened. And it must be encouraging to guilty men, to know that the way is cleared, and they may be forgiven upon their repentance. The richness of the atonement is calculated to keep the trembling penitent from despondency. Who, in sincerity, ever sought, and was disappointed?

We have reason to bless God for this consistent plan of showing mercy. In his unsearchable wisdom and goodness, he hath devised a method, in which he can be just, and yet the justifier of such as believe. None but God, who comprehends his own existence, and the immense system of creation, could have seen how the atoning sufferings of Christ could have made such display of truth, as to render it consistent to exercise mercy towards the apostate creature. Glory to God, that on earth is peace and good will towards men. In the view of these things, let us give all diligence to make our calling and election sure.   Y. Z.

Why the atoning sufferings of Christ were necessary in the gospel.

THE atoning sufferings of Christ, were necessary in the gospel scheme, for the same reason, as the eternal misery of the sinner was under the law; to make a display of God's moral character—of his righteousness as king of the universe—of his sense of the turpitude of the sinners principles and practice—and also the nature of benevolence, in its high and infinite source, Godhead himself. If God had been governed by revenge or personal resentment against the sinner, there would have been no possibility of a gospel; and the transgressor must have borne the necessary misery himself. But as the divine motive, in this matter, was solely the public benefit; and as the sinner's misery was solely to answer a public and governmental end, God might accept as a substitute, whatever would answer the same purposes in government, and equally conduce to the blessedness of the universe. Whatever would make an equal display of the same truths, might be accepted in the stead of the sinner's eternal misery. The sufferings of Christ, who was both God and man, would in a limited time make this display in a higher degree than the eternal sufferings of the whole universe; and therefore his sufferings might be accepted by God in justice to his government, in the stead of so many sinners, as infinite wisdom saw it would be best to sanctify and forgive. By the suffering of Christ, all those truths which relate to the divine character, the support of his government, and the unchangeable obligation of the law, are seen in a brighter manner, than they could be by any suffering of the sinner under the law. It is thus that the gospel opens a greater view of God and the holy system, and prepares the way for higher happiness.

THREE CONVERSATIONS,

ON

Imputation, Substitution, and Particular Redemption,

BY ANDREW FULLER.

CONVERSATION THE FIRST.

ON IMPUTATION.

PETER and James considered each other as good men, and had for several years been in the habit of corresponding on divine subjects. Their respect was mutual. Their sentiments, however, though alike in the main, were not exactly the same; and some circumstances had lately occurred, which tended rather to magnify the difference than to lessen it. Being both at the house of John, their common friend, they in his company fell into the following conversation.

I am not without painful apprehension said Peter to John, that the views of our friend James on some of the doctrines of the gospel, are unhappily diverted from the truth. I suspect he does not believe in the proper *imputation* of sin to Christ, or of Christ's righteousness to us; nor in his being our *substitute*, or representative.

John. Those are serious things; but what are the grounds, brother Peter, on which your suspicions rest?

Peter. Partly what he has published, which I cannot reconcile with those doctrines; and partly what he has said in my hearing, which I consider as an avowal of what I have stated.

John. What say you to this, brother James?

James. I cannot tell whether what I have written or spoken accords with brother Peter's ideas on these subjects: indeed I suspect it does not: but I never thought of calling either of the doctrines in question. Were I to relinguish the one or the other, I should be at a loss for ground on which to rest my salvation.—What he says of my avowing my disbelief of them in his hearing must be a misunderstanding. I did say, I suspected that *his views* of imputation and substitution were unscriptural; but had no intention of disowning the doctrines themselves.

Peter. Brother James, I have no desire to assume any dominion over your faith; but should be glad to know what are your ideas on these important subjects. Do you hold that sin was properly imputed to Christ, or that Christ's righteousness is properly imputed to us, or not?

James. You are quite at liberty, brother Peter, to ask me any questions on these subjects; and if you will hear me patiently, I will answer you as explicitly as I am able.

John. Do so, brother James; and we shall hear you not only patiently, but, I trust, with pleasure.

James. To impute,* signifies in general, to *charge, reckon,* or *place to account,* according to the different objects to which it is applied. This word, like many

---

* חשב; *Logizomai.*

others, has a *proper*, and an *improper* or figurative meaning.

First: It is applied to the *charging*, *reckoning*, or *placing to the account* of persons and things, *that which properly belongs to them*. This I consider as its *proper* meaning. In this sense the word is used in the following passages. " Eli *thought* she (Hannah) had been drunken—Hanan and Mattaniah, the treasurers, were *counted* faithful—Let a man so *account* of us as the ministers of Christ, and stewards of the mysteries of God—Let such an one *think* this, that such as we are in word by letters when we are absent, such will we be also in deed when we are present—I *reckon* that the sufferings of this present time are not worthy to be compared with the glory that shall be revealed in us."[*] Reckoning or accounting, in the above instances, is no other than judging of persons and things *according to what they are*, or *appear to be*. To impute sin in this sense is to charge guilt upon the guilty in a judicial way, or with a view to punishment. Thus Shimei besought David that his iniquity might *not be imputed to him ;* thus the man is pronounced blessed to whom the Lord *imputeth not iniquity :* and thus Paul prayed that the sin of those who deserted him might *not be laid to their charge.*[†]

In this sense the term is ordinarily used in common life. To impute treason or any other crime to a man, is the same thing as charging him with having committed it, and with a view to his being punished.

Secondly : It is applied to the *charging*, *reckoning*, or *placing to the account* of persons and things, *that*

---

[*] 1 Sam. i. 13. Neh. xiii. 13. 1. Cor. iv. 1. 2 Cor. x. 11. Rom. viii. 18.

[†] 2 Sam. xix. 19. Ps. xxxii. 2. 2 Tim. iv, 16.

Y

which does not properly belong to them, as though it did.
This I consider as its *improper*, or figurative meaning.
In this sense the word is used in the following passages—" And this your heave-offering shall be *reckoned* unto you *as though it were* the corn of the thresh-
ing-floor, and as the fulness of the wine-press—Wherefore hidest thou thy face, and *holdest* me for thine enemy—If the uncircumcision keep the righteousness of
the law, shall not his uncircumcision be *counted* for
circumcision—If he hath wronged thee, or oweth thee
aught, *put that on mine account.*"*

It is in this *latter* sense that I understand the term
when applied to justification. " Abraham believed God,
and it was *counted* unto him for righteousness—To
him that worketh not, but believeth on him that justifieth the ungodly, his faith is *counted* for righteousness." The counting, or reckoning, in these instances,
is not a judging of things *as they are ;* but *as they are
not, as though they were.* I do not think that faith here
means the righteousness of the Messiah : for it is expressly called " believing." It means believing, however, not as a virtuous exercise of the mind which God
consented to accept instead of perfect obedience, but
as having respect to the promised Messiah, and so to his
righteousness as the ground of acceptance.† Justification is ascribed to faith, as healing frequently is in the
New Testament; not as that from which the *virtue*
proceeds, but as that which *receives* from the Saviour's
fulness.

But if it were allowed that faith in these passages
really means the object believed in, still this was not

---

* Num. xviii. 27—30. Job. xiii. 24. Rom. ii. 26. Philem. 18.
† Expository Discourses on Gen. xv. 1—6. Also Calvin's
Inst. bk. iii. ch. xi. § 7.

Abraham's *own* righteousness, and could not be properly *counted* by him who judges of things as they are, as being so. It was *reckoned* unto him *as if it were* his; and the effects, or benefits of it, were actually imparted to him: but this was all. Abraham did not become meritorious, or cease to be unworthy.

" What is it to place our righteousness in the obedience of Christ (says Calvin) but to affirm that hereby only we are *accounted* righteous; because the obedience of Christ is imputed to us *as if it were our own.*"*

It is thus also that I understand the imputation of sin to Christ. He was accounted in the divine administration *as if he were,* or *had been* the sinner, that those who believe in him might be accounted *as if they were,* or *had been* righteous.

Brethren, I have done. Whether my statement be just, or not, I hope it will be allowed to be explicit.

John. That it certainly is ; and we thank you. Have you any other questions, brother Peter, to ask upon the subject?

Peter. How do you understand the apostle in 2 Cor. v. 21. *He hath made him to be sin for us, who knew no sin, that we might be made the righteousness of God in him?*

James. Till lately I cannot say that I have thought closely upon it: I have understood that several of our best writers consider the word *amartia (sin)* as frequently meaning a *sin-offering.* Dr. Owen so interprets it in his answer to Biddle,† though it seems he afterwards changed his mind. Considering the opposition between the sin which Christ was made, and the righteousness which we are made, together with the

---

* Inst. Bk. iii. ch. xi. § 2.   † p. 510.

same word being used for that which he was *made*, and that which he *knew not*, I am inclined to be of the doctor's last opinion; namely, that the sin which Christ was made means *sin itself*, and the righteousness which we are made means *righteousness itself*. I doubt not but that the allusion is to the sin-offering under the law; but not to its being *made a sacrifice*. Let me be a little more particular. There were two things belonging to the sin-offering. *First:* The imputation of the sins of the people, signified by the priest's laying his hands upon the head of the animal, and confessing over it their transgressions; and which is called " putting them upon it."* That is, it was *counted* in the divine administration *as if the animal had been* the sinner, and the only sinner of the nation. *Secondly:* Offering it in sacrifice, or " killing it before the Lord for an atonement."† Now the phrase, *made sin*, in 2 Cor. v. 21. appears to refer to the *first* step in this process in order to the last. It is expressive of what was preparatory to Christ's suffering death rather than of the thing itself, just as our being *made righteousness* expresses what was preparatory to God's bestowing upon us eternal life. But the term *made* is not to be taken literally; for that would convey the idea of Christ's being really the subject of moral evil. It is expressive of a divine *constitution*, by which our Redeemer with his own consent, stood in the sinner's place, as though he had been himself the transgressor; just as the sin-offering under the law was, in mercy to Israel, reckoned or accounted to have the sins of the people " put upon its head," with this difference; that was only a shadow, but this went really to take away sin.

---

* Lev. xvi. 21. † Lev. i. 4, 5.

Peter. Do you consider Christ as having been *pun-ished, really and properly* PUNISHED?

James. I should think I do not. But what do you mean by punishment?

Peter. An innocent person may *suffer*, but, properly speaking, he cannot be *punished*. Punishment necessarily supposes *criminality*.

James. Just so; and therefore as I do not believe that Jesus was in any sense criminal, I cannot say he was really and properly punished.

Peter. Punishment is the infliction of natural evil for the commission of moral evil. It is not necessary, however, that the latter should have been committed by the party—Criminality is supposed: but it may be either personal or imputed.

James. This I cannot admit. Real and proper punishment, if I understand the terms, is not only the infliction of natural evil for the commission of moral evil; but the infliction of the one *upon the person who committed the other, and in displeasure against him.* It not only supposes criminality, but that the party punished was literally the criminal. Criminality committed by one party, and imputed to another, is not a ground for real and proper punishment. If Paul had sustained the punishment due to Onesimus for having wronged his master, yet it would not have been real and proper punishment *to him*, but *suffering* only, as not being inflicted in displeasure against him. I am aware of what has been said on this subject, that there was a more intimate *union* between Christ and those for whom he died, than could ever exist between creatures. But be it so, it is enough for me that the union was not such as *that the actions of the one became those of the other.* Christ, even in the act of offering him-

Y 2

self a sacrifice, when, to speak in the language of the Jewish law, the sins of the people were put or laid upon him, gave himself nevertheless *the just for the unjust.*

Peter. And thus it is that you understand the words of Isaiah, *The Lord hath laid on him the iniquity of us all?*

James. Yes, he bore the punishment due to our sins, or that which, considering the dignity of his person, was equivalent to it. The phrase " He shall bear his iniquity," which so frequently occurs in the Old Testament, means, he shall bear the punishment due to his iniquity.

Peter. And yet you deny that Christ's sufferings were properly *penal.*

James. You would not deny eternal life which is promised to believers to be properly *a reward;* but you would deny its being *a real and proper reward* TO THEM.

Peter. And what then?

James. If eternal life, though it be a reward, and we partake of it, yet is really and properly the reward of Christ's obedience, and not ours; then the sufferings of Christ, though they were a punishment, and he sustained it, yet were really and properly the punishment of our sins, and not his. What he bore *was* punishment: that is, it was the expression of divine displeasure against transgressors. So what we enjoy *is* reward: that is, it is the expression of God's well-pleasedness in the obedience and death of his Son.— But neither is the one a punishment *to him,* nor the other, properly speaking, a reward *to us.*

There appears to me great accuracy in the scriptural language on this subject. What our Saviour underwent is almost always expressed by the term *suf-*

fering. Once it is called a *chastisement:* yet there he is not said to have been chastised; but " the chastisement of our peace was *upon him.*" This is the same as saying he bore *our* punishment. He was made a *curse* for us: that is, having been reckoned, or accounted the sinner, as though he had actually been so, he was treated accordingly, *as* one that had deserved to be an outcast from heaven and earth. I believe the wrath of God that was due to us was poured upon him: but I do not believe that God for one moment was angry or displeased *with him,* or that he smote him from any such displeasure.

There is a passage in Calvin's *Institutes,* which so fully expresses my mind, that I hope you will excuse me if I read it. You will find it in Bk. ii. Ch. xvi. § 10, 11. " It behooved him that he should, as it were, hand to hand, wrestle with the armies of hell, and the horrors of eternal death. The chastisement of our peace was *laid upon him.* He was smitten of his Father for our crimes, and bruised for our iniquities : whereby is meant that he was put in the stead of the wicked, as surety and pledge, yea, and *as* the very guilty person himself, to sustain and bear away all the punishments that should have been laid upon them, save only that he could not be holden of death. Yet do we not mean that God was at any time either his enemy, or angry with him. For how could he be angry with his beloved Son, upon whom his mind rested? Or how could Christ by his intercession appease his Father's wrath towards others, if, full of hatred, he has been incensed against himself? But this is our meaning—that he sustained the weight of the divine displeasure ; inasmuch as he, being stricken and tormented by the hand of God, *did feel all the tokens of God when he is angry and punisheth.*"

Peter. The words of scripture are very express—He hath *made him to be sin for us*—He was *made a curse for us.*—You may, by diluting and qualifying interpretations, soften what you consider as intolerable *harshness.* In other words, you may choose to correct the language and sentiments of inspiration, and teach the apostle to speak of his Lord with more decorum, lest his personal purity should be impeached, and lest the odium of the cross, annexed by divine law, remain attached to his death: but if you abide by the obvious meaning of the passages, you must hold with *a commutation of persons*, the *imputation* of sin and righteousness, and a *vicarious punishment*, equally pregnant with *execration* as with *death.*

John. I wish brother Peter would forbear the use of language which tends not to convince, but to irritate.

James. If there be any thing convincing in it, I confess I do not perceive it. I admit with Mr. *Charnock,* " That Christ was " made sin" *as if he had* sinned all the sins of men; and we are " made righteousness," *as if we had* not sinned at all." What more is necessary to abide by the obvious meaning of the words? To go further must be to maintain that Christ's being *made sin* means that he was literally rendered wicked, and that his being *made a curse* is the same thing as his being punished for it according to his deserts. Brother Peter, I am sure, does not believe this shocking position: but he seems to think there is a medium between his being treated *as if he were* a sinner, and his *being one.* If such a medium there be, I should be glad to discover it: at present it appears to me to have no existence.

Brother Peter will not suspect me, I hope, of wishing to depreciate his judgment, when I say, that he appears to me to be attached to certain terms without having sufficiently weighed their import. In most cases I should think it a privilege to learn of him : but in some things I cannot agree with him. In order to maintain the *real* and *proper punishment* of Christ, he talks of his being " guilty by imputation." The term *guilty,* I am aware, is often used by theological writers for *an obligation to punishment,* and so applies to that voluntary obligation which Christ came under to sustain the punishment of our sins : but strictly speaking, guilt is the *desert* of punishment ; and this can never apply but to the offender. It is the opposite of innocence. A voluntary obligation to endure the punishment of another is not guilt, any more than a consequent exemption from obligation in the offender, is innocence. Both guilt and innocence are transferable in their effects, but in themselves they are untransferable. They say that Christ was *reckoned* or *counted* in the divine administration *as if he were* the sinner, and came under an obligation to endure the curse or punishment due to our sins, is one thing : but to say he *deserved* that curse, is another. Guilt, strictly speaking, is the inseparable attendant of transgression, and could never therefore for one moment occupy the conscience of Christ. If Christ by imputation became *deserving* of punishment, we by non-imputation cease to deserve it ; and if our demerits be literally transferred to him, his merits must of course be the same to us : and then, instead of approaching God as *guilty* and *unworthy,* we might take consequence to ourselves before him, as not only guiltless, but meritorious beings.

Peter. Some who profess to hold that believers are justified by the righteousness of Christ, deny, nevertheless, that his *obedience itself* is imputed to them :

for they maintain that the scripture represents believers as receiving only the *benefits,* or effects of
Christ's righteousness in justification, or their being
pardoned and accepted for Christ's *righteousness sake.*
But it is not merely *for the sake* of Christ, or of what
he has done, that believers are accepted of God, and
treated as completely righteous; but it is IN him as
their Head, Representative, and Substitute; and by
the imputation of that *very obedience.* which as such he
performed to the divine law, that they are justified.

James. I have no doubt but that the imputation of
Christ's righteousness presupposes a *union* with him;
since there is no perceivable fitness in bestowing benefits on one *for another's sake* where there is no union
or relation subsisting between them. It is not such a
union, however, as that *the actions of either become
those of the other.* That " the scriptures represent believers as *receiving* only the benefits or the effects of
Christ's righteousness in justification," is a remark of
which I am not able to perceive the fallacy: nor does
it follow that his obedience itself is not imputed to
them. Obedience itself may be and is imputed, while
its effects only are *imparted,* and consequently *received.*
I never met with a person who held the absurd notion
of imputed benefits, or imputed punishments; and
am inclined to think there never was such a person.
Be that however as it may, sin on the one hand, and
righteousness on the other, are the proper objects of
imputation; but that imputation *consists* in charging
or reckoning them to the account of the party in such
a way as to *impart* to him their evil or beneficial effects.

Peter. The doctrine for which I contend as taught
by the apostle Paul, is neither novel, nor more strongly expressed than it has formerly been by authors of
eminence.

James. It may be so. We have been told of an old protestant writer who says, that "In Christ, and by him, every true christian may be called *a fulfiller of the law:*" but I see not why he might not as well have added, Every true christian may be said to have been slain, and, if not to have redeemed himself by his own blood, yet to be worthy of all that blessing, and honour, and glory, that shall be conferred upon him in the world to come.—What do you think of Dr. Crisp's Sermons? Has he not carried your principles to an extreme?

Peter. I cordially agree with Witsius, as to the impropriety of calling Christ *a sinner, truly a sinner, the greatest of sinners,* &c. yet I am far from disapproving of what Dr. Crisp, and some others, *meant* by those exceptionable expressions.

James. If a christian may be called *a fulfiller of the law,* on account of Christ's obedience being imputed to him, I see not why Christ may not be called *a transgressor of the law,* on account of our disobedience being imputed to him. Persons and things *should be called what they are.* As to the *meaning* of Dr. Crisp, I am very willing to think he had no ill design: but my concern is with the meaning which his words convey to his readers. He considers God in charging our sins on Christ, and accounting his righteousness to us, as reckoning of things *as they are.* (p. 280.) He contends that Christ was *really* the sinner, or guilt could not have been laid upon him. (p. 272.) Imputation of sin and righteousness, with him, is literally and actually *a transfer of character;* and it is the object of his reasoning to persuade his believing hearers that from henceforward Christ is the sinner, and not they. "Hast thou been an idolater," says he, "a blasphemer, a despiser of God's word, a profaner of

his name and ordinances, a thief, a liar, a drunkard—
If thou hast part in Christ, *all these transgressions of
thine become actually the transgressions of Christ, and
so cease to be thine ; and thou ceasest to be a transgressor from the time they were laid upon Christ, to the last
hour of thy life :* so that now thou art *not* an idolater,
a persecutor, a thief, a liar, &c.—thou art *not* a sinful
person. Reckon whatever sin you commit, when as
you have part in Christ, you are all that Christ was,
and Christ is all that you were."*

If the *meaning* of this passage be true and good, I
see nothing exceptionable in the expressions. All
that can be said is, that the writer explicitly states his
principle and avows its legitimate consequences. I
believe the principle to be false.—(1.) Because neither
sin nor righteousness are *in themselves* transferable.
The act and deed of one person may *affect* another in
many ways, but cannot possibly become his act and
deed.—(2.) Because the scriptures uniformly declare
Christ to be sinless, and believers to be sinful creatures.—(3.) Because believers themselves have in all
ages *confessed* their sins, and applied to the mercy-
seat for *forgiveness.* They never plead such an union
as shall render their sins not theirs, but Christ's ; but
merely such a one as affords ground to apply for pardon *in his name,* or *for his sake ;* not as worthy claimants, but as unworthy supplicants.

Whatever reasonings we may give into, there are
certain times in which *conscience* will bear witness,
that notwithstanding the imputation of our sins to
Christ, *we are actually the sinners ;* and I should have
thought no good man could have gravely gone about
to overturn its testimony. Yet this is what Dr. Crisp

* p. 270.

has done. " Believers *think*, says he, that they find their transgressions in their own consciences, and they *imagine* that there is a sting of this poison still behind, wounding them : but, beloved, if this principle be received for a truth, that God hath laid thy iniquities on Christ, how can thy transgressions, belonging to Christ, be found in thy heart and conscience ?—Is thy conscience Christ ?" p. 269.

Perhaps no man has gone further than Dr. Crisp in his attempts at consistency ; and admitting his principle, that imputation consists in a transfer of character, I do not see who can dispute his conclusions.— To have been perfectly consistent, however, he should have proved that all the confessions and lamentations of believers, recorded in scripture, arose from their being under the *mistake* which he labours to rectify ; that is, *thinking* sin did not cease to be theirs, even when under the fullest persuasion that the Lord would not impute it to them, but would graciously cover it by the righteousness of his Son.

John. I hope, my brethren, that what has been said in this free conversation will be reconsidered with candour ; and that you will neither of you impute designs or consequences to the other which are not avowed.

————◆————

CONVERSATION THE SECOND.

ON SUBSTITUTION.

JOHN. I think, brother Peter, you expressed at the beginning of our last conversation, a strong suspicion that brother James denied the *substitution of Christ*, as well as the proper imputation of sin and

Z

righteousness. What has passed on the latter subject would probably tend either to confirm or remove your suspicions respecting the former.

Peter. I confess I was mistaken in some of my suspicions. I consider our friend as a good man ; but am far from being satisfied with what I still understand to be his views on this important subject.

John. It gives me great pleasure to hear the honest concessions of brethren, when they feel themselves in any measure to have gone too far.

Peter. I shall be glad to hear brother James's statement on *substitution,* and to know whether he considers our Lord in his undertaking as having sustained the character of a *Head,* or *Representative ;* and if so, whether the persons for whom he was a substitute were the elect only, or mankind in general.

James. I must acknowledge that on this subject I feel considerably at a loss. I have no consciousness of having ever called the doctrine of substitution in question. On the contrary, my hope of salvation rests upon it ; and the sum of my delight, as a minister of the gospel, consists in it. If I know any thing of my own heart, I can say of my Saviour as laying down his life *for, or instead of* sinners, as was said of Jerusalem by the captives—*If I forget* THEE, *let my right hand forget : If I do not remember* THEE, *let my tongue cleave to the roof of my mouth !*

[James here paused, and wept ; and both John and Peter wept with him. After recovering himself a little, he proceeded as follows—]

I have always considered the denial of this doctrine as being of the essence of Socinianism. I could not have imagined that any person whose hope of acceptance with God rests not on any goodness in himself, but entirely on the righteousness of Christ, imputed

to him *as if it were his own*, would have been accounted to disown his substitution. But perhaps, my dear
brother (for such I feel him to be, notwithstanding our
differences) may include in his ideas of this subject,
that Christ was so our *head* and *representative*, as that
what he did and suffered, we did and suffered in him.
[To this Peter assented.] If no more were meant by
this, resumed James, than that what he did and suffered is graciously accepted on our behalf *as if it were
ours*, I freely, as I have said before, acquiesce in it.
But I do not believe, and can hardly persuade myself
that brother Peter believes, the obedience and sufferings of Christ to be so ours, as that we can properly
be said to have obeyed and suffered.

Christ was and is our *head*, and we are his members : the union between him and us, however, is not
in all respects the same as that which is between the
head and the members of the natural body : for that
would go to explain away all distinct consciousness
and accountableness on our part.

As to the term *representative*, if no more be meant
by it than that Christ so personated us as to die in our
stead, that we, believing in him, should not die, I have
nothing to object to it. But I do not believe that Christ
was so our representative, as that what he did and suffered, we did and suffered ; and so became meritorious, or deserving of the divine favour.—But I feel myself in a wide field, and must entreat your indulgence
while I take up so much of the conversation.

Peter and John. Go on, and state your sentiments
without apology.

James. I apprehend then that many important mistakes have arisen from considering the interposition of
Christ under the notion of *paying a debt*. The blood
of Christ is indeed the *price* of our redemption, or that

for the sake of which we are delivered from the curse
of the law: but this metaporical language, as well as
that of *head and members*, may be carried too far, and
may lead us into many errors. In cases of debt and
credit among men, where a surety undertakes to *represent* the debtor, from the moment his undertaking
is accepted, the debtor is free, and may claim his liberty, not as a matter of favour, at least on the part of the
creditor, but of strict justice. Or should the undertaking be unknown to him for a time, yet as soon as
he knows it, he may demand his discharge, and, it may
be, think himself hardly treated by being kept in bondage so long after his debt had been actually paid. But
who in their sober senses will imagine this to be analogous to the redemption of sinners by Jesus Christ?—
Sin is a debt only in a metaphorical sense: properly
speaking, it is a *crime*, and satisfaction for it requires
to be made not on pecuniary, but on moral principles.
If Philemon had accepted of that part of Paul's offer
which respected property, and had placed so much to
his account as he considered Onesimus to have " owed" him, he could not have been said to have *remitted*
his debt; nor would Onesimus have had to thank him
for remitting it. But it is supposed of Onesimus that
he might not only be in debt to his master, but have
" wronged" him. Perhaps he had embezzled his
goods, corrupted his children, or injured his character. Now for Philemon to accept of that part of the
offer, were very different from the other. In the one
case he would have accepted of a pecuniary representative; in the other of a moral one; that is, of a mediator. The satisfaction in the one case would annihi-
late the idea of remission; but not in the other.—
Whatever satisfaction Paul might give to Philemon
respecting the wound inflicted upon his character and

honour as the head of a family, it would not supersede
the necessity of pardon being sought by the offender,
and freely bestowed by the offended.

The reason of this difference is easily perceived.
Debts are transferrable ; but crimes are not. A third
person may cancel the one ; but he can only oblite-
rate the *effects* of the other ; the *desert* of the criminal
remains. The *debtor* is accountable to his creditor as
a *private* individual, who has power to accept of a
surety, or if he please, to remit the whole, without
any satisfaction. In the one case he would be just ;
in the other merciful : but no place is afforded by either of them for the *combination* of justice and mercy
in the same proceeding. The *criminal,* on the other
hand, is amenable to the magistrate, or to the head of
a family, as a *public* person, and who, especially if the
offence be capital, cannot remit the punishment without
invading law and justice, nor in the ordinary discharge
of his office, admit of a third person to stand in his
place. In extraordinary cases, however, extraordinary expedients are resorted to. A satisfaction may be
made to law and justice, as to the *spirit* of them, while
the *letter* is dispensed with. The well-known story of
Zaleucus, the Grecian law giver, who consented to
lose one of his eyes to spare one of his son's eyes,
who by transgressing the law had subjected himself
to the loss of both, is an example. Here, as far as it
went, *justice and mercy were combined* in the same act :
and had the satisfaction been much fuller than it was,
so full that the authority of the law, instead of being
weakened, should have been abundantly magnified
and honoured, still it had been *perfectly consistent with
free forgiveness.*

Finally: In the case of the debtor, satisfaction be-ing once accepted, justice *requires* his complete dis-charge : but in that of the criminal, where satisfaction is made to the wounded honour of the law, and the authority of the lawgiver, justice, though it *admits* of his discharge, yet no otherwise *requires* it than as it may have been matter of promise to the substitute.

I do not mean to say that cases of this sort afford a competent representation of redemption by Christ.— That is a work which not only ranks with extraordi-nary interpositions, but which has no parallel : it is a work of God, which leaves all the petty concerns of mortals infinitely behind it. All that comparisons can do, is to give us some idea of the *principle* on which it proceeds.

If the following passage in our admired *Milton* were considered as the language of the law of innocence, it would be inaccurate—

> "——————— Man disobeying,
> . . . .
> He with his whole posterity must die :
> Die he, or justice must; unless for him
> Some other able, and as willing, pay
> The rigid satisfaction, death for death."

Abstractly considered, this is true ; but it is not ex-pressive of what was the revealed law of innocence.— The law made no such condition, or provision ; nor was it indifferent to the lawgiver who should suffer, the sinner, or another on his behalf. The language of the law to the transgressor was not *thou shalt die, or some one on thy behalf;* but simply *thou shalt die :* and had it literally taken its course, every child of man must have perished. The sufferings of Christ in our stead, therefore, are not a punishment inflicted in the ordinary course of distributive justice; but an extraordinary interposition of infinite wisdom and love : not contrary to, but rather above the law, deviating from the letter, but more than preserving the spirit of it.— Such, brethren, as well as I am able to explain them, are my views of the substitution of Christ.

Peter. The objection of our so stating the substitution of Christ, as to leave no room for the free pardon of sin, has been often made by those who avowedly reject his satisfaction ; but for any who really consider his death as an atonement for sin, and as essential to the ground of a sinner's hope, to employ the objection against us, is very extraordinary, and must, I presume, proceed from inadvertency.

James. If it be so, I do not perceive it. The grounds of the objection have been stated as clearly and as fully as I am able to state them.

John. What are your ideas, brother James, with respect to the persons for whom Christ died as a substitute ? Do you consider them as the elect only, or mankind in general ?

James. Were I asked concerning the gospel when it is introduced into a country, *For whom was it sent ?* If I had respect only to the revealed will of God, I should answer, It is sent for men, not as elect, or non-elect, but as *sinners.* It is written and preached, "that they might believe that Jesus is the Christ the Son of God, and that believing they might have life through his name." But if I had respect to the appointment of God, with regard to its application, I should say, If the divine conduct in this instance accord with what it has been in other instances, he hath visited that country to "*take out of them* a people for his name."

In like manner, concerning the death of Christ, if I speak of it irrespective of the purpose of the Father

and the Son as to the objects who should be saved by
it; referring merely to what it is in itself sufficient
for, and declared in the gospel to be adapted to, I
should think I answered the question in a scriptural
way in saying, It was *for sinners, as sinners.* But if
I have respect to the purpose of the Father in giving his Son to die, and to the design of Christ in laying down his life, I should answer, It was *for his elect
only.*

In the *first* of these views, I find the apostles and
primitive ministers (leaving the consideration of God's
secret purpose as a matter belonging to himself, not to
them) addressing themselves to sinners without distinction, and holding forth the sacrifice of Christ as a
ground of faith to all men. On this principle, the servants sent forth to bid guests to the marriage-supper,
were directed to invite them, saying, " Come, for all
things are ready." On this principle the ambassadors
of Christ besought sinners to be reconciled to God :
for, said they, " He hath made him to be sin for us,
who knew no sin, that we might be made the righteousness of God in him."

In the *last* view, I find the apostles ascribing to the
purpose and discriminating grace of God all their success—" As many as were ordained to eternal life believed"—teaching believers also to ascribe every thing
that they were, or hoped to be, to the same cause ; addressing them as having been before the foundation of
the world, *beloved* and *chosen* of God ; the *children* or
sons, whom it was the design of Christ in becoming incarnate to bring to glory ; the *church* of God, which he
purchased with his own blood, and for which he gave
himself, that he might sanctify and cleanse it with the
washing of water by the word, that he might present it

to himself a glorious church, not having spot or wrinkle, or any such thing.

If the substitution of Christ consist in his dying *for*, *or instead* of others, *that they should not die*, this, as comprehending the designed end to be answered by his death, is strictly applicable to none but the elect: for whatever ground there is for sinners as sinners to believe and be saved, it never was the purpose or design of Christ to impart faith to any other than those who were given him of the Father. He therefore did not die with the intent that any others should not die.

Whether I can perfectly reconcile these statements with each other, or not, I embrace them as being both plainly taught in the scriptures. I confess, however, I do not at present perceive their inconsistency. If I be not greatly mistaken, what apparent contradiction may attend them, arises chiefly from that which has been already mentioned, namely, the considering of Christ's substitution as an affair between *a creditor and a debtor*, or carrying the metaphor to an extreme. In that view the sufferings of Christ would require to be exactly proportioned to the nature and number of the sins which were laid upon him; and if more sinners had been saved, or those who are saved had been greater sinners than they are, he must have borne a proportionable increase of suffering. To correspond with pecuniary satisfactions this must undoubtedly be the case. I do not know that any writer has so stated things; but am persuaded that such ideas are at the bottom of a large part of the reasonings on that side of the subject.

In atonement, or satisfaction for *crime*, things do not proceed on this calculating principle. It is true there was a *designation* of the sacrifices offered up by Heze-

kiah: they were offered not only for Judah, but for
those that remained of the ten tribes: " for so the king
commanded, that the burnt-offering and the sin-offering should be made *for all Israel.*"* But the sacrifices
themselves were the same for both as they would have
been for one, and required to be the same for one as
they were for both. It was their *designation* only that
made the difference.

Thus I conceive it is in respect of the sacrifice of
Christ. If fewer had been saved than are, to be consistent with justice, it required to be by the same perfect atonement; and if more had been saved than are,
even the whole human race, there needed no other.—
But if the satisfaction of Christ was *in itself* sufficient
for the whole world, there is no further propriety in
asking, " Whose sins were imputed to Christ? or,
For whom did he die as a substitute?" Than as it is
thereby inquired, Who were the persons whom he intended finally to save?

That which is equally necessary for few as for many,
must, in its own nature, be equally sufficient for many
as for few; and could not proceed upon the principle of
the sins of some being laid on Christ rather than others,
any otherwise than as it was the *design* of the Father
and the Son, through one all-sufficient medium, to pardon the elect, while the rest are left to perish, notwithstanding, in their sins.

It seems to be as consonant with truth to say, a certain number of Christ's acts of obedience become ours,
as that a certain number of our sins become his. In
the former case his one undivided obedience, stamped
as it is with divinity, affords a ground of justification
to any number of believers: in the latter, his one

* 2 Chron. xxix. 24.

atonement, stamped also as it is with divinity, is sufficient for the pardon of any number of sins, or sinners. Yet as Christ laid not his life down but *by covenant;* as the elect were given him to be the purchase of his blood, or the fruit of the travail of his soul, he had respect, in all he did and suffered, to this recompense of reward. 'Their salvation was the joy that was set before him. It was for the covering of *their* transgressions that he became obedient unto death. To *them* his substitution was the same *in effect* as if their sins had by number and measure been literally imparted to him.

I am not aware that any principle which I imbibe is inconsistent with Christ's laying down his life *by covenant,* or with his being the *Surety* of that covenant, pledging himself for the *certain* accomplishment of whatever he undertook: as that all that were given him should come to him, should not be lost, but raised up at the last day, and be presented without spot and blameless. All this I consider as included in the *design* of the Father and the Son, with respect to the application of the atonement.

John. I have heard it objected to your views of the *sufficiency* of the atonement, to this effect—" How does this principle afford a ground for general invitations, if the *design* was confined to his elect people? If the benefits of his death were never *intended* for the non-elect, is it not just as inconsistent to invite them to partake of them, as if there were a want of sufficiency? This explanation therefore seems only to be shifting the difficulty."

James. Pharaoh was exhorted to let Israel go; and had he complied, he had saved his own life, and that of a great number of his people: yet, all things considered, it was not God's intention to save Pharaoh's life, nor that of the Egyptians. And is there no difference between this, and his being exhorted under a promise in which the object promised had no existence?

It is a fact that the scriptures rest the general invitations of the gospel upon the atonement of Christ.* But if there were not a sufficiency in the atonement for the salvation of sinners without distinction, how could the ambassadors of Christ beseech them to be reconciled to God, and that from the consideration of his having been made sin for us who knew no sin, that we might be made the righteousness of God in him? What would you think of the fallen angels being invited to be reconciled to God, from the consideration of an atonement having been made for fallen *men?*— You would say, It is inviting them to partake of a benefit which *has no existence,* the obtaining of which, therefore, is *naturally impossible.* Upon the supposition of the atonement being insufficient for the salvation of any more than are actually saved by it, the non-elect, however, are in the same state, with respect to a being reconciled to God through it, as the fallen angels; that is, the thing is not only morally, but *naturally impossible.* But if there be an objective fulness in the atonement of Christ, sufficient for any number of sinners, were they to believe in him, there is no other impossibility in the way of any man's salvation, to whom the gospel comes at least, than what arises from the state of his own mind. The intention of God not to remove this impossibility, and so not to save him, is a purpose to withhold not only that which he was not obliged to bestow, but that which is never represented in the scriptures as necessary to the consistency of exhortations or invitations.

* 2 Cor. v. 19—21. Matt. xxii. 4. John iii. 16.

I do not deny that there is *difficulty* in these statements; but it belongs to the general subject of reconciling the purposes of God with the agency of man: whereas, in the other case, God is represented as inviting sinners to partake of what has no existence, and which therefore is physically impossible. The one, while it ascribes the salvation of the believer in every stage of it to mere grace, renders the unbeliever inexcusable, which the other, I conceive, does not. In short, we must either acknowledge an objective fulness in Christ's atonement, sufficient for the salvation of the whole world, were the whole world to believe in him; or, in opposition to scripture and common sense, confine our invitations to believe, to such persons as have believed already.

John. May I ask you, brother Peter, whether, on a review of what has passed, you consider brother James as denying the doctrines of *imputation*, and *substitution*, or either of them?

Peter. Though I consider brother James's statements as containing various mistakes; and though I am exceedingly averse from the necessary consequences of certain tenets, which, if I rightly understand him, are avowed in them; yet I am now convinced that respecting those doctrines, he did not intend what I supposed he did. It behooves me therefore frankly to acknowledge, that I have unintentionally misrepresented his sentiments respecting them, for which I am truly sorry.

John. I hope, brother James, you are satisfied with this acknowledgment.

James. Perfectly so; and, shall be happy to hear brother Peter's remarks on those particulars in which he may still consider me as in the wrong.

A a

CONVERSATION THE THIRD.

————

ON PARTICULAR REDEMPTION.

————

PETER. Notwithstanding what our brother James has stated, I am far from being satisfied with his views as they affect the doctrine of *Particular Redemption.* If I understand him, his sentiment may be expressed in this position: *The particularity of the atonement consists in the sovereign pleasure of God with regard to its application.*

James. I should rather say, *The particularity of redemption consists in the sovereign pleasure of God with regard to the application of the atonement ; that is, with regard to the persons to whom it shall be applied.*

John. It is to be understood then, I presume, that you both believe the doctrine of particular redemption, and that the only question between you is, wherein it consists?

James. So I understand it.

Peter. I consider the aforementioned position as merely a reconciling expedient, or compromise between principles which can never be reconciled.

James. I am not conscious of embracing it for any such purpose—but let me hear your objections against it.

Peter. It places the particularity of redemption in application. I understand indeed, that by application you include not only what the New Testament denominates *receiving the atonement—the sprinkling of the blood of Jesus Christ*—and *faith in his blood;* but also the *absolute intention* of Christ in his death to save all those who shall be finally happy. But notwithstanding the unauthorised latitude of meaning which is here claimed for a particular term, to render the position more plausible, various and cogent reasons may be urged against it. Among others, it confounds the atonement itself with its application to the sinner.—Whereas, though the former completely ascertain the latter, yet not being the same fruit of divine favour, they must not be identified. The term application always supposes the *existence* of whatever is applied. The atonement therefore must be considered as existing, either actually, or in the divine decree, before it can be applied to the sinner. The application of a thing to any person, or for any purpose, ought not to be confounded with the thing itself. Hence in former times hardly any distinction was more common among theological writers, than that between what they denominated the *impetration* and the *application* of redemption. To represent the *intention* of Christ in his death to save Paul, for instance, and not Judas, under the notion of *applying* the atonement to the one and not to the other, is to me at least a perfectly novel sense of the word application, and was, I presume, adopted to meet the necessities of this hypothesis.

James. The whole of what you have said rests upon a mistake at the outset. You say, the position in question " places the particularity of redemption in *application.*" Whereas, if you recollect yourself, you will find that it places it *in the sovereign pleasure of God with regard to application.* The difference between this and the other is as great as that between election and vocation. Instead of my confounding redemption or atonement, therefore, with application, I have just

cause to complain of you for having confounded application with the sovereign pleasure of God respecting
it, and for having loaded me with the consequences.

Peter. But have you never made use of the term
application, so as to include the divine *intention ?*

James. I am not aware of having done so; but
whether I have or not, you were not animadverting on
what I may have said at other times, but on the position which you yourself had stated, which position affirms the very opposite of what you allege. Allowing
you to animadvert, however, on other words than those
contained in the position, and admitting that I may
have spoken or written in the manner you allege, still
it has been merely to distinguish what the death of
Christ is *in itself sufficient for,* from what it was *the
design of the Father and the Son actually to accomplish
by it:* This distinction is neither novel, nor liable to
the objection of confounding the impetration of redemption with its application. I have no other meaning, that I am aware of, than that of Dr. Owen in the
following passage—" Sufficient, we say, was the sacrifice of Christ for the redemption of the whole world,
and for the expiation of all the sins of all and every
man in the world. The sufficiency of his sacrifice
hath a two-fold rise. First, The dignity of the person
that did offer, and was offered. Secondly, The greatness of the pain he endured, by which he was able to
bear, and did undergo the whole curse of the law,
and wrath of God due to sin. And this sets forth *the
innate, real, true worth and value of the bloodshedding
of Jesus Christ.* This is its own true internal perfection and sufficiency. That it should be APPLIED unto
any, made a *price* for them, and become *beneficial* to
them, according to the worth that is in it, is *external*

to it, doth not arise from it, but merely depends upon the intention and will of God."

Peter. Intention enters into the nature of atonement. Christ was voluntary in his sufferings, and his being so was essential to his death as a sacrifice and an atonement His death detached from these considerations, would be merely that of a martyr. It was the effect of the highest degree of love, and of the kindest possible intention respecting the objects beloved; for otherwise it might well be demanded, To what purpose this *waste* of love?

James. Intention of some kind doubtless does enter into the essence of Christ's laying down his life a sacrifice: but that it should be beneficial to this person rather than that, appears to me, as Dr. Owen expresses it, "external to it, and to depend entirely on the will of God." And as to a *waste* of love, we might as well attribute a waste of goodness to the divine providence in its watering rocks and seas, as well as fruitful valleys, with the showers of heaven; or to our Lord for his commissioning his apostles to preach the gospel to every creature, while he never expected any others to believe and be saved by it than those who were *ordained* to eternal life. It accords with the general conduct of God to impart his favours with a kind of profusion which to the mind of man that sees only one or two ends to be answered by them, may have the appearance of waste: but when all things are brought to their intended issue, it will be found that God hath done nothing in vain.

John. Placing the particularily of redemption as you do, in the sovereign pleasure of God with regard to the application of the atonement, or the persons to whom it shall be applied; wherein is the difference between that doctrine and the doctrine of election?

James. I do not consider particular redemption as
being so much a doctrine of itself, as a branch of the
great doctrine of election, which runs through all God's
works of grace. If this branch of election had not been
more opposed than others, I reckon we should no more
have thought of applying the term *particular* to it than
to vocation, justification, or glorification. The idea
applies to these as well as to the other. *Whom* he did
fore-know, he did predestinate: *whom* he did predestinate, he called: *whom* he called, he justified; and
whom he justified, he glorified.

John. This would seem to agree with the apostle's
account of spiritual blessings in his epistle to the Ephesians—"He hath blessed us with all spiritual blessings
in heavenly places in Christ, ACCORDING *as he hath
chosen us in him before the foundation of the world.*"

Peter. I have some questions which I wish to put
to brother James on the difference which he appears
to make between atonement and redemption. If I understand him, he considers the latter as the *effect* of
the former.

James. There are few terms, whether in the scriptures or elsewhere, that are always used in the same
sense. *Reconciliation* sometimes means a being *actually in friendship with God, through faith in the blood of
Christ:* but when used synonymously with atonement,
it denotes *the satisfaction of justice only,* or the opening
of a way by which mercy may be exercised consistently with righteousness. In both these senses the word
occurs in Rom. v. 10. "For if when we were enemies
we *were reconciled* to God by the death of his Son;
much more *being reconciled,* we shall be saved by his
life." On this passage Dr. Guyse very properly remarks, "*Reconciled to God by the death of his Son,* in
first clause, seems to relate to Christ's having

worked out our reconciliation, or completed all in a way of merit by his death that was necessary to appease the wrath of God, and make way for the riches of his grace to be communicated to us in full consistence with the honour of all his perfections, and of his law and government, which the apostle had called (ver. 6. and 8.) *dying for the ungodly*, and *dying for us*: but *being reconciled*, in the last clause, seems to relate to the reconciliation's taking effect upon us, or to our being brought into a state of *actual* reconciliation and peace with God, through faith in Christ's blood, which the apostle had spoken of in ver. 1 and 9. and which in the verse after this is called *receiving the atonement.*"— Thus also the term *redemption* is sometimes put for the *price* by which we are redeemed; namely, the blood-shedding of Christ. In this sense it appears to be used by the apostle, in Rom. iii. 24. " Being justified freely by his grace, through the *redemption* that is in Jesus Christ." To be justified *through his redemption* is the same thing, I should think, as being *justified by his blood*. But the term properly and ordinarily signifies not that for the sake of which we are delivered from the curse of the law, but the deliverance itself.— Viewing reconciliation, or atonement, as a satisfaction to divine justice, and redemption as the deliverance of the sinner, the latter appears to me to be an *effect* of the former.

Peter. I am far from being convinced that redemption is an effect of atonement, any more than that atonement is an effect of redemption: both are the immediate effects of Christ's death, viewed in different points of light.

James. I freely admit that both are effects of Christ's death; but in such order as that one is the consequence of the other. I can conceive of the deliverance of the criminal arising from the satisfaction made to the judge ; but not of satisfaction to the judge arising from the deliverance of the criminal.

Peter. To view the atonement as merely a satisfaction to divine justice, or as a *medium* by which mercy may be exercised consistently with the divine perfections, without considering sinners as *actually reconciled to God* by it, is to retain little if any thing more than the *name* of atonement.

James. I see no grounds for calling that which was wrought for us while we were yet enemies *actual* reconciliation. Actual reconciliation appears to me, as it did to Dr. Guyse, to consist in that which is accomplished through faith, or as receiving the atonement. The reconciliation which is synonymous with atonement, is expressed in 2 Cor. v. 18. " All things are of God, who hath *reconciled us to himself* by Jesus Christ." But this is not supposed by the apostle, important as it was, to have brought sinners into a state of *actual* friendship with God : for if so, there had been no occasion for " the ministry of reconciliation," and for " beseeching sinners *to be reconciled* to him." Nor do I see how a state of *actual* reconciliation could consist with the uniform language of the New Testament concerning unbelievers, whether elect or non-elect, that they are under *condemnation.* I never understood that you held with justification before believing : but *actual* reconciliation seems to amount to this. Neither have I understood that you have ever attempted to explain away the duty of ministers to beseech sinners to be reconciled to God. On the contrary, if I mistake not, you have pleaded for it. I am surprised therefore at your speaking of them as being *actually* reconciled to God while they are yet enemies.

John. What are your ideas, brother James, of that *reconciliation* which was effected while we were yet enemies?

James. I conceive it to be that *satisfaction to the divine justice* by virtue of which nothing pertaining to the moral government of God hinders any sinner from returning to him; and that it is upon this ground that sinners are indefinitely invited so to do. Herein I conceive is the great difference at present between their state and that of the fallen angels. To them God is absolutely inaccessible; no invitations whatever being addressed to them, nor the gospel preached to them: but it is not so with fallen men. Besides this, as "Christ gave himself for us *that he might redeem us from all iniquity, and purify unto himself a peculiar people,*" I consider the actual reconciliation of the elect in the fulness of time as hereby *ascertained.* It was promised him as the reward of his sufferings that he should "see of the travail of his soul, and be satisfied."

Peter. Is there any thing in the atonement, or promised to it, which infallibly ascertains its application to *all* those for whom it was made?

James. If by this you mean all for whose salvation it was *sufficient*, I answer, There is not. But if you mean all for whose salvation it was *intended*, I answer, There is.

Peter. You consider the *principal design* of our Lord's atonement to be the manifestation of God's hatred to sin, in order to render the exercise of mercy consistent with justice: but though this idea is supposed, yet it is far from being the first, the most prominent, the characteristic idea of our Lord's death: the grand idea suggested to an enlightened mind by the atonement of Christ, is not God's hatred to sin, but his love to sinners.

James. I hope we shall none of us pretend to be more enlightened than the apostle Paul, and I am mistaken if he does not suggest the idea against which you militate. He represents God as *setting forth* his Son as a *propitiation* to *declare* or *demonstrate his righteousness in the remission of sins.** It is marvellous to me that I should be suspected of holding up God's hatred of sin to the disparagement of his love to sinners, when the former is supposed to have been manifested *to prepare the way for the latter.* Were I to say, the *principal design* of David in restoring Absalom at the instance of Joab, rather than by sending for him himself, was, that even in pardoning the young man he might show some displeasure against his sin, and save his own honour as the head of a family and of a nation, I should not be far from the truth. Yet I might be told, The grand, the prominent, the characteristic idea suggested by the king's consent, was *love;* for his " soul longed to go forth to Absalom." Love to Absalom doubtless accounts for David's *desiring his return:* but love to righteousness accounts for his desiring it *in that particular manner.* So if the question were, Why did God give his Son to die for sinners, *rather than leave them to perish in their sins?* The answer would be, Because he *loved them.* But if the question be, Why did he give his Son to be an atonement for sinners, *rather than save them without one?* The answer would be, Because he loved righteousness, and hated iniquity.

Peter. On the principle I oppose, the love of God in *applying* the atonement is much greater than in giving his Son to *be* an atonement, since the latter is mere

* Rom. iii. 25.

general benevolence; but the former is *particular* and *effectual.*

James. You should rather have said, the love of God is greater in giving his Son to be a sacrifice *in respect of those for whose salvation it was his pleasure to make it effectual,* than in merely giving him, as he is said to have done, to some who never received him.* If there was a particularity of design in the gift of Christ, it cannot be ascribed merely to general benevolence. And *so far as it is so,* we have no right to depreciate it on account of its not issuing in the salvation of sinners in general. It was no diminution to the love of God to Israel in bringing them out of Egypt, that the great body of them transgressed and perished in the wilderness:† nor could it be truly said that the bringing of Caleb and Joshua into the land of promise was a greater expression of love than that which had been bestowed upon them, and the whole body of their cotemporaries, in liberating them from the Egyptian yoke. And let me intreat you to consider whether your principles would not furnish an apology for the unbelieving Israelites. "There was little or no love in God's delivering us, unless he intended withal to prevent our sinning against him, and actually to bring us to the good land: but there was no good land for us—Would to God we had died in Egypt!" To this, however, an apostle would answer, "*They could not enter in because of unbelief.*"‡ And as this language was written for the warning of professing christians, whose inclination to relinquish the gospel resembled that of their fathers to return into Egypt, we are warranted to conclude from it that though the salvation of the saved be entirely of grace, yet the failure of others will be ascribed to themselves.

* John vi. 32. i. 11.   † Deut. vii. 8.   ‡ Heb. iii. 19.

They shall not have the consolation to say, "Our salvation was a *natural impossibility* :" or, if they were to utter such language, they would be repelled by scripture and conscience, which unite in declaring, *They could not enter in because of unbelief.*

Peter. I remember an old non-conformist minister says; "If any man be found to believe Christ's satisfaction sufficient to justify him for whom it was never paid, he is bound to believe an untruth. God will never make it any man's duty to rest for salvation on that blood that was never shed for him, or that satisfaction that was never made for him."

James. This reasoning of the old non-conformist may, for aught I know, be just on his principles; but it is not so on mine. If satisfaction was made on the principle of debtor and creditor, and that which was paid was just of sufficient value to liquidate a given number of sins, and to redeem a given number of sinners, and no more; it should seem that it could not be the duty of any but the elect, nor theirs till it was revealed to them that they were of the elect, to rely upon it: for *wherefore should we set our eyes on that which is not?* But if there be such a fulness in the satisfaction of Christ as is sufficient for the salvation of the whole world, were the whole world to believe in him; and if the particularity of redemption lie only in the purpose or sovereign pleasure of God to render it effectual to some rather than others, no such consequence will follow: or if it do, it will also follow, that divine predestination and human accountableness are utterly inconsistent, and therefore that we must either relinquish the former in favour of Arminianism, or give up the latter to the Antinomians. But though the ideas of my much respected brother on the subject of redemption, cannot be very different from those of his old non-conformist, yet I should not have supposed he would have adopted his reasoning as his own.

Peter. Why not?

James. Because it is your avowed persuasion, *that sinners* AS SINNERS *are invited to believe in Christ for salvation.* Thus you have interpreted the invitations in Isai. lv. 1—7. and various others ; carefully and justly guarding against the notion of their being addressed to *renewed,* or as some call them, *sensible sinners.*— Thus also you interpret 2 Cor. v. 20. of God's beseeching sinners by the ministry of the word to be reconciled to him. But your old friend would tell you that God will never invite a sinner to rest for salvation on that blood that was never shed for him, or on that satisfaction that was never made for him.—I should have thought too, after all that you have said of the warrant which sinners *as sinners* have to believe in Christ, you would not have denied it to be their *duty,* nor have adopted a mode of reasoning which, if followed up to its legitimate consequences, will compel you to maintain either the possibility of knowing our election before we believe in Christ, or that in our first reliance on his righteousness for acceptance with God we are guilty of presumption.

John. I conceive, my dear brethren, that you have each said as much on these subjects as is likely to be for edification. Permit me after having heard, and candidly attended to all that has passed between you, to assure you both of my esteem, and to declare that, in my opinion, the difference between you ought not to prevent your feeling towards and treating each other as brethren. You are agreed in all the great doctrines of the gospel; as the necessity of an atonement, the ground of acceptance with God, salvation by grace only,

B b

&c. &c. and with respect to particular redemption, you both admit the thing, and I would hope both hold it in a way consistent with the practice of the primitive ministers; or if it be not altogether so, that you will reconsider the subject when you are by yourselves. The greater part of those things wherein you seem to differ, may be owing either to a difference in the manner of expressing yourselves, or to the affixing of consequences to a principle which yet are unperceived by him that holds it. I do not accuse either of you with doing so intentionally: but principles and their consequences are so suddenly associated in the mind, that when we hear a person avow the former, we can scarcely forbear immediately attributing to him the latter. If a principle be proposed to us *for acceptance,* it is right to weigh the consequences: but when forming our judgment of the *person* who holds it, we should attach nothing to him but what he perceives and avows. If by an exchange of ideas you can come to a better understanding, it will afford me pleasure: meanwhile it is some satisfaction that your visit to me has not tended to widen, but considerably to diminish your differences. Brethren, there are many adversaries of the gospel around you, who would rejoice to see you at variance: Let there be no strife between you. You are both erring mortals; but both, I trust, the sincere friends of the Lord Jesus. Love one another!

THE CONSISTENCY OF THE

CHRISTIAN DOCTRINE,

Particularly that of Salvation through a Mediator, with

SOBER REASON;

BY ANDREW FULLER.

IF there be a God who created us ; if we have all sinned against him; and if there be reason to believe that he will call us to account for our conduct, all which principles are admitted by Mr. Paine ;[*] a gloomy prospect must needs present itself, sufficient, indeed, to render man " the slave of terror." It is not in the power of this writer, nor of any man living who rejects the bible, to assure us that pardon will have any place in the divine government; and however light he may make of the scripture docrine of hell, He that calls men to account for their deeds, will be at no loss how or where to punish them. But allowing that God is disposed to shew mercy to the guilty, the question is, Whether his doing so by or without a mediator be most consistent with what we know of fitness or propriety ?

That pardon is bestowed through a mediator in a vast variety of instances among men, cannot be denied; and that it is proper it should be so, must be evident to every thinking mind. All who are acquainted with the common affairs of life, must be aware of the ne-

---

[*] Age of Reason, Part L p. 1. Part II. p. 100.

. cessity of such proceedings, and the good effects of them upon society.*

It is far less *humbling* for an offender to be pardoned at his own request, than through the interposition of a third person : for in the one case he may be led to think that it was his virtue and penitence which influenced the decision ; whereas in the other he is compelled to feel his own unworthiness ; and this may be one reason why the mediation of Christ is so offensive. It is no wonder indeed that those who deny humility to be a virtue,† should be disgusted with a doctrine, the professed object of which is to abase the pride of man.

As forgiveness without a mediator is less humbling to the offender, so it provides less for the *honour* of the offended, than a contrary proceeding. Many a compassionate heart has longed to go forth, like David towards Absalom ; but, from a just sense of wounded authority, could not tell how to effect it ; and has greatly desired that some common friend would interpose, and save his honour. He has wished to remit the sentence ; but has felt the want of a mediator, at the instance of whom he might give effect to his desires, and exercise mercy without seeming to be regardless of justice. An offender who should object to a mediator, would be justly considered as hardened in impenitence, and regardless of the honour of the offended : and it is difficult to say what other construction can be put upon the objections of sinners to the mediation of Christ.

Again : To exercise pardon without a mediator, would be fixing no such *stigma upon the evil of the of-*

* See Pres. Edwards' Remarks on important Theological Controversies, Chap. VI.

† Volney's Law of Nature, p. 49.

fence, as is done by a contrary mode of proceeding.—
Every man feels that those faults which may be over-
looked on a mere acknowledgment, are not of a very
heinous nature ; they are such as arise from inadvert-
ence rather than from ill design ; and include little
more than an error of the judgment. On the other
hand, every man feels that the calling in of a third
person, is making much of the offence ; treating it as
a serious affair, a breach that is not to be lightly passed
over. This may be another reason why the mediation
of Christ is so offensive to the adversaries of the gospel. It is no wonder that men who are continually
speaking of moral evil under the palliating names of
error, frailty, imperfection, and the like, should spurn
at a doctrine, the implication of which *condemns** it
to everlasting infamy.

Finally : To bestow pardon without a mediator,
would be treating the offence as *private,* or passing
over it as a matter unknown, an affair which does not
affect the well-being of society, and which therefore
requires no public manifestation of displeasure against
it. Many a notorious offender would doubtless wish
matters to be thus conducted, and from an aversion to
public exposure, would feel strong objections to the
formal interposition of a third person. Whether this
may not be another reason of dislike to the mediation of Christ, I shall not decide; but of this I am
fully satisfied, that the want of a proper sense of the
great evil of sin, as it affects the moral government
of the universe, is a reason why its adversaries see no
necessity for it, nor fitness in it. They prove by all
their writings that they have no delight in the moral

* Rom. viii. 3.

B b 2

excellency of the divine nature, no just sense of the glory of moral government, and no proper views of the pernicious and wide extended influence of sin upon the moral sytem : Is it any wonder, therefore, that they should be unconcerned about the plague being stayed by a sacrifice? Such views are too enlarged for their selfish and contracted minds.   The only object of their care, even in their most serious moments, is to escape punishment: for the honour of God, and the real good of creation, they discover no concern.

The amount is this : If it be indeed improper for a guilty creature to lie low before his Creator ; if it be unfit that any regard should be . paid to the honour of his character ; if the offence committed against him be of so small account that it is unnecessary for him to express any displeasure against it ; and if it.have been so private and insulated.in its operations as in no way to affect the well-being of the moral system, the. doctrine of forgiveness through a mediator is unreasonable.   But if the contrary be true ; if it be proper for a guilty creature to lie in the dust before his offended Creator ; if the honour of the divine character deserve the first and highest regard ; if moral evil be the greatest of all evils, and require, even where it is forgiven, a strong expression of divine displeasure against it ; and if its.pernicious influence be such that if suffered to operate according to its native tendency, it would dethrone the Almighty, and desolate the universe ; the doctrine in question must accord with the plainest dictates of reason.

The sense of mankind, with regard to the necessity of a mediator, may be illustrated by the following similitude.   Let us suppose a division in the army of ne of the wisest and best of kings, through the evil unsel of a foreign enemy, to have been disaffected

to his government; and that without any provocation
on his part, they traitorously conspired against his
crown and life. The attempt failed; and the offenders were seized, disarmed, tried by the laws of their
country, and condemned to die. A respite however
was granted them, during his majesty's pleasure. At
this solemn period, while every part of the army, and
of the empire, was expecting the fatal order for execution, the king was employed in meditating mercy.
But how could mercy be shewn? " To make light of
a conspiracy," said he to his friends, " would loosen
the bands of good government: other divisions of the
army might be tempted to follow their example; and
the nation at large might be in danger of imputing it
to tameness, fear, or some unworthy motive."

Every one felt in this case the necessity of a mediator, and agreed as to the general line of conduct
proper for him to pursue. " He must not attempt,"
say they, " to compromise the difference by dividing
the blame: that would make things worse. He must
justify the king, and condemn the outrage committed
against him; he must offer, if possible, some honourable expedient, by means of which the bestowment of
pardon shall not relax, but strengthen just authority;
he must convince the conspirators of their crime, and
introduce them in the character of supplicants; and
mercy must be shewn to them out of respect to him,
or for his sake."

But who could be found to mediate in such a cause?
This was an important question. A work of this kind,
it was allowed on all hands, required singular qualifications. " He must be *perfectly clear of any participa-
tion in the offence*," said one, " or inclination to favour
it: for to pardon conspirators at the intercession of one

who is friendly to their cause, would be not only making light of the crime; but giving a sanction to it."

" He must," said another, " be one who, on account of his character and services, *stands high in the esteem of the king and of the public :* for to mediate in such a cause is to become, in a sort, responsible for the issue. A mediator, in effect, pledges his honour that no evil will result to the state from the granting of his request. But if a mean opinion be entertained of him, no trust can be placed in him, and consequently no good impression would be made by his mediation on the public mind."

" I conceive it is necessary," said a third, " that the weight of the mediation, should bear a proportion to the magnitude of the crime, and to the value of the favour requested; and that for this end it is proper he should be a person of *great dignity.* For his majesty to pardon a company of conspirators at the intercession of one of their former comrades, or of any other obscure character, even though he might be a worthy man, would convey a very diminutive idea of the evil of the offence."

A fourth remarked, that " he must possess a *tender compassion* towards the unhappy offenders, or he would not cordially interest himself on their behalf."

Finally : It was suggested by a fifth, " that for the greater fitness of the proceeding, it would be proper that some *relation* or *connection* should subsist between the parties. We feel the propriety," said he, " of forgiving an offence at the intercession of a father, or a brother; or, if it be committed by a soldier, of his commanding officer. Without some kind of previous relation or connection, a mediation would have the appearance of an arbitrary and formal process, and prove but little interesting to the hearts of the community."

Such were the resonings of the king's friends; but where to find the character in whom these qualifications were united, and what particular expedient could be devised by means of which, pardon, instead of relaxing, should strengthen just authority, were subjects too difficult for them to resolve.

Meanwhile the king and his son, whom he greatly loved, and whom he had appointed generalissimo of all his forces, had retired from the company, and were conversing about the matter which attracted the general attention.

"My son!" said the benevolent sovereign, "what can be done in behalf of these unhappy men? To order them for execution, violates every feeling of my heart: yet to pardon them is dangerous. The army, and even the empire would be under a strong temptation to think lightly of rebellion. If mercy be exercised, it must be through a mediator; and who is qualified to mediate in such a cause? And what expedient can be devised by means of which pardon shall not relax, but strengthen just authority? Speak, my son, and say what measures can be pursued?"

"My father!" said the prince, "I feel the insult offered to your person and government, and the injury thereby aimed at the empire at large. They have transgressed without cause, and deserve to die without mercy. Yet I also feel for them. I have the heart of a soldier. I cannot endure to witness their execution. What shall I say? On me be this wrong! Let me suffer in their stead. Inflict on me as much as is necessary to impress the army and the nation with a just sense of the evil, and of the importance of good order and faithful allegiance. Let it be in their presence, and in the presence of all assembled. When this is done, let them be permitted to implore and receive your majesty's pardon in my name. If any man refuse so to implore, and so to receive it, let him die the death!"

" My son!" replied the king, " You have expressed my heart! The same things have occupied my mind; but it was my desire that you should be voluntary in the undertaking. It shall be as you have said. I shall be satisfied; justice itself will be satisfied; and I pledge my honour that you also shall be satisfied, in seeing the happy effects of your disinterested conduct. Propriety requires that I stand aloof in the day of your affliction; but I will not leave you utterly, nor suffer the beloved of my soul to remain in that condition. A temporary affliction on your part will be more than equivalent to death on theirs. The dignity of your person and character will render the sufferings of an hour of greater account, as to the impression of the public mind, than if all the rebellious had been executed: and by how much I am known to have loved you, by so much will my compassion to them, and my displeasure against their wicked conduct be made manifest. Go, my son, assume the likeness of a criminal, and suffer in their place!"

The gracious design being communicated at court, all were struck with it. Those who had reasoned on the qualifications of a mediator, saw that in the prince all were united, and were filled with admiration: but that he should be willing to suffer in the place of rebels, was beyond all that could have been asked or thought. Yet seeing he himself had generously proposed it, would survive his sufferings, and reap the reward of them, they cordially acquiesced. The only "ficulty that was started was amongst the judges of the realm. They, at first, questioned whether the proceeding were admissible. "The law," said they, "makes provision for the transfer of debts, but not of crimes. Its language is, *The soul that sinneth shall die.*" But when they came to view things on a more enlarged scale, considering it as an expedient on an extraordinary occasion, and perceived that the *spirit* of the law would be preserved, and all the *ends* of good government answered, they were satisfied. "It is not a measure," said they, "for which the law provides: yet it is not contrary to the law, but above it."

The day appointed arrived. The prince appeared, and suffered as a criminal. The hearts of the king's friends bled at every stroke, and burned with indignation against the conduct which rendered it necessary. His enemies, however, even some of those for whom he suffered, continuing to be disaffected, added to the affliction, by deriding and insulting him all the time. At a proper period, he was rescued from their outrage. Returning to the palace, amidst the tears and shouts of the loyal spectators, the suffering hero was embraced by his royal father; who, in addition to the natural affection which he bore to him as a son, loved him for his singular interposition at such a crisis.— "Sit thou," said he, "at my right hand! Though the threatenings of the law be not literally accomplished, yet the spirit of them is preserved. The honour of good government is secured, and the end of punishment more effectually answered than if all the rebels had been sacrificed. Ask of me what I shall give thee! No favour can be too great to be bestowed, even upon the unworthiest, nor any crime too aggravated to be forgiven, in thy name. I will grant thee according to thine own heart! Ask of me, my son, what I shall give thee!"

my life be spared: but this I say, If he had not made this or some other kind of provision, I should have thought him a tyrant."

"You are all wrong," says a fifth: "I comprehend the design, and am well pleased with it. I hate the government as much as any of you: but I love the mediator; for I understand it is his intention to deliver me from its tyranny. He has paid the debt, the king is satisfied, and I am free. I will sue out my right, and demand my liberty!"

In addition to this, one of the company observed, he did not see what the greater part of them had to do with the proclamation, unless it were to give it a hearing, which they had done already. "For," said he, "pardon is promised only to them who are *willing* to submit, and it is well known that many of us are unwilling; nor *can* we alter our minds on this subject."

After a while, however, some of them were brought to relent. They thought upon the subject matter of the proclamation, were convinced of the justness of its statements, reflected upon their evil conduct, and were sincerely sorry on account of it. And now the mediation of the prince appeared in a very different light.— They cordially said *Amen* to every part of the proceeding. The very things which gave such offence while their hearts were disaffected, now appeared to them fit, and right, and glorious. "It is fit," said they, "that the king should be honoured, and that we should be humbled; for we have *transgressed without cause.* It is right that no regard should be paid to any petition of ours for its own sake; for we have done deeds worthy of death. It is glorious that we should be saved at the intercession of so honourable a personage. The dignity of his character, together with his surprising condescension and goodness, impresses us more than any thing else, and fills our hearts with penitence, confidence, and love. That which in the proclamation is called grace *is* grace; for we are utterly unworthy of it; and if we had all suffered according to our sentence, the king and his throne had been guiltless. We embrace the mediation of the prince, not as a reparation for an injury, but as a singular instance of mercy.— And far be it from us that we should consider it as designed to deliver us from our original and just allegiance to his majesty's government! No, rather it is intended to restore us to it. We love our intercessor, and will implore forgiveness in his name; but we also love our sovereign, and long to prostrate ourselves at his feet. We rejoice in the satisfaction which the prince has made, and all our hopes of mercy are founded upon it: but we have no notion of being freed by it previously to our acquiescence in it. Nor do we desire any other kind of freedom than that which, while it remits the just sentence of the law, restores us to his majesty's government. O that we were once clear of this hateful and horrid conspiracy, and might be permitted to serve him with affection and fidelity all the days of our life! We cannot suspect the *sincerity* of the invitation, or acquit our companions on the score of *unwillingness*. Why should we? We do not on this account acquit ourselves. On the contrary, it is the remembrance of our unwillingness that now cuts us to the heart. We well remember to what it was owing that we *could not* be satisfied with the just government of the king, and afterwards *could not* comply with the invitation of mercy: it was because we were under the dominion of a *disaffected spirit*; a spirit which, wicked as it is in itself, it would be more wicked to justify. Our counsel is, therefore, the same as that of his majesty's messengers, with whom we now take our stand. Let us lay aside this cavilling humour, repent, and sue for mercy in the way prescribed, ere mercy be hid from our eyes!"

The reader, in applying this supposed case to the mediation of Christ, will do me the justice to remember that I do not pretend to have perfectly represented it. Probably there is no similitude fully adequate to the purpose. The distinction between the Father and the Son is not the same as that which exists between a father and son amongst men: the latter are two separate beings; but to assert this of the former would be inconsistent with the divine unity. Nor can any thing be found analogous to the doctrine of divine influence, by which the redemption of Christ is carried into effect. And with respect to the innocent voluntarily suffering for the guilty, in a few extraordinary instances this principle may be adopted; but the management and application of it generally require more wisdom and more power than mortals possess. We may by the help of a machine collect a few sparks of the electrical fluid, and produce an effect somewhat resembling that of lightning: but we cannot cause it to blaze like the Almighty, nor *thunder with a voice like Him.*

Imperfect, however, as the foregoing similitude may appear in some respects, it is sufficient to show the fallacy of Mr. Paine's reasoning. " The doctrine of redemption," says this writer, " has for its basis an idea of pecuniary justice, and not that of moral justice. If I owe a person money, and cannot pay him, and he threatens to put me in prison, another person can take the debt upon himself, and pay it for me. But if I have committed a *crime,* every circumstance of the case is changed. Moral justice cannot take the innocent for the guilty, even if the innocent would offer *itself.* To suppose justice to do this, is to destroy the

principle of its existence, which is the thing itself.—
It is then no longer justice: but indiscriminate revenge."* This objection, which is the same for substance as has been frequently urged by socinians as
well as deists, is founded in misrepresentation. It is
not true that redemption has for its basis the idea of
pecuniary justice, and not that of moral justice. That
sin is called a *debt*, and the death of Christ a *price*, a
ransom, *&c.* is true; but it is no unusual thing for moral obligations and deliverances to be expressed in language borrowed from pecuniary transactions. The
obligations of a son to a father are commonly expressed
by such terms as owing and paying: he *owes* a debt of
obedience, and in yielding it he *pays* a debt of gratitude. The same may be said of an obligation to punishment. A murderer *owes* his life to the justice of
his country; and when he suffers, he is said to *pay* the
awful debt. So also if a great character by suffering
death could deliver up his country, such deliverance
would be spoken of as obtained by the *price* of blood. No
one mistakes these things by understanding them of
pecuniary transactions. In such connections, every
one perceives that the terms are used not literally, but
metaphorically; and it is thus that they are to be understood with reference to the death of Christ. As sin
is not a pecuniary, but a moral debt; so the atonement
for it is not a pecuniary, but a moral ransom.

There is doubtless a sufficient analogy between pecuniary and moral proceedings to justify the use of
such language, both in scripture and in common life:
and it is easy to perceive the advantages which arise
from it; as besides conveying much important truth,
it renders it peculiarly impressive to the mind. But
it is not always safe to reason from the former to the

* Age of Reason. Part I. p. 20.

latter; much less is it just to affirm that the latter has for its basis every principle which pertains to the former. The deliverance effected by the prince in the case before stated might with propriety be called a *redemption;* and the recollection of it under this idea would be very impressive to the minds of those who were delivered. They would scarcely be able to see or think of their commander in chief, even though it might be years after the event, without being reminded of the *price* at which their pardon was obtained, and dropping a tear of ingenuous grief over their unworthy conduct on this account. Yet it would not be just to say that this redemption had for its basis an idea of pecuniary justice, and not that of moral justice. It was moral justice which in this case was satisfied; not however in its ordinary form, but as exercised on an extraordinary occasion; not the letter, but the spirit of it.

The scripture doctrine of atonement being conveyed in language borrowed from pecuniary transactions, is not only improved by unbelievers into an argument against the truth of the gospel, but has been the occasion of many errors amongst the professors of christianity. Socinus on this ground attempts to explain away the necessity of a satisfaction. " God," says he, " is our *creditor.* Our sins are *debts* which we have contracted with him; but every one may yield up his right, and more especially God, who is the supreme Lord of all, and extolled in the scriptures for his liberality and goodness. Hence then it is evident that God can pardon sins without any satisfaction received."[*] *Others,* who profess to embrace the doctrine of satisfaction, have on the same ground perverted and abused it; objecting to the propriety of humble and continued applications for mercy, and presuming to claim the

[*] Treatise of Jesus Christ the Saviour, Pt. III. Ch. I.

forgiveness of their sins, past, present, and to come, as their legal right, and what it would be unjust in the Supreme Being, having received complete satisfaction, to withhold.

To the reasoning of Socinus, Dr. Owen judiciously replies by distinguishing between right as it respects *debts,* and as it respects *government.* The former he allows may be given up without a satisfaction, but not the latter. " Our sins," he adds, " are called debts, not properly, but metaphorically."* This answer equally applies to those who pervert the doctrine, as to those who deny it : for though in matters of debt and credit a full satisfaction from a surety excludes the idea of *free* pardon on the part of the creditor, and admits of a *claim* on the part of the debtor, yet it is otherwise in relation to crimes. In the interposition of the prince as stated above, an honourable expedient was adopted, by means of which the sovereign was sa-tisfied, and the exercise of mercy rendered consistent with just authority: but there was no less grace in the act of forgiveness than if it had been without a satisfaction. However well pleased the king might be with the conduct of his son, the freeness of pardon was not at all diminished by it; nor must the criminals come before him as claimants, but as supplicants, im-ploring mercy in the mediator's name.

Such are the leading ideas which the scriptures give us of redemption by Jesus Christ. The apostle Paul especially teaches this doctrine with great precision— *Being justified freely by his grace, through the redemp-tion that is in Jesus Christ : Whom God hath set forth to be a propitiation, through faith in his blood, to de-clare his righteousness for the remission of sins that are*

* Dissertation on Divine Justice, Ch. IX. § vii. viii.

just, through the forbearance of God ; to declare, I say, *at this time his righteousness, that he might be just, and the justifier of him that believeth in Jesus.** From this passage we may remark, First: That the *grace* of God, as taught in the scripture, is not that kind of liberality which socinians and deists ascribe to him, which sets aside the necessity of a satisfaction. Free grace, according to Paul, requires a *propitiation,* even the shedding of the Saviour's *blood,* as a medium through which it may be honourably communicated. Secondly: Redemption by Jesus Christ was accomplished not by a satisfaction that should preclude the exercise of grace in forgiveness, but in which the displeasure of God against sin being manifested, mercy to the sinner might be exercised without any suspicion of his having relinquished his regards for righteousness   *in setting forth Jesus Christ to be a propitiation,* he declared *his righteousness for the remission of sins.* Thirdly: The righteousness of God was not only declared when Christ was made a propitiatory sacrifice ; but continues to be manifested in the acceptance of believers through his name. He appears as *just* while acting the part of a justifier towards every one that *believeth in Jesus.* Fourthly: That which is here applied to the blessings of forgiveness and acceptance with God, is applicable to all other spiritual blessings: all, according to the scriptures, are freely communicated through the same distinguished medium. See Ephes. i.†

* Rom. iii. 24—26.

† The christian reader, it is presumed, may from hence obtain a clear view of the ends answered by the death of Christ ; a subject which has occupied much attention amongst divines. Some have asserted that Christ by his satisfaction accomplished this only, "That God now, consistently with

These remarks may suffice to shew, not only that Mr. Paine's assertion has no truth in it, but that all those professors of christianity who have adopted his principle, have so far deviated from the doctrine of redemption as it is taught in the scriptures.

the honour of his justice, may pardon (returning) sinners, if he willeth so to do." This is doubtless true as far as it goes : but it makes no provision for the return of the sinner. This scheme therefore leaves the sinner to perish in impenitence and unbelief, and the Saviour without any security of seeing of the travail of his soul. For how can a sinner return without the power of the Holy Spirit ? And the Holy Spirit, equally with every other spiritual blessing, is given in consideration of the death of Christ.—Others, to remedy this defect, have considered the death of Christ as *purchasing* repentance and faith, as well as all other spiritual blessings, on behalf of the elect. The writer of these pages acknowledges he never could perceive that any clear or determinate idea was conveyed by the term *purchase*, in this connection ; nor does it appear to him to be applicable to the subject, unless it be in an improper or figurative sense. He has no doubt of the atonement of Christ being a perfect satisfaction to divine justice ; nor of his being *worthy* of all that was conferred upon him, and upon us for his sake ; nor of that which to *us* is sovereign mercy being to *him* an exercise of remunerative justice : but he wishes it to be considered, Whether the moral Governor of the world was laid under such a kind of obligation to shew mercy to sinners as a creditor is under to discharge the debtor, on having received full satisfaction at the hands of a surety ? If he be, the writer is unable to perceive how there can be any room for free forgiveness on the part of God ; or how it can be said that justice and grace harmonize in a sinner's salvation.—Nothing is farther from his intention than to depreciate the merit of his Lord and Saviour : but he considers merit as of two kinds ; either on account of a *benefit* conferred, which on the footing of justice requires an equal return ; or of something done or suffered which is *worthy of being rewarded* by a Being who is

As to what Mr. Paine alleges, that the innocent suffering for the guilty, even though it be with his own
consent, is contrary to every principle of moral justice,
he affirms the same of God's *visiting the iniquities of*

distinguished for his love of righteousness. In the first sense,
it cannot, as he supposes, be exercised towards an infinite,
and perfect Being. The goodness of Christ himself, in this
way, *extendeth not to him.* It is in the last sense that the
scriptures appear to him to represent the merit of the Redeemer. That he, " who was in the form of God, should
take upon him the form of a servant, and be made in the
likeness of men, and humble himself, and become obedient
unto death, even the death of the cross," was so glorious an
undertaking, and so acceptable to the Father, that on this
account he " set him at his own right hand in the heavenly
places, far above all principality and power, and might and
dominion, and every name that is named, not only in this
world, but also in that which is to come : and hath put all
things under his feet, and gave him to be the Head *over all*
things to the church." Nor was this all : so *well pleased* was
he with all that he did and suffered, as to reward it not only
with honours conferred on himself, but with blessings on
sinners for his sake. Whatever is asked *in his name,* it is
given us.

It is thus, as the writer apprehends, that *a way was open-*
ed by the mediation of Christ, for the free and consistent exer-
cise of mercy in all the methods which sovereign wisdom saw
fit to adopt.

There are *three* kinds of blessings in particular, which God
out of regard to the death of his Son bestows upon men.—
First : He sends forth the gospel of salvation, accompanied
with a free and indefinite invitation to embrace it, and an assurance that whosoever complies with the invitation (for
which there is no ability wanting in any man who possesses
an honest heart) shall have everlasting life. This favour is
bestowed on sinners as sinners: *God giveth the true*
bread from heaven in this way to many who never receive it.
He inviteth those to the gospel supper who refuse and *make*
light of it. John vi. 32, 36. Matt. xxii. 4, 5.—Secondly : He

the fathers upon the children.*   But this is a truth evident by universal experience. It is seen every day, in every part of the world. If Mr. Paine indulge in intemperance, and leave children behind him, they may feel the consequences of his misconduct when he is in the grave. The sins of the father may thus be visited upon the children, to the third and fourth generation. It would, however, be their affliction only, and not their punishment. Yet such visitations are wisely ordered as a motive to sobriety. Nor is it between parents and children only that such a connection exists, as that the happiness of one depends upon the conduct of others : a slight survey of society, in its various relations, must convince us that the same principle pervades creation. To call this injustice, is to fly in the face of the Creator. With such an objector I have nothing to do : *He that reproveth God, let him answer it.*

If the idea of the innocent suffering in the room of the guilty were in all cases inadmissible, and utterly

bestows his Holy Spirit to renew and sanctify the soul ; gives a new heart, and a right spirit, and takes away the heart of stone. *Christ is exalted to give repentance,* Acts v. 31. *Unto us it is given in behalf of Christ, to believe in him,* Phil. i. 29. *We have obtained like precious faith through the righteousness of God, and our Saviour Jesus Christ,* 2 Pet. i. 1. This favour is conferred on ELECT SINNERS. See Acts xiii. 48. Rom. viii. 28—30.—Thirdly : Through the same medium is given the free pardon of all our sins, acceptance with God, power to become the sons of God, and the promise of everlasting life. *Your sins are forgiven you for his name's sake,* 1 John ii. 12. *God for Christ's sake hath forgiven you,* Ephes. iv. 32.— *We are accepted in the beloved,* Ephes. i. 6. *By means of his death we receive the promise of eternal inheritance,* Heb. ix. 15. This kind of blessings is conferred on BELIEVING SINNERS.

* Age of Reason, Part 1. p. 4. Note.

repugnant to the human understanding, How came the use of *expiatory sacrifices* to prevail as it has, in every age and nation? Whether the idea first proceeded from a divine command, as christians generally believe, or whatever was its origin, it has approved itself to the minds of men ; and not of the most uncultivated part of mankind only, but of the most learned and polite. The sacrifices of the gentiles, it is true, were full of superstition, and widely different as might be expected, from those which were regulated by the scriptures; but the general principle is the same : all agree in the idea of the displeasure of Deity being appeasable by an innocent victim being sacrificed in the place of the guilty. The idea of expiatory sacrifices, and of a mediation founded upon them, is beautifully expressed in the book of Job ; a book not only of great antiquity, but which seems to have obtained the approbation of Mr. Paine, having, as he supposes, been written by a gentile.—" And it was so, that, after the Lord had spoken these words unto Job, the Lord said to Eliphaz the Temanite, My wrath is kindled against thee, and against thy two friends ; for ye have not spoken of me the thing that is right, as my servant Job hath. Therefore take unto you now seven bullocks and seven rams, and go to my servant Job, and offer up for yourselves a burnt-offering, and my servant Job shall pray for you ; for him will I accept : lest I deal with you after your folly, in that ye have not spoken of me the thing which is right, like my servant Job. So Eliphaz the Temanite, and Bildad the Shuite, and Zophar the Naamathite, went and did according as the Lord commanded them : the Lord also accepted Job." Job xlii. 7—9. The objections which are now made to the sacrifice of Christ, equally apply to all expiatory sacrifices ; the offering up of which, had not the former superseded them, would have continued to this day.

If an innocent character offers to die in the room of a guilty fellow-creature, it is not ordinarily accepted, nor would it be proper that it should. For he may have no just right to dispose of his life ; or if he have, he has no power to resume it : there may likewise be no such relation between the parties, as that the suffering of the one should express displeasure against the conduct of the other. Besides this, there may be no great and good end accomplished by such a substitution, to society : the loss sustained by the death of the one, might be equal if not superior to the gain from the life of the other. If the evil to be endured might be survived; if the relation between the parties were such, that in the sufferings of the one, mankind would be impressed with the evil of the other; and if by such a proceeding, great advantage would accrue to society ; instead of being accounted inadmissible, it would be reckoned right, and wise, and good. If a dignified individual, by enduring some temporary severity from an offended nation, could appease their displeasure, and thereby save his country from the destroying sword, who would not admire his disinterested conduct ? And if the offended, from motives of humanity, were contented with expressing their displeasure by transferring the effect of it from a whole nation to an individual who thus stepped forward on their behalf, Would their conduct be censured as " indiscriminate revenge ?" The truth is, The atonement of Christ affords a display of justice on too large a scale, and on too humbling a principle, to approve itself to a contracted, selfish, and haughty mind.

D d

SCRIPTURE DOCTRINE

OF ELECTION STATED.

(From the Vermont Adviser.)

IT is a very plainly revealed truth, of great importance in the christian system, that some of our fallen
race were, "from the beginning, chosen to salvation,
through sanctification of the Spirit, and belief of the
truth;" or, elected, "according to the foreknowledge
of God the Father, through sanctification, unto obedience, and sprinkling of the blood of Jesus Christ."
It is not true, as many seem to hold, that some are
chosen to salvation, because they were previously
sanctified; but, they were "chosen to salvation, *through*
sanctification." They are elected, not because they
were previously obedient; but, "unto obedience."—
As this doctrine of election makes the salvation of
sinners depend, not on him that willeth, nor on him
that runneth, but, on the sovereign electing grace of
God, it is very offensive to the carnal heart, and has,
perhaps, been opposed with more unchristian zeal and
virulence, than almost any other truth of the gospel.
nor has it always been easy, even for apparently humble disciples of the Lord Jesus to perceive the entire
consistency of this, with other plainly revealed truths.
Perhaps, too, this doctrine has sometimes been so

stated, by very pious and learned advocates for the doctrines of grace, in their zeal for the sovereignty of
God, as to be an occasion of stumbling to their friends,
while it has given their adversaries some advantage.

A leading objection to this doctrine has ever been,
that, if it be true, then no grace has been manifested
to the non-elect, in the gift of a Saviour; in the atonement he has made; or in the offer of salvation to
them, in the gospel; whereas the scripture representation certainly is, that great grace has been manifested in these things. Could this objection be fairly sub-
stantiated, it would, indeed, go so far towards invalida-
ting the truth of the doctrine. If, then, the doctrine be
so stated, by its advocates, that this objection will lie,
unanswerably, against their statement, great advantage
is given to the adversary.

It has not been uncommon for those, who have undertaken to defend the doctrines of grace, to represent
the elect as being chosen, not merely, as the scriptures express it, " to salvation, through sanctification
of the Spirit, and belief of the truth;" but, also, as
chosen, that Christ might die for them, and make
atonement for their sins, and for theirs only. But it
must be very obvious, that, if the atonement made by
Christ were for the sins of the elect only, then, in making the atonement, there could be no act of grace to
the non-elect. Besides, if Christ were set forth a propitiation for the sins of the elect only, then, in what he
has done and suffered, no provision has been made, in
any sense, for the salvation of the non-elect; and, surely, then, there can be no grace in the gospel offer of
salvation to them. In this case, were they even to
repent and believe the gospel, they could not be
saved by Christ. Against this view of election, therefore, it seems evident, the objection must be valid.—

Hence we may safely conclude, that this view of the doctrine is not agreeable to scripture. It is readily concluded, however, that, had it seemed good in the sight of God to exercise his holy sovereignty in this way, it could have been no ground of objection against his glorious character. If, contemplating men merely as transgressors of his law, he had elected some, and determined to give his Son to die for them only, leaving others to perish, without making any provision for them, in any sense, he would have done the latter no injustice. He might still have appeared glorious in holiness. But, what is contended for is, that, in this case, there could be no grace to the non-elect, in the gift of the Saviour, in the atonement made by him, or in an offer of salvation to them, through him. And, therefore, that it is evident this is not the way, in which he has exercised his sovereignty, in regard to the redemption and salvation of sinners. Because, according to the scriptures, he has done this in a way, which is consistent with a gracious offer of salvation to the non-elect.

When we open the Bible, we there find, that "God so loved the *world*, that he gave his only begotten Son, that whosoever believeth in him should not perish, but have everlasting life." That Christ "gave himself a ransom for all." That, "by the grace of God he should taste death for every man" And that an apostle, addressing his christian brethren, says, "He is the propitiation for our sins; and not for our sins only, but also for the sins of the whole world." Accordingly, the gracious invitation is addressed to all, indiscriminately. "Come unto me, all ye that labour, and are heavy laden, and I will give you rest." "Whosoever *will*, *let* him take of the water of life freely." And, *the* promise is, "Him that cometh to me, I will in no wise cast out." We are also plainly taught, that, if sinners now perish, it will be, not because no atonement has been made for their sins, and no door of salvation opened before them ; but, because they will not come unto Christ, that they might have life. It is " he, who believeth not," who " shall be damned." In all this, it is evidently implied, that there is great grace manifested, even to those who will finally perish, in the provisions of the gospel, and in the offer of salvation to them. Unquestionably, the scripture doctrine of election perfectly harmonizes with these things, and is, therefore, consistent with this manifestation of grace to the non-elect.

Those who urge the objection in question, against the doctrine of election, sometimes concede, and no one, surely, can reasonably deny, that, had God sent his Son into the world, to die, and make atonement for the sins of all men, and had he offered salvation to all men, on the terms on which it is offered in the gospel, without doing any thing more to effect their salvation, this would have been an act of grace, even though all had refused the offer, and perished in their sins. Now, whatever may be the truth, respecting election, so much at least, God has actually done. He has given his Son to die, as a propitiation for the sins of the whole world ; and, through him, salvation is freely offered.— The invitation given is universal. It is also true, that, this being done, sinners universally reject the salvation offered. They all, with one consent, begin to make excuses, and will not come unto Christ, that they may have life. Hence, if nothing more were done, to effect the salvation of sinners, they would all certainly perish together. Unless God were pleased to make farther displays of grace, to these rebellious and un-

grateful creatures, not one of them would be saved.—
If, in these circumstances, God were pleased to send
forth his Spirit to renew the hearts of all men, and to
grant them repentance unto salvation, this would be
another great display of grace to all; but it would neither increase, nor diminish, the grace, which he has
already manifested, in giving his Son to be a propitiation for their sins, and offering salvation to them,
through him. This would remain the same. If, then,
instead of sending his Spirit to renew the hearts of all
men, and to bring them into a state of salvation, he be
pleased to send him to renew the hearts of part of them
only, and to grant salvation unto them, leaving others
to follow the natural inclinations of their hearts, and to
continue in their ungrateful rejection of Christ, and his
salvation; here is another wonderful act of grace to
those, in whom this good work is effected, in which
those, who are left to their own chosen way, do not
share. Still, however, the grace already manifested
to them, in the gift of a Saviour, in the atonement he
has made, and in the offer of salvation to them, remains the same. It is not diminished, surely, by the
farther displays of grace, which God is pleased to
make, in the actual salvation of others. What God
does for others, lays no bar in the way of their coming
to Christ, and obtaining salvation. Nothing hinders
this, but the wicked perverseness and obstinacy of
their own evil hearts. Now, this representation is not
mere hypothesis; it is according to fact. As has been
stated already, men are all sinners, and under condemnation. Christ has been set forth a propitiation for the
sins of the whole world. Through him, salvation is
freely offered; and, when offered, it is universally and
most ungratefully rejected. In view of these circumstances, God says, concerning the ungrateful and guilty

race, "I will have mercy on whom I will have mercy."
He sends his Spirit to renew the hearts of some, and
to form them " vessels of mercy prepared unto glory ;"
and he leaves others to their own choice, who continue
to reject the salvation offered, and after their hardness,
and impenitent heart, treasure up unto themselves
wrath, against the day of wrath, and revelation of the
righteous judgment of God. Those, on whom God
thus has mercy, are the elect. They are "chosen unto
salvation, through sanctification of the Spirit, and belief of the truth." But, the election is made, not from
among men, viewed merely as transgressors of the
law, and under condemnation ; but, from among men,
viewed as having rejected salvation, when graciously
offered. Hence, it is not an election of some, that
Christ might die for them in particular, while, in making atonement, others are passed by ; but, it is an election of some, from among all, for whom atonement has
been made, and who have refused to obey the calls of
the gospel, " unto obedience, and sprinkling of the
blood of Jesus Christ."

But, here, some may inquire, What, then, becomes
of eternal election? The answer is easy. " Known
unto God are all his works, from the beginning of the
world." The election of some unto salvation, therefore, was, " from the beginning." Those, whom God
blesses " with all spiritual blessings in heavenly places,"
or things, " in Christ," he so blesses, "according as
he hath chosen" them " in him, before the foundation
of the world, that" they " should be holy, and without
blame before him in love." But, though they were
" chosen before the foundation of the world," the
choice was made in view of such circumstances as God
foresaw would actually exist. Those, who would have
it that some were chosen, not only to salvation, but

that atonement might be made particularly for them, must admit, that, in making the election, God contemplated men as fallen, and under condemnation. What is now contended for is, that he contemplated them, not merely as fallen, and under condemnation; but, as fallen creatures, to whom salvation has been offered, and by whom it has been rejected.

These different views of the subject assign to election different places, in the order of divine purposes. It is true, the purposes of God, being all eternal, are necessarily co-existent. In the order of time, no one purpose could have existence, in his all-comprehensive mind, prior to another. In the order of nature, however, one divine purpose may be considered as preceding another. The purpose to give existence to men, for example, must have been prior, in the order of nature, to the purpose of giving Christ to redeem and save men. According to those, who maintain that some were elected, that Christ might die for them, in particular, the order of nature, in the divine purposes effecting the salvation of men, must be as follows :— God determined to create men; foreseeing that they would fall into sin, he determined to give his Son to die for some of them only; and then made his election of the individuals, to whom this favour should be granted. But, as the subject has now been contemplated, the order is this : God determined to create men; foreseeing that they would fall into sin, he determined to give his Son to be a propitiation for the sins of the whole world, and that, through him, salvation should be freely offered, only on condition of repentance and faith in Christ; and, foreseeing that the gracious offer would be, universally, ungratefully rejected, he said, " I will have mercy, on whom I will have mercy," and, accordingly, chose some " unto salvation through sanctification of the Spirit, and belief of the truth."

The order, first stated, not only leaves no room for any manifestation of grace, in the offer of salvation, to the non-elect; but it gives opposers opportunity to urge against the doctrine of election, arguments drawn from such passages of scripture, as speak of the atonement of Christ as made for the sins of all, and from those, also, in which the invitations of the gospel are addressed to all, with very great effect, if not unanswerably. Besides, it does not well harmonize with the order of events.

Against the order last stated, no such objections can lie. It takes out of the hands of opposers all arguments drawn from the universality of the atonement, and the general invitations of the gospel, and leaves them, in producing these arguments, to fight, " as one that beateth the air." For, the universality of the atonement, and the general invitations of the gospel notwithstanding, sinners reject the offer of salvation, and, from among those who reject, God has chosen some to salvation ; and his purpose, according to election, must stand. It perfectly harmonizes, also, with the order of events. Man was created before he fell ; he fell, before salvation was offered, through Christ ; salvation was offered, before rejected ; and it was rejected, before the Spirit was sent to communicate " all spiritual blessings," to some, " according as they were chosen in Christ, before the foundation of the world, that they should be holy." According to this view of the subject, too, there is the same grace manifested to the non-elect, as to the elect, in the gift of a Saviour; in the atonement, which he has made, by his obedience, and sufferings, and death, and in the offer of salvation. But, when all ungratefully re-

fuse the salvation offered, God has " mercy on whom
he will have mercy ;" and it is true, that, in their election to salvation ; in the renovation of their hearts ; in
being enabled to persevere in holiness, and in being
brought home to glory, the elect do receive, from the
fulness there is in Christ, and " grace upon grace," in
which the non-elect do not share.

TROPHIMUS.

GENERAL ATONEMENT.

AN EXTRACT

From the CHRISTIAN OBSERVER's *Review of the Bishop
of Lincoln's Charge, Vol. II. p.* 544, *considered by
many respectable persons the most able periodical work
ever published.*

THE doctrine of *universal* or *general redemption* is
unquestionably contained in the sacred scriptures, and
is taught in the articles, homilies, and liturgy of our
church (church of England.) The Irish articles of
religion compiled in the reign of James I. are most
explicitly Calvinistic, having the Lambeth articles in-
corporated into them ; now it is well known that they
were digested and reduced into form principally by
the labours of the learned Usher ; yet this eminent
prelate maintained, most unequivocally, the doctrine
of general redemption. The English divines who attended the Synod of Dort, and assented to the tenets
of predestination, and the divine decrees, as taught
by Calvin, nevertheless contended for the doctrine in

question. And not to multiply authorities on so plain
a subject, many of the most learned among the Puri-
tans, who agreed with Calvin in matters of discipline,
as well as in the tenets of predestination, were, nevertheless, strenuous advocates for the doctrine of general redemption. Upon this point, we believe his lord-
ship will meet with few opponents among those whom
he may call Calvinistic clergymen; few among the
more learned and respectable, who will deny that
" Christ made a full satisfaction and complete atonement for the sins of the whole world."

Nay, Calvin himself, in commenting on Rom. v. 18,
admits that *Christ suffered for the sins of the whole
world,* and is *offered indiscriminately to all men by the
goodness of God.* And we believe that among our
English divines of the present day, who incline to the
views of that reformer, there are few who do not adopt
the language of our church upon this point. In a sermon now before us, written by the Rev. Thomas Scott,
late chaplain of the Lock Hospital, in which he en-
deavours to prove, that the doctrines of election and
final perseverance are scriptural, and that they consist with exhortatory and practical preaching, and conduce to holiness of life, we find the following passage:
" But what is the general purport of this commission
(viz. Christ's?) Let us hear the word of God: ' This
is a faithful saying, and worthy of all acceptation, that
Jesus Christ came into the world to save *sinners.*'—
' God so loved *the world* that he gave his only begotten Son, that whosoever believeth in him should not
perish, but have everlasting life; for God sent not his
Son into the world to condemn *the world* but that *the
world* through him might be saved.' ' His blood is the
propitiation for our sins, and not for ours only, but for
the sins of *the whole world.*" He then proceeds to ob-

serve—" For my part, I dare not use any arts of criticism to narrow the obvious sense of these and similar texts; and as I hope this day, previously to receiving and administering the Lord's Supper, to use the following terms in solemn prayer, Christ 'by his own oblation of himself once offered, made a full, perfect, and sufficient sacrifice, oblation, and satisfaction for the sins of the whole' world;' I would no more contradict this solemn profession from the pulpit, than I would preach against the seventeenth article respecting predestination.   The compilers of our liturgy evidently thought both true and consistent with each other; and I am happy to coincide in sentiment with these venerable characters."

EXTRACT

From the 31st Article of the Church of England.

THE offering of Christ once made, is that perfect redemption, propitiation, and satisfaction for all the sins of the whole world, both original and actual; and there is none other satisfaction for sin but that alone.

EXTRACT FROM THE
HEIDELBURGH CATECHISM.

XVth Lord's Day.

CHRIST " sustained in body and soul, the wrath of God against the sins of all mankind, that so by his passion, as the only propitiatory sacrifice, he might redeem our body and soul from everlasting damnation, and obtain for us the favour of God, righteousness and eternal life."

The Necessity of Atonement, and the consistency between that and Free Grace, in Forgiveness.

ILLUSTRATED IN THREE SERMONS,
Delivered at New-Haven, Oct. 1785,
BY JOHNATHAN EDWARDS, *D. D.*
PRESIDENT OF UNION COLLEGE.

SERMON I.

EPHESIANS i. 7.

In whom we have redemption through his blood, the forgiveness of sins, according to the riches of his grace.

THE doctrine of the forgiveness of sins is a capital doctrine of the gospel, and is much insisted on by the writers of the New Testament: above all, by the author of this epistle. In our text he asserts that we are forgiven *according to the riches of grace:* not merely in the exercise of *grace,* as the very term *forgiveness,* implies : but in the exercise of *the riches of grace :* importing that forgiveness is an act of the most *free and abundant* grace. Yet he also asserts that this gratuitous forgiveness is in consequence of a *redemption by the blood of Christ.* But how are these two parts of the proposition consistent? If we be in the literal sense forgiven in consequence of a redemp-

away sin, by the *sacrifice* of himself." 1 Cor. v. 7.
Eph. v. 2. Heb. ix. 26. As the ancient Israelites
could obtain pardon in no other way than by those
sacrifices; this teaches us that we can obtain it only
by the sacrifice of Christ.

The positive declarations of the New Testament
teach the same truth still more directly; as Luke
xxiv. 25, 26. "O fools, and slow of heart to believe
all that the prophets have spoken! *Ought* not Christ
to have suffered these things, and to enter into his
glory?" verse 46. "Thus it behoved Christ to suffer,
and to rise from the dead the third day." Rom. iii. 25,
26. "Whom God hath set forth to be a propitiation
through faith in his blood, to declare his righteousness—*that he might be just,* and the justifier of him
which believeth in Jesus." It seems that God could
not have been just in justifying the believer, had not
Christ been made a propitiation. John iii. 14, 15.
"As Moses lifted up the serpent in the wilderness, so
must the son of man be lifted up." Heb. ix. 22.
"Without shedding of blood is no remission." 1 Cor.
iii. 11. "Other foundation can no man lay, than that
is laid, which is Jesus Christ." Acts iv. 12. "Neither
is there salvation in any other: for there is no other
name, under heaven, given among men, whereby we
must be saved."

The necessity of the death and atonement of Christ
sufficiently appears by the bare event of his death.—
If his death were not necessary, he died in vain. But
we cannot suppose that either he or his father would
have consented to his death, had it not been absolutely necessary. Even a *man* of common wisdom and
goodness, would not consent either to his own death or
that of his son, but in a case of necessity, and in order
to *some* important and valuable end. Much less can

we suppose, that either Christ Jesus the Son would
have consented to his own death, or that the infinitely
wise and good father would have consented to the death
of his only begotten and dearly beloved Son, in whom
his soul was well pleased, and who was full of grace
and truth, the brightness of his own glory, and the express image of his person, the chiefest among ten thousand, and altogether lovely, if there had not been the
most urgent necessity. Esspecially as this most excellent Son so earnestly prayed to the Father, to except
him from death; Matt. xx. 39. "O my Father, if it
be possible, let this cup pass from me! Nevertheless,
not as I will, but as thou wilt." The Son himself hath
told us, John xi. 42. " That the father heareth him
always:" and therefore we may be sure, that if the
condition of his pathetic petition had taken place; if
it had been possible, that the designs of God in the salvation of sinners should be accomplished, without the
death of Christ; Christ's prayer, in this instance, would
have been answered, and he would have been exempted
from death. And since he was not exempted, we have
clear evidence, that his death was a matter of absolute
necessity.

The necessity of the atonement of Christ, is clearly
taught also by the apostle, Gal. ii. 21. " If righteousness come by the law, then Christ is dead in vain." It
is to no purpose to pretend that *the law*, in this passage, means the *ceremonial* law; because he tells us,
chap. iii. 21. " That if there had been a law given,
which could have given life, verily righteousness should
have been by the law." But the moral law was a law
which had been given; and since no law which had
been given could give life, it follows, that forgiveness
and life could not be by the moral law, any more than

E e 2

by the *ceremonial*, and that if they could, Christ is dead in vain.

II. Our next inquiry is, what is the *reason* or *ground* of this mode of forgiveness? or *why* is an atonement necessary in order to the pardon of the sinner? I answer, it is necessary on the same ground, and for the same reasons, as punishment would have been necessary, if there had been no atonement made. The ground of both is the same. The question then comes to this: why would it have been necessary, if no atonement had been made, that punishment should be inflicted on the transgressors of the divine law? This, I suppose, would have been necessary, *to maintain the authority of the divine law.* If that be not maintained, but the law fall into contempt, the contempt will fall equally on the legislator himself; his authority will be despised and his government weakened. And as the contempt shall increase, which may be expected to increase, in proportion to the neglect of executing the law; the divine government will approach nearer and nearer to a dissolution, till at length it will be totally *annihilated.*

But when moral creatures are brought into existence, there must be a moral government. It cannot be reconciled with the wisdom and goodness of God, to make intelligent creatures and leave them at random, without moral law and government. This is the dictate of reason from the nature of things. Besides the nature of things, we have in the present instance *fact*, to assist our reasoning. God hath *in fact* given a moral law and established a moral government over his intelligent creatures. So that we have clear proof, that infinite wisdom and goodness judged it to be necessary, to put intelligent creatures under moral law and government. But in order to a moral law, there must be a penalty; otherwise it would be mere advice;

but no law. In order to support the authority and vigour of this law, the penalty must be inflicted on transgressors. If a penalty be denounced indeed, but never inflicted; the law becomes no law, as really as if no penalty had been annexed to it. As well might no law have been made or published, as that a law be published, with all the most awful penalties, and these never be inflicted. Nay, in some respects it would be much better and more reconcileable with the divine perfections. It would be more consistent, and show that the legislator was not ignorant, either of his own want of power to carry a law into effect, or of the rights of his subjects, or of the boundaries between right and wrong. But to enact a law and not execute it, implies a weakness of some kind or other: either an error of judgment, or a consciousness of a depraved design in making the law, or a want of power to carry it into effect, or some other defect. Therefore such a proceeding as this is dishonourable and contemptible; and by it, both the law and legislator not only *appear in a contemptible light,* but *really are* contemptible.

Hence, to execute the threatening of the divine law, is necessary to preserve the dignity and authority of the law, and of the author of it, and to the very existence of the divine moral government. It is no impeachment of the divine power and wisdom, to say, that it is impossible for God himself to uphold his moral government, over intelligent creatures, when once his law hath fallen into contempt. He may indeed govern them by *irresistible force,* as he governs the material world: but he cannot govern them *by law,* by rewards and punishments.

If God maintain the authority of his law, by the infliction of the penalty, it will appear, that he acts consistently in the legislative and executive parts of his government. But if he were not to inflict the penalty, he would act and appear to act, an inconsistent part; or to be inconsistent with himself. If the authority of the divine law be supported by the punishment of transgressors, it will most powerfully tend to restrain all intelligent creatures from sin. But if the authority of the law be not supported, it will rather encourage and invite to sin, than restrain from it.

For these reasons, which are indeed all implied in supporting the dignity and authority of the divine law, it would have been necessary, had no atonement for sin been made, that the penalty of the law be inflicted on transgressors.

If in this view of the matter, it should be said, though for the reasons before mentioned, it is necessary that the penalty of the law, in *many* instances, or in *most* instances, be inflicted; yet why is it necessary, that it should be inflicted in *every* instance? Why could not the Deity, in a sovereign way, without any atonement, have forgiven at least some sinners? Why could not the authority of the law have been sufficiently supported, without the punishment of every individual transgressor? We find that such strictness is not *necessary* or even *subservient* to the public good, in human governments: and why is it necessary in the divine? To these inquiries I answer, by other inquiries. Why, on the supposition of no atonement, would it have been necessary, that the penalty of the law should be inflicted in *any* instance? Why could not the Deity, in a sovereign way, without any atonement, have pardoned all mankind? I presume it will be granted, for the reasons before assigned, that such a proceeding as this, would be inconsistent with the dignity and authority of the divine law and government. And the same consequence, *in a degree,* follows from every instance of pardon in this mode. It is true the ends of human governments are tolerably answered, though in some instances the guilty are suffered to pass with impunity. But as imperfection attends all human affairs; so it attends human governments in this very particular, that there are *reasons of state* which require, or the public good requires, that gross criminals, in some instances, be dismissed with impunity, and without atonement. Thus, because the government of David was weak, *and the sons of Zeruiah were too hard for him*, Joab, a most atrocious murderer, could not, during the life of David, be brought to justice. In other instances, atrocious criminals are pardoned, in order to obtain information against others still more atrocious, and dangerous to the community. In many instances, the *principals* only in certain high crimes, are punished: the rest being led away by artifice and misrepresentation, are not supposed to deserve punishment. And it is presumed, that in every instance, wherein it is really for the good of the community, to pardon a criminal, without proper satisfaction for his crime; it is because of either some weakness in the particular state of the government, under which the pardon is granted; or some imperfection in the laws of that state, not being adapted to the particular case; or some imperfection attending all human affairs. But as not any of these is supposable in the divine government, there is no arguing conclusively, from pardons in human governments, to pardons in the divine.

It may be added, that in every instance in human governments, in which just laws are not strictly executed, the government is so far weakened, and the character of the rulers, either legislative or executive, suffers, either in point of ability or in point of integrity. If it be granted that the law is just, and condemns sin to no greater punishment than it deserves, and if God were to pardon it without atonement, it would seem, that he did not hate sin in every instance, nor treat it as being what it really is, infinitely vile.

For these reasons it appears that it would have been necessary, provided no atonement had been made, that the penalty of the law should have been inflicted, even in every instance of disobedience: and for the same reasons doubtless was it necessary, that if any sinners were to be pardoned, they should be pardoned only in consequence of an *adequate* atonement. The atonement is the substitute for the punishment threatened in the law; and was designed to answer the same ends of supporting the authority of the law, the dignity of the divine moral government, and the consistency of the divine conduct in legislation and execution. By the atonement it appears that God is determined that his law shall be supported; that it shall not be despised or transgressed with impunity; and that it is an evil and a bitter thing to sin against God.

The very idea of an atonement or satisfaction for sin, is something which, to the purposes of supporting the authority of the divine law, and the dignity and con-sistency of the divine government, is equivalent to the punishment of the sinner, according to the literal threatening of the law. That which answers these purposes being done, whatever it be, atonement is made, and the way is prepared for the dispensation of pardon. In any such case, *God can be just and yet the justifier of the sinner.* And that that which is sufficient to answer these purposes, has been done for us accord-ing to the gospel plan, I presume none can deny, who believe, that the eternal word was made flesh, and dwelt among us, and that he, the only begotten and well beloved Son of God, John i. 14, bare our sins in his own body on the tree, i. Peter ii. 24, and gave himself a sacrifice to God for us, Eph. v. 2.

But perhaps some who may readily grant that what Christ hath done and suffered, is undoubtedly sufficient to atone for the sins of his people; may also suppose that if God had seen fit so to order it, we might have made a sufficient atonement for our own sins. Or whether they believe in the reality and sufficiency of the atonement of Christ or not, they may suppose that we might have atoned, or even now may atone, for our own sins. This hypothesis therefore demands our attention.

If we could have atoned, by any means, for our own sins, it must have been either by our *repentance* and *reformation*, or by *enduring* a *punishment*, less in degree or duration, than that which is threatened in the law as the wages of sin. No other way for us to atone for our own sins appears to be conceivable. But if we attend to the subject, we shall find that we can make no proper atonement in either of these ways.

1. We could not make atonement for our sins by repentance and reformation. Repentance and reformation are a mere return to our duty, which we ought never to have forsaken or intermitted. Suppose a soldier deserts the service into which he is enlisted, and at the most critical period not only forsakes his general and the cause of his country, but joins the enemy and exerts himself to his utmost in his cause, and in direct opposition to that of his country; yet after twelve months spent in this manner, he repents and returns to his duty and his former service: will this repentance and reformation atone for his desertion and rebellion? will his repentance and return, without punishment, support the authority of the law against desertion and rebellion, and deter others from the like conduct equal-

ly as the punishment of the delinquent according to
law? It cannot be pretended. Such a treatment of the
soldier would express no indignation or displeasure of
the general at the conduct of the soldier: it would by
no means convince the army or the world, that it was a
most heinous crime to desert and join the standard of
the enemy. Just so in the case under consideration:
The language of forgiving sinners barely on their repentance is, that he who sins shall repent; that the
curse of the law is repentance; that he who repents
shall suffer, and that he deserves, no further punishment. But this would be so far from an effectual tendency to discourage and restrain from sin, that it would
greatly encourage to the commission and indulgence
of it; as all that sinners would have to fear, on this supposition, would be not the wrath of God, nor any thing
terrible, but the greatest blessing to which any man in
this life can attain, repentance. If this were the condition of forgiving sinners, not only no measures would
be taken to support the divine law, but none to vindicate the character of God himself, or to show that he
acts a consistent part, and agreeably to his own law;
or that he is a friend to virtue and an enemy to vice.
On the other hand, he would rather appear as a friend
to sin and vice, or indifferent concerning them. What
would you think of a prince who should make a law
against murder, and should threaten it with a punishment properly severe; yet should declare that none
who should be guilty of that crime and should repent,
should be punished? or if he did not positively declare
this, yet should in fact suffer all murderers who repented of their murders, to pass with impunity? Undoubtedly you would conclude that he was either a very
weak or a very *wicked* prince; either that he was unable to protect his subjects, or that he had no real regard

to their lives or safety, whether in their individual or collective capacity.

2. Neither could we make atonement by any sufferings short of the full punishment of sin. Because the very idea of atonement is something done, which to the purpose of supporting the authority of the law, the dignity and consistency of divine government and conduct, is fully equivalent to the curse of the law, and on the ground of which, the sinner may be saved from that curse. But no sufferings endured *by the sinner himself*, short of the curse of the law, can be to these purposes equivalent to that curse; any more than a less number or quantity can be equal to a greater. Indeed a less degree or duration of suffering endured by *Christ the Son of God*, may, on account of the infinite dignity and glory of his person, be an equivalent to the curse of the law endured by *the sinner :* as it would be a far more striking demonstration of a king's displeasure, to inflict, in an ignominious manner, on the body of his own son, forty stripes save one; than to punish some obscure subject with death. But when the person is the same, it is absurd to suppose that a less degree or duration of pain can be equal to a greater, or can equally strike terror into the minds of spectators, and make them fear and no more do any such wickedness. Deut. xiii. 11.

Besides; if a less degree or duration of punishment, inflicted on the sinner, would answer all the purposes of supporting the authority of the divine law, &c. equally as that punishment which is threatened in the law; it follows that the punishment which is threatened in the law is too great, is unjust, is cruel and oppressive : which cannot be as long as God is a just being.

F f

Thus it clearly appears, that we could never have atoned for our own sins. If therefore atonement be made at all, it must be made by some other person: and since as we before argued, Christ the Son of God hath been appointed to this work, we may be sure, that it could be done by no other person of inferior dignity.

It may be inquired of those who deny the necessity of the atonement of Christ, whether the *mission, work and death* of Christ were at all *necessary* in order to the salvation of sinners. If they grant that they were necessary, as they exhibit the strongest motives to repentance, I ask further, could not God by any revelation or motives otherwise, whether externally or internally, exhibited, lead sinners to repentance? We find he did in fact, without the mission, work and death of Christ, lead the saints of the Old Testament to repentance. And doubtless in the same way, he might have produced the same effect, on men of modern times. Why then doth the scripture say, " Other foundation can no man lay, than that is laid, which is Jesus Christ:" and, " neither is there salvation in any other?" If it be said that these texts are true, as God hath *seen fit* to adopt and establish this mode of salvation: It occurs at once, that then it may with equal truth be said, concerning those who were converted by the preaching of Paul; other foundation could no man lay, for their salvation, than the apostle *Paul.* In this sense too every event which ever takes place, is equally necessary as the mission and death of Christ: and it was in no other sense necessary, that Christ should be sent and die, than that *a sparrow should fall, or not fall, to the ground.* In short to say, that the mission and death of Christ were necessary, because God had made this constitution, is to resolve all into the sovereignty of God, and to confess that no *reason* of Christ's mission and death is assignable.

Besides, if the mission, death and resurrection of Christ, and the knowledge of them, be, by divine constitution, made necessary to the salvation of sinners; this will seem to be wholly inconsistent with the fundamental principle of the system of those who deny the atonement of Christ; I mean the principle, that it is not reconcilable with the perfections of God, to refuse a pardon to any who repent. If bare repentance and reformation be the ground of pardon, doubtless all who repent, though ever so ignorant of Christ, his death and resurrection, and of the motives to repentance therein exhibited, are entitled to pardon; and if so, in what sense will the socinians say, the mission and death of Christ are necessary to pardon? Not surely as purchasing salvation, for even those who are ignorant of them; this is abhorrent to their whole system. Not as exhibiting the strongest motives to repentance; because in the case now supposed, these motives are perfectly unknown. And they will not say, it is impossible for any to repent, who are ignorant of Christ.*

Again, how is it more consistent with the divine perfections, to confine pardon and salvation to the narrow limits of those who know and are influenced by the motives to repentance, implied in the death and resurrection of Christ; than to the limits of those who repent and depend on the atonement of Christ?

* "It is certainly the doctrine of reason, as well as of the 'Old Testament, that God is merciful to the *penitent*, and no thing is requisite to make men, *in all situations*, the object of his favour, but such *moral conduct* as he has made them *capable of.*" Priestly's Corruptions of Christianity, page

It may be further inquired of those gentlemen mentioned above, whether the pardon of the penitent, be according to the divine *law*. or according to the *gospel.* If it be a constitution of the *law*, that every penitent be pardoned, what then is the *gospel?* And wherein does *the grace* of the latter, exceed that of the former? Besides, is it not strange, to suppose. that *bare law* knows any thing of *repentance* and of the *promise* of *pardon* on repentance? surely such a law must be a very *gracious* law : and a *very gracious law*, and a *very gracious gospel*, seem to be very *nearly* one and the same thing. It has been commonly understood that the divine *law* is the rule of *justice.* If so, and it be a provision of the law, that every penitent be acquitted from punishment ; then surely there is *no grace* at all in the acquittal of the penitent, as the gentlemen to whom I now refer, pretend there is none on the supposition of the satisfaction of Christ.—Again, if the law secure impunity to all penitents, then all the terror or punishment which the law threatens, is either repentance itself, or that wise and wholesome discipline which is necessary to lead to repentance : these are the true and utmost *curse* of the law. But neither of these is any curse at all ; they are at lest *among* the greatest blessings which can be bestowed on those who need them. But if it be granted that the bare law of God does not secure pardon to the penitent, but admits of his punishment, it will follow that the punishment of the penitent would be nothing opposed to justice.— Surely God hath not made an unjust law. It also follows, that to punish the penitent would be not at all inconsistent with the divine perfections ; unless God hath made a law, which cannot in any instance be executed consistently with his own perfections.— And *if* the *punishment* of the penitent, provided no atonement had been made, would not be inconsistent with justice, or with the perfections of God, who will say, that the pardon of the penitent, on the sole footing of an atonement, is inconsistent with either?

If neither strict justice, nor the divine law founded on justice, nor the divine perfections, without an atonement, secure pardon to all who repent, what will become of the boasted argument of the socinians, against the atonement, that God will certainly pardon and save; and that it is absurd and impious to suppose, that he will not pardon and save, all who repent?— Are the socinians themselves certain, that God will not do that which eternal justice, his own law, and his own perfections allow him to do? The dilemma is this :—*eternal justice* either requires that every penitent be pardoned in consequence of his repentance merely, or it does not. If it do require this, it follows, that pardon is an act of *justice* and not of *grace :* therefore let the socinians be forever silent on this head. It also follows, that repentance answers, satisfies, fulfils, the divine law, so that, in consequence of it, the law has no farther demand on the sinner. It is therefore either the complete righteousness of the law, or the complete curse of the law : for cursed is every one that continueth not in all things written in the book of the law to do them. It also follows, that sin is no moral evil. Doubtless that which deserves no punishment, or token of the divine displeasure, is no moral evil. But the utmost that justice, on this hypothesis, requires of the sinner, is repentance, which is no token of the divine displeasure, but an inestimable blessing.—It also follows, that as eternal justice is no other than the eternal law of God, *grace* and *truth*, *life* and *immortality* came and were brought to light by Moses, since the *law* came by him; that the law contains exceeding great and precious *promises*, which promises however, *exceeding great* and *precious* as they are, are no more than assurances, that we shall not be *injured*.—It follows in the last place that *justice* and *grace*, *law* and *gospel* are perfectly synonymous terms.

Or if the other part of the dilemma be taken, that *eternal justice* does not require, that every penitent be pardoned; who knows but that God may see fit, to suffer justice, in some instances, to take place? who will say that the other divine perfections are utterly inconsistent with justice? or that wisdom, goodness and justice cannot co-exist in the same character? or that the law of God is such that it cannot be executed in any instance, consistently with the divine character?* These would be bold assertions indeed: let him who avows them, at the same time prove them. Indeed he must either prove these assertions, or own that *justice* requires the pardon of every penitent, and abide the consequences; or renounce the doctrine, that the divine perfections require that every penitent be pardoned, without an atonement.†

* That law in which Paul delighted after the inward man; which he declares to be holy, and just, and good; to be glorious too, nay, in the abstract, *glory* (Rom. vii. and 2 Cor. iii.) and which David pronounces to be *perfect*, and more desirable than gold, yea, than much fine gold: sweeter also than honey and the honey comb. Psalm xix.

† "Arguments drawn from such considerations as those of the moral government of God, the nature of things, and the general plan of revelation, will not be put off to a future time. The whole compass and force of them is within our reach, and if the mind be unbiassed, they must, I think, determine our assent." Corruptions of Christianity, Vol. I. page 278.

SERMON II.

EPHESIANS. i. 7.

In whom we have redemption through his blood, the for-
giveness of sins, according to the riches of his grace.

HAVING, in the preceding discourse, given an
answer to the two enquiries proposed concerning the
necessity, and the *ground* of the necessity of the atonement of Christ, I proceed to the third, which is,

III. Are we, notwithstanding the redemption of
Christ, forgiven *freely by grace ?*—That we should be
forgiven wholly through the redemption of Christ, and
yet by *free grace*, hath, as I observed, appeared to
many, a grand inconsistency, or a perplexing difficulty. In discoursing on this question, I shall,

1. Mention several modes in which attempts have
been made to solve this difficulty.—2. I shall suggest
some considerations which may possibly lead to the
true solution.

First. I am to mention several modes, in which attempts have been made, to solve this difficulty.

1. Some allow that there is no exercise of grace in
the *bare pardon** or *justification* of the sinner: that all
the grace of the gospel consists in the gift of Christ ;
in providing an atonement; in the undertaking of
Christ to make atonement, and in the actual making

---

* The impropriety of expression, in speaking of *pardon*
without *grace*, would need an apology, were it not common
in treatises on this subject. No more is intended, than that
the sinner is *acquitted* or *released*, without grace.

it. And as the pardon of the sinner is founded on those gracious actions ; so *that* in a more lax sense is also said to be an act of *grace.* As to this account of of the matter, I have to observe—That it is rather yielding to the objection, than answering it. It is allowed, in this state of the matter, that the *pardon* of the sinner is properly no act of grace. But this seems not to be reconcileable with the plain declarations of scripture ; as in our text ; In whom we have redemption through his blood, the forgiveness of sins, according to *the riches of his grace.* Being justified freely by his grace, through the redemption that is in Jesus Christ, Rom. iii. 24. These and such like passages seem plainly to import, that pardon itself is an act of grace, and not merely that it is founded on other acts, which *are* acts of grace. Besides the very idea of pardon or forgiveness implies *grace.* So far only is any crime pardoned, as it is pardoned *graciously.*— To pardon a crime on the footing of justice, in the proper sense of the word *justice,* is a direct contradiction.

Again : It is not proper to say, that the pardon of the sinner is an act of grace, merely because it is founded on the gracious gift of Christ, and his gracious act in making atonement. It is not proper to say, that any act is an act of grace, merely because it is founded on another act, which is really an act of grace. As well we may say, that if a creditor, by a third person, furnish his debtor with money sufficient to discharge his debt, when the debtor has paid, in this way, the full debt, it is an act of grace in the creditor to give up the obligation. Whereas, who does not see that the furnishing of the money, and the giving up of the obligation, are two distinct acts, and ~wever the former is indeed an act of grace ; yet the latter is no more an act of grace, than if the money had been paid to some other creditor, and he had given up an obligation for the same sum. If it be an act of grace in the creditor, to deliver up an obligation, for which he hath received the full sum, because the money paid was originally furnished by himself, then it would be consistent with justice in the creditor, to retain the obligation, after he has received the full sum for which it was given ; or to reject the money, and cast the debtor into prison, though he tenders payment. But neither of these, I presume, will be pretended to be just.

2. Some have attempted to relieve the difficulty now under consideration, in this manner : They say, The pardon of the sinner is no act of grace to *Christ*, because *he* has paid the debt for the sinner : but that it is an act of grace to the *sinner*, because the debt was paid, not by the sinner himself, but by Christ. Nor was Christ so much as *delegated* by the sinner to pay his debt. Concerning this I observe, in the *first place* : That if the atonement of Christ be considered as the payment of a debt, the release of the sinner seems not to be an act of grace, although the payment be made by Christ, and not by the sinner personally. Suppose any one of you, my auditors, owes a certain sum : he goes and pays the full sum himself personally. Doubtless all will agree, that the creditor, in this case, when he gives up the obligation, performs a mere act of justice, in which there is no grace at all. But in what respect would there have been more grace in giving up the obligation, if the money had been sent by a servant, by a friend, or by a third person ? Here I am sensible an objection will arise to this effect ; But we did not send the payment of our debt to God, by the hand of Christ as our friend : we did not delegate him

to make atonement for us; he was graciously appointed and given by God.   To this I answer, That this objection places the whole grace of the gospel in *providing* the Saviour, not in the *pardon* of sin.   Besides, if
by *delegating* Christ, he meant such a sincere consent
and earnest desire, that Christ should make atonement
for us, as a man may have, that his friend should discharge a debt in his behalf; without doubt every true
christian, in this sense, delegates Christ to make atonement for his sins.   Did not Abraham and all the saints
who lived before the incarnation of Christ, and who
were informed that atonement was to be made for them
by Christ, sincerely consent to it, and earnestly desire
it? and though now Christ has actually made atonement, yet every one who walks in the steps of the faith
of Abraham, is the subject of the like sincere consent
to the office and work of Christ, and the like earnest
desire, that by his atonement, a reconciliation may be
effected between God and himself.   So that if Christ
have, in the proper sense of the words, *paid the debt*
for his people, his people do as truly send him to make
this payment, as a man ever sends his friend to make
payment to his creditor.

Nor is any thing wanting to make any man, or all
men, in this sense, delegate Christ to make atonement for them, but the gift of repentance or a new
heart.   And if God had not prevented them by previously appointing Christ to the work of redemption,
all mankind being brought to repentance, and being
informed that Christ, on their consent and delegation,
would make atonement for their sins, would freely
have given their consent, and delegated him to the
work.

But what if the people of Christ did not, in any
sense, delegate him to this work? would this cause

the payment of their debt by Christ, to be at all more
consistent with free grace in their discharge? Suppose
a man without any delegation, consent, or knowledge
of his friend, pays the full demand of his creditor, it
is manifest, that the creditor is obliged in justice to
discharge the debtor, equally as if the agent had acted
by delegation from the debtor. Or if we had in every
sense delegated and commissioned Christ, still our pardon would be an act of grace, as still we should be
treated more favourably than our personal characters
deserve.

Now to apply the whole of this to the subject before us: If Christ have, in the proper sense of the
words, paid the debt which we owed to God, whether
by a delegation from us or not; there can be no more
grace in our discharge, than if we had paid it ourselves.

But the fact is, that Christ has not, in the *literal* and
proper sense, paid the debt for us. It is indeed true,
that our deliverance is called a *redemption*, which refers
to the deliverance of a prisoner out of captivity, commonly effected by paying a certain sum as the price of
his liberty. In the same strain, Christ is said to give
himself a *ransom* for many, and christians are said to
be *bought* with a *price*, &c. All which scripture expressions bring into view the payment of money, or
the discharge of a debt. But it is to be remembered,
that these are metaphorical expressions, therefore not
literally and exactly true. We had not deprived God
of his property; we had not robbed the treasury of
heaven. God was possessed of as much property after
the fall as before: the universe and the fulness thereof
still remained to be his. Therefore when Christ made
satisfaction for us, he *refunded* no property. As none
had been *taken away*, none *needed* to be refunded. But

we had *rebelled* against God, we had practically despised his law and authority, and it was necessary, that his authority should be supported, and that it should be made to appear, that sin shall not go without proper tokens of divine displeasure and abhorrence; that God will maintain his law; that his authority and government shall not be suffered to fall into contempt; and that God is a friend to virtue and holiness, and an irreconcileable enemy to transgression, sin and vice.— These things were necessary to be made manifest, and the clear manifestation of these things, if we will use the term, was *the debt* which was due to God. This manifestation was made in the sufferings and death of Christ. But Christ did not, *in the literal sense*, pay the debt we owed to God; if he had paid it, all grace would have been excluded from the pardon of the sinner.— Therefore,

3. Others seeing clearly that these solutions of the difficulty are not satisfactory, have said, that the atonement of Christ consisted, not in the payment of a debt, but in the *vindication of the divine law and character*: that Christ made this vindication, by practically declaring the justice of the law, in his active obedience, and by submitting to the penalty of it, in his death: that as what Christ did and suffered in the flesh, was a declaration of the rectitude of the divine law and character, so it was a declaration of the evil of sin; and the greater the evil of sin appears to be, the greater the grace of pardon appears to be. Therefore the atonement of Christ is so far from diminishing the grace of pardon, that it magnifies it. The sum of this is, that since the atonement consists not in the payment of a debt, but in the vindication of the divine law and character: therefore it is not at all opposed to free grace in pardon.

Concerning this stating of the matter, I beg leave to observe; that if by *a vindication of the divine law and character*, be meant, proof given that the law of God is just, and that the divine character is good and irreproachable; I can by no means suppose, that the atonement consisted in a vindication of the law and character of God. The law is no more proved to be just, and the character of God is no more proved to be good, by the perfect obedience and death of Christ, than the same things are proved by the perfect obedience of the angels, and by the torments of the damned. But I shall have occasion to enlarge on this point by and by.

Again; if by *vindication of the divine law and character*, be meant, proof given that God is determined to support the authority of his law, and that he will not suffer it to fall into contempt; that he will also support his own dignity, will act a consistent part in legislation and in the execution of his law, and will not be disobeyed with impunity, or without proper satisfaction: I grant, that by Christ the *divine law and character are vindicated;* so that God can now consistently with his own honour, and the authority of his law, forgive the sinner. But how does this make it appear that there is any grace in the pardon of the sinner, when Christ as his substitute, hath made full atonement for him, by vindicating the law and character of God? what if *the sinner himself*, instead of *Christ*, had by obedience and suffering, vindicated the law and character of God; and in consequence had been released from farther punishment? Would his release in this case, have been by *grace*, or by *justice?* Doubtless by the latter and not by the former: for " to him that worketh, is the reward reckoned, not of grace, but of debt." Rom. iv. 4. Therefore why is it not equally an act of justice, to release the sinner, in consequence of the same vindication made by *Christ ?* Payment of debt equally precludes grace, when made by a *third person*, as when made by the debtor himself. And since the vindication of the divine law and character, made by the sinner himself, precludes grace from the release of the sinner ; why does not the same vindication as effectually preclude it, when made by a *third person ?*

Those authors who give us this solution of the difficulty under consideration, seem to suppose that it is a sufficient solution to say that the atonement consists, not in the payment of debt, but in the vindication of the divine law and character ; and what they say, seems to imply, that however or by whomsoever, that vindication be made, whether by the sinner himself, or any other person, it is not at all opposed to the exercise of grace in the release of the sinner. Whereas it appears by the text just now quoted, and by many others, that if that vindication were made by the sinner himself, it would shut out all grace from his release. And I presume this will be granted by those authors themselves, on a little reflection. To say otherwise, is to say, that though a sinner should endure the curse of the law, yet there would be grace in his subsequent release.— It seems then that the grace of pardon depends, not barely on this, that the atonement consists in a vindication of the law and character of God ; but upon this particular circumstance attending the vindication, that it be made by a *third person.* And if this circumstance will leave room for grace in the release of the sinner, why is there not as much grace in the release of the sinner, though the atonement of Christ be a payment of the sinner's debt : since the payment is attended with the same *important* and *decisive* circumstance, that it is made by a *third person ?*

Objection. But we could not vindicate the law and character of God; therefore it is absurd to make the supposition, and to draw consequences from the supposition, that we had made such a vindication. Answer: It is no more absurd to make this supposition, than it is to make the supposition, that we had paid the debt to divine justice; for we could no more do this than we could make the vindication in question. And if it follows from this circumstance, that we neither have vindicated nor could vindicate the divine character, that our release from condemnation is an act of grace; why does it not also follow from the circumstance, that we neither have paid nor could pay the debt to divine justice, that our release is an act of grace, even on the supposition, that Christ has in the literal sense paid the debt for us?

Thus, not any of these modes of solving this grand difficulty, appears to be satisfactory. Even this last, which seemed to bid the fairest to afford satisfaction, fails. Therefore,

Secondly. I shall suggest some considerations, which may possibly lead to the true solution. The question before us, is, whether pardon through the atonement of Christ be an act of *justice* or of *grace.*— In order to a proper answer to this question, it is of primary importance, that we have clear and determinate ideas affixed to the words *justice* and *grace.*

I find the word *justice* to be used in three distinct senses: sometimes it means *commutative* justice, sometimes *distributive* justice, and sometimes what may be called *general* or *public* justice.

Commutative justice respects property and matters of commerce solely, and secures to every man his own property. To treat a man justly in this sense, is not to deprive him of his property, and whenever it fall into our hands, to restore it duly, or to make due payment of debts. In one word, commutative justice is to violate no man's property.

Distributive justice consists in properly rewarding virtue or good conduct, and punishing crimes or vicious conduct; and it has respect to a man's personal moral character or conduct. To treat a man justly in this sense, is to treat him according to his personal character or conduct. Commutative justice in the recovery of debts, has no respect at all to the character or conduct of the debtor, but merely to the property of the creditor. Distributive justice in the punishment of crimes, has no respect at all to the property of the criminal; but merely to his personal conduct: unless his property may, in some instances, enhance his crimes.

General or *public* justice comprehends all moral goodness: and though the word is often used in this sense, it is really an improper use of it. In this sense, whatever is *right*, is said to be *just*, or an act of *justice ;* and whatever is *wrong* or improper to be done, is said to be *unjust*, or an act of *injustice*. To practise justice in this sense, is to practise agreeably to the dictates of general benevolence, or to seek the glory of God and the good of the universe. And whenever the glory of God is neglected, it may be said, that God is *injured* or *deprived of his right*. Whenever the general good is neglected or impeded, the universe may be said to suffer an *injury*. For instance; if Paul were now to be cast down from heaven, to suffer the pains of hell, it would be wrong, as it would be inconsistent with God's covenant faithfulness, with the designed exhibition of his glorious grace, and with the good of the universe. In this sense, it would not be *just*. Yet in the sense of *distributive* justice, such a treatment of Paul would be

perfectly just, as it would be no more than correspondent to his personal demerits.

The term *grace*, comes now to be explained. *Grace*
is ever so opposed to justice, that they mutually limit
each other. Wherever *grace* begins, *justice* ends ;
and wherever *justice* begins, *grace* ends. Grace, as opposed to commutative justice, is gratuitously to relinquish your property, or to forgive a man his debt.—
And commutative *injustice* is to demand more of a man
than your own property. Grace as opposed to justice
in the distributive sense, is to treat a man more favourably or mildly, than is correspondent to his personal
character or conduct. To treat him *unjustly* is to use
him with greater severity, than is correspondent to his
personal character. It is to be remembered, that in
personal character I include punishment endured, as
well as actions performed. When a man has broken
any law, and has afterwards suffered the penalty of that
law ; as he has, by the transgression, treated the law
with contempt, so by suffering the penalty, he has supported the authority of it : and the latter makes a part
of his personal character, as he stands related to that
law, as really as the former.

With regard to the *third* kind of justice, as this is
improperly called justice, and as it comprehends all
moral goodness, it is not at all opposed to *grace ;* but
comprehends that, as well as every other virtue, as
truth, faithfulness, meekness, forgiveness, patience,
prudence, temperance, fortitude, &c. All these are
right and *fit*, and the contrary tempers or practices are
wrong, and *injurious* to God and the system : and therefore in this sense of justice are *unjust*. And even *grace*
itself, which is favour to the ill-deserving, so far as it is
wise and proper to be exercised, makes but a part of
this kind of justice.

We proceed now to apply these explanations to the solution of the difficulty under consideration. The question is this, Is the pardon of the sinner, through the atonement of Christ, an act of justice or of grace? To which I answer, That with respect to *commutative* justice, it is neither an act of justice nor of grace.— Because commutative justice is not concerned in the affair. We neither owed money to the Deity, nor did Christ pay any on our behalf. His atonement is not a payment of our debt. If it had been, our discharge would have been an act of mere justice, and not of grace. To make the sinner also pay the debt, which had been already paid by Christ, would be manifestly injurious, oppressive, and beyond the bounds of commutative justice, the rule of which is, that every man retain and recover his own property, and that only.— But a debt being paid, by whomsoever it be paid, the creditor *has* recovered his property, and therefore has a right to nothing further. If he extort, or attempt to extort, any thing further, he proceeds beyond his right and is guilty of injustice. So that if Christ had paid the debt for the believer, he would be discharged, not on the footing of grace, but of strict justice.

With respect to *distributive* justice, the discharge of the sinner is wholly an act of grace. This kind of justice has respect solely to the personal character and conduct of its object. And then is a man treated justly, when he is treated according to his personal moral character. If he be treated more favourably than is correspondent to his personal character, he is the object of grace. I say *personal* character; for distributive justice has no respect to the character of a *third* person, or to any thing which may be done or suffered by another person, than by him, who is the object of this justice, or who is on trial, to be rewarded or punished. And with regard to the case now before us, what if Christ has made atonement for sin? This atonement constitutes no part of the personal character of the sinner: but his personal character is essentially the same, as it would have been, if Christ had made no atonement. And as the sinner, in pardon, is treated, not only more favourably, but infinitely more favourably, than is correspondent to his personal character, his pardon is wholly an act of infinite grace. If it were, in the sense of *distributive justice,* an act of justice: he would be injured, if a pardon were refused him.— But as the case is, he would not be injured, though a pardon were refused him; because he would not be treated more unfavourably than is correspondent to his personal character.

Therefore though it be true, that if a *third* person pay a debt, there would be no grace exercised by the creditor, in discharging the debtor, yet when a *third* person atones for a crime, by suffering in the stead of a *criminal,* there is entire grace in the discharge of the criminal, and *distributive justice* still allows him to be punished in his own person. The reason is, what I have mentioned already, that justice in punishing crimes, respects the personal character only of the criminal: but in the payment of debts, it respects the recovery of property only. In the former case, it admits of any treatment which is according to his personal character: in the latter, it admits of nothing beyond the recovery of property.

So that though Christ has made complete atonement for the sins of all his disciples, and they are justified wholly through his redemption; yet they are justified wholly by grace. Because they *personally* have not made atonement for their sins, or suffered the curse of the law. Therefore they have no claim to a discharge on account of their own personal conduct and suffering. And if it is objected, that neither is a debtor discharged on account of any thing which he hath done personally, when he is discharged on the payment of his debt by a third person: yet justice does not admit, that the creditor recover the debt again from the debtor himself: why then does it admit, that a magistrate inflict the punishment of a crime on the criminal himself, when atonement has been made by a substitute? The answer is, that justice in these two cases is very different, and respects very different objects. In *criminal* causes, it respects the personal conduct or character of the criminal, and admits of any treatment which is correspondent to that conduct. In *civil* causes, or matters of debt, it respects the restitution of property only, and this being made, it admits of no further demand.

In the *third* sense of justice before explained, according to which any thing is just, which is right and best to be done; the pardon of the sinner is entirely an act of *justice*. It is undoubtedly most conducive to the divine glory, and general good of the created system, that every believer should be pardoned; and therefore, in the present sense of the word, it is an act of justice. The pardon of the sinner is equally an act of *justice*, if, as some suppose, he be pardoned not on account of the death of Christ, considered as an equivalent to the curse of the law denounced against the sinner; but merely on account of the positive obedience of Christ. If this be the mode and the condition of pardon established by God, doubtless pardon granted in this mode and on this condition, is most conducive to the divine glory and the general good.— Therefore it is, in the sense of justice now under consideration, an act of *justice;* insomuch that if pardon were not granted in this mode, the divine glory would be tarnished, and the general good diminished, or the universe would suffer an injury. The same would be true, if God had in fact granted pardon, without any atonement, whether by suffering or obedience. We might have argued from that fact, that infinite wisdom saw it to be most conducive to the divine glory and the general good, to pardon without an atonement; and of course that if pardon had not been granted in this way, both the divine glory and general good, would have been diminished, and injustice would have been done to the universe. In the same sense the gift of Christ, to be our saviour, his undertaking to save us, and every other gift of God to his creatures, are acts of *justice*. But it must be remembered, that this is an improper sense of the word *justice*, and is not at all opposed to grace, but implies it. For all those divine acts and gifts just mentioned, though in this sense they are acts of *justice*, yet are at the same time, acts of *pure grace*.

In this sense of *justice*, the word seems to be used by the apostle Paul, Rom. iii. 26. " To declare his *righteousness* (or *justice*) that he might be *just* and the justifier of him which believeth in Jesus." That God might be just *to himself* and to the *universe*. Again in Psalm lxxxv. 10. " Mercy and truth are met together, *righteousness* and peace have kissed each other."— *Righteousness*, in the *distributive* sense, hath not kissed peace with respect to the sinner; but so far as it speaks any thing, calls for his punishment. But the public good, and the divine glory admit of peace with the sinner. In the same sense the word occurs in the version of the psalms in common use among us, where it is said, " justice is pleased and peace is given."— Again in the catechism of the assembly of divines, where they say, "Christ offered up himself a sacrifice to satisfy divine *justice.*"

Thus it appears, that the pardon of the sinner, in reference to *distributive* justice, which is the only proper sense of the word, with respect to this matter, is entirely an act of grace, and that although he is pardoned wholly through the redemption of Jesus Christ.

It is in the same sense an act of grace, as the gift of Christ, or any other most gracious act of God.— Though the sinner is pardoned wholly through the redemption of Christ, yet his pardon is an act of pure grace, because in it he is treated inconceivably more favourably than is correspondent to his personal character.

The pardon of the sinner, on this plan of the redemption or the atonement of Christ, is as entirely an act of grace, as if it had been granted on an atonement made, not by the sufferings of Christ, but merely by his active obedience. For if we suppose, that the atonement of Christ consists wholly in the obedience of Christ, not in his sufferings, in what sense would the pardon of the sinner be an act of grace, in which it is not an act of grace, on the hypothesis concerning the atonement which hath been now stated? Pardon is no more procured by the payment of the sinner's debt, in the one case, than in the other. If it be said that Christ's suffering the curse of the law is the payment of the debt; I answer, this is no more a payment of the debt, than the obedience of Christ. If it be said that Christ's *obedience* only honours and magnifies the law, I answer, No more is done by the *sufferings* of Christ. It is true, that if the sinner be pardoned on account of Christ's obedience, he is treated more favourably than is correspondent to his personal character. The same is true, if he be pardoned on

account of Christ's sufferings. If it be said, that in
the one case, Christ suffers, as the substitute of the
sinner; I answer, In the other case, he obeys as the
substitute of the sinner. In the one case, Christ has
by his sufferings made it consistent with the general
good, to pardon the sinner; in the other case, he hath
made the same thing consistent with the general good,
by his *obedience*. And if this circumstance, that the
pardon of the sinner is consistent with the general
good, abolishes grace from his pardon in the one
case, the same circumstance is productive of the same
effect, in the other. The truth is, that in both cases,
the whole grace of pardon consists in *this*, and *this
only*, that the sinner is treated infinitely more favourably, than is correspondent to his personal character.

Again: According to this scheme of the atonement, the pardon of the sinner, is as wholly an act
of grace, as if he had been pardoned without any
atonement at all. If the sinner had been pardoned
without any atonement, he would have been treated
more favourably than is correspondent to his own character: so he is, when pardoned through the atonement of Christ. In the former case, he would be
pardoned, without a payment of his debt: so he is in
the latter. If the measures taken by God, to secure
the public good, those measures consisting neither in
any personal doing or suffering of the sinner, nor in
the payment of debt, be inconsistent with grace in the
pardon of the sinner, in the one case; doubtless whatever measures are taken by God, to secure the public
good in the other case, are equally inconsistent with
grace in pardon. And no man will pretend, that if
God do pardon the sinner without an atonement, he
will pardon him in a way which is inconsistent with the
public good. In this view of the objection, either the

bare circumstance that the pardon of the sinner is consistent with the public good, is that which abolishes the grace of pardon ; or it is the particular mode, in which the consistence of pardon and the public good, is brought about. If the bare circumstance of the consistence of pardon and the public good, be that which abolishes the grace of pardon ; then it seems, that in order that any pardon may be gracious, it must be *inconsistent* with the public good ; and therefore the pardon of the sinner without any atonement, being by the concession of the objector, a gracious act, is inconsistent with the general good of the universe, and with the glory and perfections of God, and therefore can never be granted by God, as long as he is possessed of infinite perfection and goodness, whereby he is necessarily disposed to seek the good of the universal system, or of his own kingdom.

Or if it be said, that it is the *particular mode,* in which the consistence between pardon and the public good is brought about, which abolishes the grace of pardon ; in this case it is incumbent on the objector, to point out what there is in the *mode,* which is opposed to grace in pardon. He cannot pretend, that in this mode, the debt of the sinner is paid; or that in repentance the sinner's personal character is so altered, that he now *deserves* no punishment. If this were the case, there would certainly be no grace in his pardon. It is no *grace,* and no *pardon,* not to punish a man who *deserves* no punishment. If the objector were to hold, that the personal character of the sinner is so altered by repentance, that he no longer *deserves* punishment, he would at once confute his own scheme of *gracious* pardon.

Neither can it be pretended, by the advocates for pardon without atonement, that there is any grace in pardon, in any other view than this, that the sinner is treated more favourably, than is correspondent to his personal character. And pardon on such an atonement as Christ hath made, is, in the same view, an act of grace. So that if the true idea of *grace*, with respect to this subject be, a treatment of a sinner more favourably than is correspondent to his personal character; the pardon of the sinner through the atonement of Christ, is an act of *pure grace*. If this be not the true idea of grace, let a better be given, and I am willing to examine it; and presume that on the most thorough examination of the matter, it will be found, that there is as much grace in the pardon of the sinner, through the atonement of Christ, as without any atonement at all. Surely it will not be pleaded, that it is no act of grace to treat a sinner more favourably than is correspondent to his own personal character; if such treatment be not more favourable than is correspondent to the personal character of some other man, or some other being; and that it is no act of grace in a prince to pardon a criminal, from respect to the merits of the criminal's father; or, that if Capt. Asgill had been the murderer of Capt. Huddy, there would have been no grace exercised in the pardon of Asgill, from respect to the intercession of the court of France.

On every hypothesis concerning the mode or condition of pardon, it must be allowed, that God dispenses pardon, from regard to some circumstance, or juncture of circumstances, which renders the pardon both consistent with the general good, and subservient to it: and whatever this be, whether the death of Christ, or any thing else, provided it be not the payment of money, and provided the personal character

H h

of the sinner be the same, it is equally consistent or inconsistent with grace in pardon.

In short, the whole strength of this objection, in which the socinians have so much triumphed, that complete atonement is inconsistent with grace in the pardon of the sinner, depends on the supposition, that the atonement of Christ consists in the literal payment of a debt which we owed to God; and this groundless supposition being set aside, the objection itself appears equally groundless, and vanishes like dew before the sun.

Whatever hypothesis we adopt concerning the pardon of the sinner, whether we suppose it to be granted on account of the death of Christ; or on account of the obedience of Christ; or absolutely without any atonement; all will agree in this, that it is granted in such a way, or on such conditions only, as are consistent with the general good of the moral system; and from a regard to some event or circumstance, or juncture of circumstances, which causes pardon to be consistent with the general good. And that circumstance or juncture of circumstances, may as well be called the *price* of pardon, the *ransom* of the sinner, &c. as the death of Christ. And whereas it is objected, that if God grant a pardon from respect to the atonement of Christ, we are under no obligation to God for the grace of pardon; I answer that whenever God grants a pardon, from respect to the circumstance or juncture of circumstances before mentioned, it may as well be pleaded, that the sinner *so* pardoned, is under no obligations of gratitude to God, *on account of his pardon;* for that it was granted from regard to the general good, or to that circumstance which rendered it consistent with the general good, and not from any gracious regard to *him;* or that if he be under any obligation to God, it is to him

as the author of that circumstance or juncture of circumstances, which renders his pardon consistent with
the general good, and not to him, as the dispenser of
his pardon : as it is objected, that if, on the scheme
of pardon through the atonement of Christ, we be
under any obligation to God at all, it is merely on account of the provision of the atonement, and not on
account of pardon itself.

Perhaps some, loath to relinquish this objection, may
say, Though it be true, that the pardon of the sinner,
on account of the atonement of Christ, be a *real* act of
grace ; would it not have been an act of *greater* grace,
to pardon absolutely, without an atonement ?—This
question is capable of a twofold construction. If the
meaning be, Whether there would not have been more
grace manifested *towards the sinner*, if his pardon had
been granted, without any atonement? I answer, by
no means ; because to put the question in this sense,
is the same as to ask, Whether the favour of pardon
granted without an atonement, would not be greater
in comparison with the sinner's personal character,
than it is when granted on account of the atonement of
Christ? Or whether there would not have been a
greater distance between the good of pardon, and the
demerit of the sinner's personal character, if his pardon had been granted without an atonement, than if it
be granted on account of the atonement of Christ? But
the good, the safety, the indemnity of pardon, or of deliverance from condemnation, is the very same, in
whatever way it be granted, whether through an atonement or not, whether in a way of grace or in a way of
debt, whether from a regard to the merits of Christ, or
the merits of the sinner himself. Again, the personal
character of the sinner is also the same, whether he be
pardoned through an atonement or not. If his pardon

be granted without an atonement, it makes not the de-. merit of his personal character and conduct the greater: or if it be granted on account of the atonement of Christ, it makes not the demerit of his personal character the less. Therefore as the good of pardon is the same, in whatever way it be granted; and the personal character of the sinner pardoned is the same; the distance between the good of pardon, and the demerit of the sinner's character is also the same, whether he be pardoned on account of the atonement of Christ, or absolutely, without any atonement. Of course the pardon of the sinner is not an act of greater grace *to him personally*, if granted without regard to any atonement, than if granted from regard to the atonement of Christ.

But perhaps the meaning of the question stated above, is, Whether, if the sinner had been pardoned, without an atonement, it would not have exhibited greater grace, *in the divine mind*, or greater goodness *in God*; and whether in this mode of pardon, greater good would not have accrued to the universe. The answer to this question wholly depends on the *necessity* of an atonement, which I have endeavoured briefly to show, in the preceding discourse. If an atonement be necessary to support the authority of the law and of the moral government of God, it is doubtless necessary to the public good of the moral system, or to the general good of the universe and to the divine glory. This being granted or established, the question just now stated, comes to this simply; whether it exhibits greater grace and goodness in the divine mind, and secures greater good to the universe, to pardon sin in such a mode, as is consistent with the general good of the universe; or in such a mode as is inconsistent with that important object?—a question which no man, from regard to his own reputation would choose to propose.

SERMON III.

EPHESIANS i. 7.

In whom we have redemption through his blood, the for-giveness of sins, according to the riches of his grace.

HAVING, in the preceding discourses, consider-ed the particulars at first proposed, which were, That we can obtain forgiveness in no other way, than through the redemption of Christ—The reason or ground of this mode of forgiveness—and the consistency be-tween the complete atonement of Christ, and *free grace* in forgiveness—The way is prepared for the fol-lowing inferences and reflections :

If the atonement of Christ be a substitute for the punishment of the sinner according to the divine law, and were designed to support the authority of that law, equally as the punishment of hell ; then we may infer, that the atonement of Christ does not consist *in shew-ing, that the divine law is just.*—With regard to this, I venture to assert two things—That the obedience and death of Christ do not prove, that the divine law is just—That if they did prove this, still merely by that circumstance they would make no atonement.

1. The obedience and death of Christ do not prove, that the divine law is a just law. The sufferings of Christ no more prove this, than the punishment of the damned proves it. The former are the substitute of the latter, and were designed for substance to prove and exhibit the same truths, and to answer the same

H h 2

ends. But who will say that the torments of the
damned prove the justice of the divine law? No more
is this proved by the sufferings of Christ. If the justice of the divine law be called in question, the justice
and moral perfection of God is of course equally called in question. This being the case, whatever he can
say, whether by obedience or suffering, to testify the
justice of the law, must be considered as the testimony
of a party in his own cause; and also as the testimony of a
being whose integrity is as much disputed, as the justice of the law. It cannot therefore be received as
proof in the case. The testimony of God, whether
given in obedience or suffering, so long as his character is disputed, as it will be, so long as the justice of
his law is disputed, proves neither that the law is just,
in *reality*, nor that it is so in *his own estimation*. A being of a disputed character may be supposed to testify,
both contrary to reality, and contrary to his *own knowledge*. And as the character of the *Deity* is disputed,
by those who dispute the justice of the divine law; so
there is the same foundation to dispute the character
and testimony of *the Son* of God. Therefore the obedience and death of Christ do not prove, that the divine law is just.

2. If the obedience and death of Christ did prove
that the law is just; still by this circumstance, they
would make no atonement for sin. If it were a truth,
that the obedience and death of Christ did prove the
divine law to be just, and merely *on that account* made
atonement, the ground of this truth would be, that
whatever makes it manifest that the law is just, makes
atonement. The essence of the atonement, on this
hypothesis, is placed in the manifestation of the justice
of the divine law. Therefore this manifestation, however, or by whomsoever it be made, is an atonement.

But as the law is really just, it was doubtless in the power of infinite wisdom to manifest the justice of it, to rational creatures, without either the obedience or the death of Christ, or of any other person. If it were not in the power of infinite wisdom to manifest the justice of the divine law, without the death of Christ; then if Christ had not died, but all men had perished according to the law, it never would have appeared that the law is just. But bare attention to the law itself, to the reason, ground, and necessity of it, especially when this attention is excited, and the powers of the mind are aided, by even such a divine influence, as God does in fact sometimes give to men of the most depraved characters; is sufficient to convince of the justice of the law. But there can be no dispute, whether the sanctifying and savingly illuminating influences of the spirit of God, without the obedience and death of Christ, would convince any man of the justice of the law. We have no more reason to dispute this, than to dispute, whether the angels who kept their first estate, did believe the justice of the law, before they were informed of the incarnation and death of Christ. According to this hypothesis therefore, all that was necessary to make atonement for mankind, was to communicate to them sanctifying grace, or to lead them to repentance: and as to Christ, he is dead in vain.

Besides; if the obedience and death of Christ did ever so credibly manifest the justice of the law, what atonement, what satisfaction for sin, would this make? how would this support the authority of the law? how would this make it to appear, that the transgressor may expect the most awful consequences from his transgression? or that transgression is infinitely abominable in the sight of God? And how would the manifestation of the justice of the law, tend to restrain men from transgressing that law? Whatever the effect of such manifestation may be on the minds of those innocent creatures, who have regard to justice or moral rectitude; yet on the minds of those who are disposed to transgress, and have lost the proper sense of moral rectitude, the manifestation would have no effectual tendency to restrain *them* from transgression : therefore would in no degree answer the ends of the punishment threatened in the law, nor be any atonement for sin.

Perhaps some may suppose, that what hath now been asserted, that the death or atonement of Christ does not prove the justice of God and of his law, is inconsistent with what hath been repeatedly suggested in the preceding discourses, that it is an end of the death or atonement of Christ, to manifest how hateful sin is to God. If the death of Christ manifest God's hatred of sin, it seems, that the same event must also manifest God's love of holiness and justice. In answer to this, I observe ; that the death of Christ manifests God's hatred of sin and love of holiness, in the same sense as the damnation of the wicked manifests these, viz. on the supposition that the divine law is just and holy. If it be allowed the divine law is just and holy, then every thing done to support and execute that law, is a declaration in favour of holiness and against sin ; or a declaration of God's love of holiness and of his hatred of iniquity. Both the punishment of the damned, and the death of Christ declare God's hatred of all *transgressions* of his law. And if that law be holy, to hate the transgressions of it, is to hate sin, and at the same time to love holiness. But if the law be not holy, no such consequence will follow : it cannot, on that supposition, be inferred from the divine hatred of *trans-gression*, that God either hates *sin* or loves *holiness*.

Again ; we may infer from the preceding doctrine, that the atonement of Christ does not consist essential-ly in his active or positive obedience. By atonement I mean that which, as a substitute for the punishment which is threatened in the law, supports the authority of that law, and the dignity of the divine government. But the obedience of Christ, even in the most trying circumstances, without any tokens of the divine displeasure against the transgressors of the law, would never support the authority of the law, and the dignity of the divine government. It by no means makes it appear, that it is an evil and bitter thing to violate the law, and that the violation of it deserves, and may be expected to be followed with most awful consequences to him, who dares to violate it. A familiar example may illustrate this matter. It is the rule or law of a certain family, that a particular child shall steadily at-tend the school kept in the neighbourhood, and that if he absent himself for a day, without license, he shall feel the rod. However after some time the child be-ing weary of observing this law, does absent himself, and spend the day in play. At night the father being informed of it, arraigns the child, finds him guilty, and prepares to inflict the punishment, which he had threatened. At this instant, the brother of the offend-ing child intercedes, acknowledges the reasonableness of the law, which his brother hath transgressed, con-fesses that he deserves the penalty, but offers himself to make satisfaction for his brother's offence.—Be-ing interrogated by what means he expects to make satisfaction ; he answers, By going himself to school the next day. Now can any one suppose, that in this way the second child can make satisfaction for the offence of the first? Or that if the father were to accept the proposal, he would find the authority of his law, and the government of his family supported with dignity? Or that the offending child, or the other children of the family, would by this means be effectually deterred from future offences of the like nature? And however trying the circumstances of going to school may be, if those circumstances be no token of the father's displeasure at the disobedient child's transgression; still the going to school, of the second child, will not make the least satisfaction for the offence of the first.

I venture to say further, That not only did not the atonement of Christ consist *essentially* in his *active obedience,* but that his active obedience was *no part* of his atonement properly so called, nor essential to it,— The perfect obedience of Christ was doubtless necessary in order to the due execution of his prophetical and priestly office; in order to his intercession: and also in order that the salvation of his disciples might be a reward of his obedience. But that it was necessary to support the authority of the divine law in the pardon of sinners, does not appear. If Christ himself could possibly have been a sinner, and had first made satisfaction for his own sin; it does not appear, but that afterward he might also satisfy for the sins of his people. If the pretender to the crown of Great Britain, should wage war against king *George,* in the course of the war should be taken, should be brought to trial, and be condemned to the block; will any man say that the king of France, by becoming the substitute of the pretender, and suffering in his stead, could not make atonement for the pretender, so as effectually to support the authority of the British laws and government, *and* discourage all future groundless pretensions to the

British crown? Yet the king of France could plead no perfect obedience to the British laws. Even the sinner himself, but upon the supposition of the infinite evil of sin, could by his own sufferings, atone for his sins. Yet he could not exhibit a perfect obedience.

Beside; if the *bare obedience* of Christ have made atonement, why could not the repentance and perfect obedience of Christ's people themselves, have answered, instead of the obedience of Christ? Doubtless if they had suffered the penalty of the divine law, it would have answered to support the authority of the law, and the vigour of the divine government, as really as the death of Christ. And since the eternal sufferings of the people of Christ, would have answered the same end of supporting the authority of the law, as the sufferings of Christ; why would not the eternal perfect *repentance* and *obedience* of the people of Christ, have answered the same end, as his obedience in their behalf? If it would, both the death and obedience of Christ as our substitute, are entirely in vain. If the elect had only been converted, and made perfectly and perseveringly obedient, it would have answered every purpose both of the death and obedience of Christ.— Or if the obedience of Christ in the flesh were at all necessary, it was not necessary to support the authority of the law and government of God; but merely as it was most *wise*, that he should obey. It was necessary in the same sense only, as that the wind should, at this moment, blow from the north-east, and not from the south-west, or from any other quarter.

If the mere active obedience of Christ have made atonement for sin, it may be difficult to account for the punishment of any sinners. If obedience without any demonstration of divine displeasure at sin, will answer every purpose of the divine authority and govern-

ment, in some instances, why not in all instances?—
And if the obedience of sinners themselves will answer
as really as that of Christ, why might not all men have
been led by divine grace to repentance, and perfect
subsequent obedience, and in that way been saved from
the curse of the law? Doubtless they might: nor was
there originally, nor is there now, without any consideration of the atonement of Christ, any other necessity
of the punishment of any of mankind according to the
law, than that which results from mere sovereign wisdom: in which sense indeed it was necessary that
Christ should be given to be the saviour of sinners,
that Paul should be saved, and that every other event
should take place, just as it does take place.

From our doctrine we also learn the great gain
which accrues to the universe by the death of Christ.
It hath been objected to the idea of atonement now exhibited, that if the death of Christ be an equivalent to
the curse of the law, which was to have been inflicted
on all his people; then there is on the whole no gain,
no advantage to the universe: that all that punishment
from which christians are saved, hath been suffered
by Christ, and therefore that there is just as much misery and no more happiness, than there would have
been, had Christ not died. To this I answer,

1. That it is not true, that Christ endured an *equal
quantity* of misery, to that which would have been endured by all his people, had they suffered the curse of
the law. This was not necessary on account of the infinite dignity of his person. If a king were to condemn his son to lose an ear or a hand, it would doubtless be esteemed by all his subjects, a proof of far
greater displeasure in the king, than if he should order
some mean criminal to the gallows: and it would tend
more effectually to support the authority of the law,

for the violation of which, this punishment should b. inflicted on the prince.

2. That if it were true, that Christ endured the very same *quantity* of misery,-which was due to all his people; still by his death an infinite gain accrues to the universe. For though the misery, on this supposition, is in both cases the same, and balances itself; yet the positive happiness obtained by the death of Christ, infinitely exceeds that which was lost by Christ. As the eternal Logos was capable of neither enduring misery, nor losing happiness, all the happiness lost by the substitution of Christ, was barely that of the *man* Christ Jesus, during only thirty-three years : or rather during the *three* last years of his life : because it does not appear, but that during the rest of his life he was as happy, as men in general, and enjoyed as much or more good, than he suffered evil. But the happiness gained by the substitution of Christ, is that of a great multitude, which no man can number, of all nations, kindreds, and people and tongues; Rev. vii 9. Now if the happiness of one man for *three years*, or at most for *thirty-three* years, be equal to that of an innumerable multitude throughout eternity, with the addition of the greater happiness, which Christ himself must enjoy now that he has brought so many sons to glory, beyond what he would have enjoyed, if all these had been plunged in inconceivable and endless misery : then it may be justly said, on the present hypothesis, that by the substitution of Christ, no advantage is gained to the universe. But if the latter infinitely exceed the former, the gain to the universe, even on the supposition, that the sufferings of Christ were equal to those, to which all his people were exposed, is infinite.

I i

I may also hence take occasion to oppose an opinion which appears to me erroneous; which is, That the perfect obedience of Christ was in a great measure designed, to show us, that the divine law may be obeyed by men. It shows, indeed, that it may be obeyed by a man in personal union with the divine nature.—— But how does this show, that it may be obeyed by a mere man? If we should also allow, that it shows, that a man born into the world in perfect innocence, and who is not a fallen creature, may obey the law: yet how does this prove, that it may be obeyed by a fallen creature, dead in trespasses and sins?—It is an undoubted truth, that there is no inability in men to obey the law, except that which is of a moral nature, consisting in the disinclination or disaffection of their own hearts; which does not in the least excuse them in their disobedience. But this is manifest by other considerations, than the perfect obedience of Christ: if it were not, it would not be manifest at all.

Another remark which naturally offers itself in discoursing on this subject is, that Christ's obedience to the *precepts* of the law, without submitting to the *curse,* would by no means prove the justice of that curse. This is the idea of some: That God sent his Son into the world, to obey the precepts of the law, and that his mere obedience of these, proves the justice both of the precepts and of the penalty of the law. I have already given the reasons by which I am made to believe, that the obedience of Christ does not prove the precepts of the law to be just. But if it did prove the *precepts* to be just, it would not therefore prove the *penalty too* to be just. As the precepts of any law may be just and reasonable, yet may be enforced by a penalty which is unjust and cruel; so the proof that the precept is just, does not at all prove, but that the penalty may be unjust and cruel. Indeed as the penalty of any law is designed to support and enforce the precept of that law, so to prove the justice of the penalty, proves the justice of the precept : because not the slightest penalty can be just, when applied to enforce an unjust precept. But this rule when inverted, doth not hold good. To prove the justice of a precept, does by no means prove the justice of the penalty by which that precept is enforced. So that if Christ have proved the precepts of the divine law to be just, this by no means infers the justice of its penalty. On the other hand ; if Christ came to prove the justice of the law, and all that he has done to this effect, have an immediate reference to the precepts only ; and if he have done nothing to establish the justice of the penal part, considered by itself ; the aspect of the whole will be, that the penal part is unjustifiable, and that for this reason he did not pretend to justify it.

The subject which hath been under our consideration, also shews us, in what sense the sufferings of Christ were *agreeable* to God. It has been said, that it is incredible, that *mere pain* should be agreeable to a God of infinite goodness ; that therefore the sufferings of Christ were agreeable to God only as a proof of the strength of the virtue of Christ, or of his disposition to obey the divine law. If by *mere pain* be meant *pain abstracted from the obedience of Christ*, I cannot see why it may not be agreeable to God. It certainly is, in the damned : and for the same reason might have been, and doubtless was, in the case of our Lord. The Father was pleased with the pains of his Son, as they were necessary to support the authority of his law and government, in the salvation of sinners.

Another reflection naturally suggested by this subject is, that in punishing some sinners according to the curse of the law, and in requiring an adequate atonement, in order to the salvation of others ; God acts, not from any *contracted, selfish* motives, but from the most noble *benevolence* and regard to the public good. It hath often and long since been made a matter of objection to the doctrines of the future punishment of the wicked, and of the atonement of Christ ; that they represent the Deity as having regard merely to his own honour and dignity, and not to the good of his creatures, and therefore represent him as deficient in goodness But can it be pretended to be a proof of goodness in God, to suffer his own law, which is the perfect rule of virtue, to fall into contempt? However it might afford relief to some individuals, if God were to suffer his moral kingdom to be dissolved; can it be for the general good of the system of his creatures? Is it not manifestly necessary to the general good of the created system, that God's moral kingdom be upholden? and that therefore the authority of the divine law, and vigour of the divine goveinment be maintained? If so, then it is also necessary to the general good, that punishments be inflicted on the disobedient and lawless ; or that they be pardoned in consequence only of a proper satisfaction or atonement.

So that those very doctrines which of all others are made matter of the most objection to the divine goodness or benevolence, are clear proofs of goodness, and are absolutely necessary to it. If a prince should either make no laws for the government of his subjects, or should never execute them : but should suffer all crimes to pass with impunity : you would by no means esteem him a good prince, aiming at the good of his subjects : you would not hesitate to pronounce him either very weak or very wicked.

In reflecting on this subject, we may notice the reason, why so many, who profess to be advocates for the doctrine of atonement, yet place the atonement in that, in which it does by no means consist. The principal reason seems to be, that they have conceived, that the idea of Christ's having suffered an equivalent to the punishment, to which all his people were exposed, is inconsistent with *grace* in their pardon. But if I have been so happy as properly to state the ideas of *justice* and *grace*, it appears that there is as much grace in the pardon of sinners on account of such an atonement as that just mentioned, as there would be on account of an atonement consisting in mere obedience ; or as there would be in pardon without any atonement at all.

Hence also we see, that the death of Christ in our stead, is not useless or in vain. The opposers of Christ's substitution and atonement, assert, that no good end is answered by the sufferings of an innocent, amiable and virtuous person, in the stead of the guilty. But surely to support the authority of the law and of the moral government of God, is not a vain or unimportant end. It was not in vain that *Zaleucus*, having made a law, that all adulterers should have both their eyes put out, and his own son being the first who transgressed, put out one of his own eyes and one of his son's. Hereby he spared his son in part, and yet as effectually supported the authority of his law, as if it had been literally executed. Nor was it in vain, that during the late war, a soldier in the American army of a robust constitution, pitying his fellow soldier of a slender constitution, who was condemned to receive a certain number of stripes, petitioned to be put in the place of the criminal, and actually received the stripes.* For the authority of the martial law was effectually supported, and perhaps by this means, the life or future health and service of the criminal were preserved, which would otherwise have been lost.

Neither was the death of Christ in the stead of sinners, any injury done to an innocent person. As well may we say, that Zaleucus, or the soldier just mentioned, were injured: Or that a man is injured, when another man receives the money of him, which he voluntarily tenders in payment of the debt of a third person: Or that a man is injured, by the surgeon, who takes off his leg to preserve his life, the man himself consenting, and desiring him so to do.

Again; we may observe in what sense *justice* and *the divine law are satisfied* by the death of Christ; and in what sense the atonement of Christ is properly called a *satisfaction.* It is only the third kind of justice before mentioned, that is *satisfied* by the death of Christ. No man for the reasons already given, will pretend that *commutative* justice is satisfied by Christ; for the controversy between God and the sinner is not concerning property. Nor is *distributive* justice satisfied. If it were, there would indeed be no more grace in the discharge of the sinner, than there is in the discharge of a criminal, when he hath endured the full punishment, to which according to law, he hath been condemned. If distributive justice were satisfied, it would have no further claim on the sinner. And to punish him, when this kind of justice has no claim on him, is to treat him more unfavourably or severely than his personal character deserves. If so, the penitent believer, considered *in his own person*, deserves even according

* This I am informed was real fact.

to the strictness of the divine law, no punishment; and
that merely because he repents and believes : and if
so, repentance and faith satisfy the law, or are the curse
of it, as I have already shown. If distributive justice
be satisfied, it *admits* of no further punishment, and to
punish him further, would be as positively *unjust*, as
to continue a man's punishment, after he hath endured
the full penalty of any law. If distributive justice be
satisfied by Christ, in the behalf of sinners, then the
rule of distributive justice is not the personal character
of a man, but the character of his friend, his advocate,
or representative ; any man has a right, on the footing
of distributive justice, to be treated according to the
character of his friend or representative. Therefore
if a subject rebel against his sovereign, and procure a
man of a most unexceptionable and amiable character,
to represent him and plead his cause before his sovereign, he has a right on the footing of distributive justice, to be treated according to the character of his representative ; and if he be not thus treated, he suffers
an injury ; he is abused. On this principle, no prince
or magistrate will have a right to punish, for any
crime, a subject who can procure a man of a virtuous
life, to represent him and plead his cause.

But perhaps it will be said, that distributive justice
is satisfied by the death of Christ, because he placed
himself in our stead, and suffered in our room ; and
that whenever a person thus substitutes himself for
another, and suffers the punishment due to that other,
that other hath a right to a discharge, as distributive
justice is then satisfied. Now according to this objection, the true idea of distributive justice is, to treat a
man either according to his own sufferings, or according to the sufferings of his representative. And if according to the *sufferings* of his representative, why not,

tice or abuse. Nor is the magistrate under any obligation of distributive justice, or justice to the criminal himself, to accept a substitute.

It is true, that the circumstances of the case may be such, that it may be most conducive to the public good, that the offered substitute be accepted : in this case *wisdom* and goodness, or public justice, will require that it be accepted, and the criminal discharged.

This leads me to observe, that it hath also been said, that when Christ offered to become a substitute, and to make atonement for sinners, God was under no obligation to accept the proposal. This, I conceive, is as wide of the truth, as that he was under the same obligation to accept the proposal, as a creditor is, to accept the proposal of a third person, to pay the debt of his friend. The truth is, The glory of God and the greatest good of the moral system, did require, that Christ should become a substitute for sinners; and that his offered substitution should be accepted by God. This was dictated and recommended by both wisdom and goodness. So far therefore as wisdom and goodness could infer an obligation on the Father, to accept the substitution of his Son, he was *under obligation* to accept it. But this obligation was only that of the third kind of justice before explained, a regard to the general good.

This subject further teaches us, that that constitution which requires an atonement, in order to the pardon of the sinner, is nothing *arbitrary*. That divine constitution which is wise and good, as being necessary to the good of the moral system, is not *arbitrary*. But if an atonement was necessary, in order to support the authority of the divine law, and the honour, vigour and even existence of the divine moral government, while sinners are pardoned ; undoubtedly that constitution which requires an atonement, in order to the pardon of the sinner, is the dictate of wisdom and goodness, and by no means, of an *arbitrary* spirit.

Hence we also learn in what sense the death of Christ renders God *propitious* to sinners. It does so only as it supports the authority of his law and government, and renders the pardon of sinners consistent with the good of the system, and the glory of God.

Finally : This subject teaches the groundlessness of that objection to the doctrine of atonement, that it represents the Deity as *inexorable*. If to refuse to pardon sinners unless it be in a way which is consistent with the good of the moral system, is to be inexorable ; then that God will not pardon sinners without atonement, or in a way which is consistent with the authority of his law, and with the authority and even existence of his moral government ; is indeed a proof, that God is inexorable. But unless it be an instance of inexorability, that God will pardon sinners, unless it be in a way which is consistent with the good of the moral system, there is no ground to object to the doctrine of atonement, that it represents the Diety as inexorable. On the other hand ; that God requires an atonement in order to pardon, is an instance and proof of truly divine goodness : and if he were to pardon without an atonement, it would prove, that he is destitute of goodness, and regardless, not only of his own glory, but of the true happiness of the system of his moral creatures.

K k

UNIVERSAL REDEMPTION.

Extracted from the Christian Observer's Review of Simeon's Skeletons of Sermons, Vol. II. page 39.

WE were rather surprised at the apparent hesitation with which Mr. Simeon speaks of the extent of our Saviour's satisfaction (page 266); since our 31st Article and our sacramental service have decided the point in such strong and unequivocal language. We think the want of a necessary distinction upon this head has produced considerable confusion. The propitiation of Christ, in its value and in its offer, is universal and illimitable; but with respect to its *ultimate* effect, it is confined to a certain number.

Extracted from the Christian Observer's Review of Daubeney's Vindiciæ Anglicanæ, Vol. III. page 430.

THE strong conclusion respecting the necessary Anti-calvinism of our Church, which at page 85, and in many other parts of his work, Mr. Daubeney has drawn from the assertions in our articles and liturgy on the subject of universal redemption, will hardly be found consistent with the well known fact, that many of the most learned and pious Calvinists have been amongst the most strenuous approvers and defenders of them: witness the names of Sanderson and Beveridge, the former of whom composed the preface to the liturgy as it now stands, containing an unqualified commendation of its contents. The latter has been no less explicit in a sermon on the liturgy.

For a *modern* instance we refer the reader to that excellent work, intitled " The History of the Church of Christ." The learned and pious author would unquestionably be called a Calvinist by Mr. Daubeney. But how does Mr. Milner express himself on the subject of particular redemption ? " On occasion of the controversies, Augustine was objected to, as denying that Christ died for all. But Prosper, his admirer and follower, and as strict a predestinarian as any writer in any age, maintains that Augustine ' held that Christ gave himself a ransom for all.' Doubtless the natural and obvious sense of scripture is the same,* and the notion of particular redemption was unknown to the ancients, and I wish it had remained equally unknown to the moderns."† What language can be more decisive ? And we may add that when Dr. Haweis expressed himself " shocked that the scriptures of truth should be treated thus slightly, alluding to the above statement, the present Dean of Carlisle defended his brother by quoting the following passage—" of God our Saviour who will have *all* men to be saved, and to come unto the knowledge of the truth, For there is one God, and one Mediator between God and man, the man Jesus Christ, who gave himself a ransom for ALL." The Dean adds, " one would think that any plain man might be allowed to infer from this ' scripture of truth,' that Christ died for ALL, without shocking the nicest feelings."‡

* See particularly, 1 Tim ii.
† Vol. ii. page 445, Boston edition.
‡ Preface to second edition of first vol. omitted in Boston edition.

THE

PECULIARITY OF REDEMPTION,

From Fuller's Gospel, worthy of all Acceptation.

IT is proper to enquire, Wherein the peculiarity of redemption consists? If the atonement of Christ were considered as the literal payment of a debt; if the measure of his sufferings were according to the number of those for whom he died, and to the degree of their guilt, in such a manner as that if more had been saved, or if those who are saved had been more guilty, his sorrows must have been proportionably encreased, it might, for aught I know, be inconsistent with indefinite invitations. But it would be equally inconsistent with the free *forgiveness* of sin, and with sinners being directed to apply for mercy as *supplicants*, rather than as claimants. I conclude, therefore, that an hypothesis which in so many important points is manifestly inconsistent with the scriptures, cannot be true.

On the other hand, If the atonement of Christ proceed not on the principle of commercial, but of moral justice, or justice as it relates to *crime ;* if its grand object were to express the divine displeasure against sin,* and so to render the exercise of mercy, in all the ways wherein sovereign wisdom should determine to apply it, consistent with righteousness ;† if it be in itself equal to the salvation of the whole world, were the whole world to embrace it; and if the peculiarity which attends it, consist not in its insufficiency to save more than are saved, but in the sovereignty of its application, no such inconsistency can justly be ascribed to it.

* Rom. viii. 3.   † Rom. iii. 25.   *LB*

W. V M.

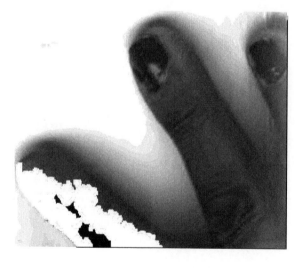